JOHN HADAMUSCIN'S

Enchanted Evenings

JOHN HADAMUSCIN'S
Enchanted Evenings

◆

DINNERS, SUPPERS, PICNICS & PARTIES

◆

PHOTOGRAPHS BY RANDY O'ROURKE

ART DIRECTION BY KEN SANSONE

HARMONY BOOKS / NEW YORK

Published by Harmony Books, a division of Crown Publishers, Inc.,
201 East 50th Street, New York, New York 10022.
Member of Crown Publishing Group.

HARMONY and colophon are trademarks of Crown Publishers, Inc.
Manufactured in Japan

Library of Congress Cataloging-in-Publication Data

Hadamuscin, John.
[Enchanted evenings]
John Hadamuscin's enchanted evenings:
dinners, suppers, picnics & parties
photographs by Randy O'Rourke.—1st ed.
p.   cm.
1. Dinners and dining.   2. Entertaining.   I. Title.
II. Title: Enchanted evenings.
TX737.H33   1990
642—dc20   89-77181
CIP
ISBN 0-517-57508-6

10   9   8   7   6   5   4   3   2   1

First Edition

ACKNOWLEDGMENTS

After having done two books, I initially thought, "this one won't be difficult at all." Well, this turned out to be the most challenging one so far, but thanks to a lot of wonderful people who shared the experience with me, working on it has been a lot of fun.

Anyone familiar with my other books will recognize the rooms I live in here, too. But again, we went out "on location" to capture different settings and moods. Many, many thanks to all those who so generously (and patiently!) welcomed us into their homes: Seth, Lynn, and Sari Abraham; Diane Cleaver; Phil and Sally Drew; Peter Duble, Jennifer Trainer, and all the Duble family; Deborah Kass; Carol and J. Barry O'Rourke; Michael Pritchard; Philip McDowell Stoehr; and Janet Sutherland.

Thanks, too, to Fred's Farm in Ghent, New York, for the hay for our hayride and to Chris Loken of Love Apple Farm for the tractor and wagon. And to my agent, Diane Cleaver, who, above and beyond the call of duty, organized all the details.

Thanks to Joyce Wadler, who a few years ago, offered an idea that evolved into this book.

I'm fortunate to have a lot of good friends who got caught up in the project and helped in many ways—from tasting new recipes to watching the cherry blossoms on a daily basis so we could photograph them in their prime. Thanks to: Ron Baker, Fred Bastian, John Coll, Genevieve Como, Pam Cucuzza, Peter A. Davis, Doris Driegert, Lisa Ekus, Raymond Ewert, all the Hadamuscins, Nancy Kenmore, Iola Keiter, Lindsay Miller, Esther Mitgang, Paula Obermiller, Lillian Olsen, Mary Ann Podesta, Bob Schmidt, Bob Schuman, Jean Sokolik, Pam Thomas, Patrick Ugaro, and Cheryl Valentine. And thanks to Thomas and Elizabeth Bartles, Foster and Penny Deveraux, Nancy Duble, Debra and John Hennessey, A.J. and Michael Meehan, and Tony Moretti, for being great party guests. Then there are the friends who offered recipes —their names are mentioned in the text. A special thanks to my old friends Ken Daniels and Nolan Drummond, who were always ready, willing, and able to help in any way when I needed an extra hand. They've given new meaning to the word "friendship."

It would be impossible to create a book like this without the support of an enthusiastic and able editor, and once again my editor and friend Harriet Bell has been my sounding board, confidante, and cheerleader. She understood what I wanted this book to be and let me do it "my way," while still offering great ideas, sound advice, and encouragement (and even testing recipes in the "Bell Labs"). All I can say is "thanks." When Harriet went on to other endeavors, she turned over the reins to Kathy Belden, who picked them up without missing a step.

And thanks to the rest of my friends on the Crown and Harmony team: production supervisor Joan Denman, who once again went that extra mile to produce a beautiful book; production editor Amy Boorstein, who continues to watch every detail with diligence and care; and managing editor Laurie Stark, who made sure we all met our deadlines (or else!!!). Thanks, too, to everyone else who continues to support my efforts, particularly Bruce Harris, Michelle Sidrane, Betty A. Prashker, Peter Guzzardi, Jo Fagan, Phyllis Fleiss, Jonathan Fox, Barbara Marks, and Hilary Bass.

Thanks to Jeanne di Giacomo of Affairs of the Heart in West Hartford, Connecticut, and the staff of La Grande Pantrie in Simsbury, Connecticut, for generously lending us extra platters and pans.

A big round of applause to "the crew," who helped me get the visions in my head onto the printed page. This book is theirs, too. Photographer Randy O'Rourke, as usual, didn't let me down. He remained good-natured and enthusiastic, even when I wanted to try "just one more shot" at 2 A.M. This is our second book and working together remains a pleasure. New mom Stephanie O'Rourke and baby Tiernan were frequently on hand and both were always ready to offer their two cents! Crown's design director Ken Sansone's artistic direction is evident on every page. He was always willing to listen to any crazy idea that might come into my head and he burned a lot of midnight oil designing this book when everyone else's work was done. A loving note of thanks to my mom, Clara Henry. It seems like she's spent most of her retirement trying out recipes for me and during the last year she made several trips to New York to spend what must have at times seemed like months in my kitchen and "on the set," helping to prepare food for the photographs. After three books, she's become quite a pro! I'm really lucky—and grateful—to be part of such a fine team.

Finally, thanks to all of you, my extended family— now that we've spent "the holidays" together and enjoyed some "special occasions," I hope this book brings you a few "enchanted evenings"!

CONTENTS

◆

INTRODUCTION
9

Spring

A RAINY NIGHT SUPPER
14

MY BIRTHDAY DINNER
18

BLOSSOM TIME
FINGER-FOODS PARTY
22

FIRST DINNER ON THE PORCH
35

DINNER IN THE HARBOR
39

WEDDING REHEARSAL
BUFFET DINNER
44

Summer

A SIMPLE CAMPFIRE SUPPER
52

BARBECUE AT THE BEACH
56

FOURTH OF JULY DINNER ON THE LAWN
62

A MIDSUMMER NIGHT'S
FINGER-FOODS PARTY
68

BAND CONCERT PICNIC ON THE GREEN
76

A FARMSTAND SUPPER
82

INDIAN SUMMER DINNER AT SUNSET
87

Fall

DINNER AWAY FROM IT ALL
92

A "BACK TO THE FIFTIES" COCKTAIL PARTY
97

SUNDAY SUPPER
105

A HAYRIDE PICNIC SUPPER
110

A THEATRE PARTY DINNER
118

AN OLD-FASHIONED WAFFLE SUPPER
124

A NATIVE FEAST OF THANKSGIVING
129

Winter

"PUTTIN' ON THE RITZ"
COCKTAIL PARTY
140

A FIRESIDE CHRISTMAS EVE SUPPER
152

A HOLIDAY DESSERT PARTY
157

WINTER VACATION BARBECUE
172

A HEARTY SKI LODGE DINNER
179

A WEEKNIGHT KITCHEN SUPPER
184

DINNER FOR AN ICY EVENING
188

A POTLUCK SUPPER
193

◆

AFTER-DINNER TREATS
210

BASIC RECIPES
220

INDEX
222

INTRODUCTION

◆

"Welcome sweet night!
The evening crowns the day."
John Ford

We all have certain times of the day that we love for different reasons—I've always loved evenings. Growing up on a farm in Ohio, I would often lie on the front lawn at sunset and listen as the stillness came over the little world around me. What enchantment it held. And I remember hayrides lit by a silvery harvest moon and skating parties under a starlit snowfall, and suppers on the lawn on warm golden summer nights.

I still find an element of excitement in the darkness of the night, and nightfall always seems to bring a little serenity after a busy day. Evening is still a time for small talk on the porch on a rainy night in spring or in front of a glowing fireplace in winter, a time for watching the stars and fireflies and listening to crickets and frogs in summer, and, most of all, a time for sharing laughter, conversation, and good food, no matter what time of year.

There's no better place to share these simple pleasures than at home, the most welcoming place of all. Having friends in for the evening has always been one of my favorite indulgences. Let's admit it—we're all a bit selfish, by pleasing and enjoying others we also please and enjoy ourselves.

• • •

Whenever I plan a party, I think of it as a theatrical production. A party, like a play, depends on a theme, lights, sets, music, and myriad other details for its success. I try to organize all of the details for the evening with one result in mind and, just as a playwright crafts a play, I try to keep things "fresh" as the evening unfolds. For example, I often use different dinnerware patterns for different courses to keep the look of the table constantly changing. Or after a dinner in the dining room, dessert and coffee may be served somewhere else, giving the guests a change of scenery and an opportunity to stretch their legs and mingle. Or I may plan a party in an unexpected place, such as a formal dinner in an attic or a picnic in a barn.

As I see it, the "backstage" part of entertaining is of the utmost importance, but requires little more than commonsense and planning. Creating a strategy for getting everything ready at the appointed hour is a major key. I start my planning with the guest list and continue with not only the menu but all the "extras" that contribute to making a party an enjoyable and memorable one. I always make lists and more lists.

It's no news to anyone that a beautifully set table in a warm and inviting environment makes even the best food more enjoyable (restaurant designers aren't paid fortunes for nothing!) The trick is the selection of accessories that enhance the food rather than overwhelm it. For any party, I always plan what tableware and accessories are to be used in advance so that the red-checkered tablecloth isn't in the laundry on the night of the party or I'm not scrounging around in the back of a closet looking for the cocktail shaker as the first guest arrives. When I'm planning, I begin by plotting a table setting in my head. Next, I set my "dress rehearsal" table. I often switch things around two or three times until the setting is just right.

More often than not, I include abundant bouquets of flowers at my parties, whether casual or formal, and I always arrange flowers myself. Even if my bouquets aren't absolutely perfect every time, they always add a personal touch. It isn't necessary to have a huge variety of vases and baskets, but it helps to have a few different shapes and sizes. A flower container might be a pitcher, a kettle, a basket, or even a big tin can. Once the container is selected it's just a matter of filling it with a variety of flowers and greens—the more the better.

There are times when other centerpieces can take the place of a big bouquet. In the fall, a variety of gourds and pumpkins can be intertwined with small branches of bittersweet and dried leaves, or in the spring a few blossoms may be placed on the table around a single hurricane-shaded candle. In the summer, a simple bowl of beautiful vegetables or fruits can do the trick, and in the winter a grouping of fat candles and pinecones.

Perhaps even more than dishes, glassware, linens, and flowers, the right lighting can set the mood for an enchanted evening. Lighting instantly changes the appearance of a table or room—even a supper of ordered-in pizza on paper plates can look quite wonderful by candlelight. I use a variety of candlesticks, old and new (and frequently unmatched), gas lamps, and even old railroad lanterns. For mood-enhancement, votive candles are at the top of my list, and I frequently place them all over a table, or better yet, all over a room. As a rule, electric lighting is kept to a minimum to allow flickering flames to cast their flattering glow.

Although the ambience of a party is important, the food should still be the star. The foods that I like best are usually fairly simple. When I cook I never stray too far from the home cooking I grew up with. The essence of good cooking is fresh ingredients, honestly prepared without too much frou-frou. While I may venture into foreign ingredients, combinations, and techniques that I've discovered as an adult living in a cosmopolitan city, the way I cook now has evolved from that basic home-style I learned growing up on a farm in Ohio. I try not to get too "fancy." There's a definite difference in cooking food to impress and cooking food to be savored and enjoyed.

The menus have been designed for the person who, like me, doesn't want to live in the kitchen. The menus and recipes aren't unnecessarily elaborate or complicated. They don't need any extraordinary skills, exotic equipment, or hired help, though one or two of the larger party menus can be easier to prepare and more fun with the help of a friend or two. Each menu is introduced with a section called "Getting Ready" that plots out the cooking schedule, including as much advance preparation as possible.

Since this book is arranged seasonally, the menus and recipes emphasize the use of fresh seasonal ingredients, but if a menu calls for asparagus and it doesn't look its best at the market, buy green beans instead. Try to be flexible. Do try to use fresh herbs when the recipe specifies; in many cases I've listed alternative quantities for dried herbs, where they won't harm the flavor of the finished dish. (But I never use dried parsley or dried dill, which look and taste like green sawdust.)

As far as other ingredients go, I've tried to use only ingredients that are readily available. For the most part, I don't want to spend hours and hours scouting out some oddball ingredient just to be different, and I don't think anyone else does either.

Since the recipes in this book are intended for special occasions rather than everyday fare, here I'm not overly concerned about calories or cholesterol. I do use less butter than I once did and I never use much salt, but I heartily agree with Julia Child, who'd rather eat just a few bites of something "sinful" and delicious than a whole plateful of something "healthy" and bland. So in the recipes here I do use real butter, cream, eggs, and so on. Anyone who cooks for those on restricted diets knows how to make appropriate substitutions.

People often ask me what I think of microwave cooking. I don't own a microwave oven, but I have used microwaves in other people's kitchens. I've found the microwave to be helpful for defrosting fro-

ABOVE: Over the years I've acquired quite a varied collection of containers for flowers. I use vases, baskets, pitchers, bottles, bowls, and even tin cans.

BELOW: Candlelight adds a warm glow to any evening gathering. I use a wide variety of candles and holders for different kinds of occasions.

zen foods, melting butter and chocolate, reheating, and other simple tasks, but it seems to me that most microwave cooking—where something needs to be added, stirred, or tossed every few minutes—is more trouble than it's worth. I guess I'm old fashioned, but for me much of the pleasure of cooking is seeing, smelling, and tasting all the way.

•   •   •

As we photographed the events in this book I was careful not to do anything I don't or wouldn't do in real life. The food is all real, prepared "by the book," and the presentation and garnishes are simple and easily accomplished. I've also tried to keep all the settings realistic and practical. The photographs were taken in real homes, especially my own. The dishes, glasses, flatware, and linens are mostly mine, many of them tag sale and flea market finds, none of them particularly costly. Many items have been used in different combinations, just as we all do in real life. Often, formal elements appear side by side with rustic ones. And since I have only a few pieces of any particular pattern, for the most part, I mix rather than match, which makes for a more visually interesting table. My aim is for the photographs to be used as jumping-off points, as suggestions meant to be changed and expanded, not to be followed to the letter.

One of the most important parts of any party is something that can't be photographed—the music. There are two schools of thought about music at dinnertime: some find it to be an intrusion or distraction and some, including me, think it enhances and adds the finishing touch. I've offered a few suggestions for several of the menus in the book, but for the most part, I've left it up to the individual hosts. But for starters, how about that song from *South Pacific?*

•   •   •

Finally, the most important part of a party is the host. The host is the producer, director, designer, and stage manager (and, usually, even the most critical critic). It's up to the host to set the tone as the curtain goes up when the first guest arrives. Once a warm and welcoming atmosphere is established, the party is already a hit. Perhaps the most wonderful "review" is when, at the end of the evening, guests linger, not wanting the party to end, and everyone is already planning to get together again soon. It's been an evening to remember.

John

JOHN HADAMUSCIN

S
P
R
I
N
G

A RAINY NIGHT SUPPER

for 8

◆

Menu

HERB-MARINATED MOZZARELLA WITH TOASTS

· · ·

GARLICKY OVEN-BRAISED BEEF WITH
PAN-ROASTED VEGETABLES

CABBAGE, FENNEL, AND APPLE SALAD WITH
WALNUT VINAIGRETTE

· · ·

GRANDMA WYNN'S LEMON PUDDING CAKE
WITH BERRIES

W hen the spring rains came to our farm, it was a sure sign that the long winter was finally over and that nature was preparing the earth for planting. On those cool rainy nights, while Mom was fixing a hearty supper, we kids would sneak out onto the porch to listen to the rain and thunder, watch the lightning, and smell the wonderful green freshness in the air. Our kitchen, built as an addition onto the back of our old farmhouse, had a tin roof. When suppertime came we'd go in to the kitchen, where the pitter-patter of the rain on the roof tried to drown out our suppertime conversation. After doing homework or playing some parlor games, it was off to bed, where the rain would lull us to sleep.

Nowadays, I still love rainy evenings. This supper of comforting foods was planned as a prelude to a few rounds of Scrabble with a couple of close friends. And after everyone's gone home, I still like falling asleep listening to the sound of the rain pitter-pattering on the roof.

GETTING READY Prepare the marinated mozzarella up to 24 hours in advance and store in the refrigerator. The bread can be sliced and toasted up to a few days ahead and stored in a tightly covered container.

The beef should be prepared a day in advance up to the end of step 3, or prepare the entire dish a day in

ABOVE: Marinated mozzarella, flecked with pepper and herbs, is served on a green reproduction majolica platter.

ABOVE: The hearty main course is garnished with herbs and served family-style from a big ironstone platter.

BELOW: Lemon pudding cake is dusted with confectioners' sugar and garnished with lemon slices and raspberries.

advance up to the middle of step 6 and follow the recipe for reheating.

Prepare the salad and the dressing early in the day and store the salad in the refrigerator. Dress and toss the salad just before serving.

The lemon pudding cake is best when freshly baked and served warm. Mix the batter and put the cake into the oven just before serving the main course, or bake the cake early in the day and rewarm it in a slow oven.

BEVERAGES I like to serve a hearty red, such as a Cabernet, with both the first and main courses. Strongly brewed Earl Grey tea goes well with the cake. After dessert, serve more tea with a drop of brandy.

*H*ERB-MARINATED MOZZARELLA WITH TOASTS

·

SERVES 8

The vivid flavors of olive oil, oregano, basil, hot pepper, and a hint of garlic enhance the bland mozzarella wonderfully. Fresh mozzarella is a must here—the rubbery texture of the packaged kind doesn't make it much fun to eat, and it won't absorb the flavors of the marinade. I serve the cheese with toasted thin slices of baguette—long, slender French bread.

2 pounds fresh mozzarella, cut into ¼-inch slices
¼ cup extra-virgin olive oil
1 teaspoon lemon juice
1 small garlic clove, crushed
2 tablespoons chopped basil or parsley
1 tablespoon chopped fresh oregano leaves
    or 1 teaspoon dried oregano
¼ teaspoon cracked black peppercorns
½ teaspoon dried red pepper flakes
Fresh basil leaves, for garnish
Thin slices of baguette, toasted and cooled

1. Arrange the mozzarella in a shallow bowl. Combine all the remaining ingredients in a small bowl and pour over the cheese. Cover with plastic wrap and refrigerate several hours, turning once or twice.

2. Bring the mozzarella to room temperature 1 hour before serving and remove the garlic clove. Arrange the cheese on a serving plate and garnish with basil leaves. Serve with the toasted bread.

"There is no place more delightful than home." —Cicero

*G*ARLICKY OVEN-BRAISED BEEF WITH PAN-ROASTED VEGETABLES

·

SERVES 8, WITH LEFTOVERS

2 large heads garlic, separated into cloves and
    peeled
4 medium onions, sliced horizontally into rings
2 bay leaves
1 teaspoon salt
1 tablespoon crushed black peppercorns
2 tablespoons Dijon mustard
1 5- to 6-pound beef bottom round roast, rump
    roast, or thick-cut brisket
1½ cups beef stock
½ cup Scotch whiskey

3 tablespoons olive oil
6 large carrots, peeled and diagonally cut into
    ¼-inch slices
2 pounds medium russet potatoes, scrubbed and
    quartered
12 ounces medium button mushrooms, cleaned
1 tablespoon all-purpose flour
¼ cup tomato paste
1 tablespoon chopped fresh sage leaves
    or 1 teaspoon dried sage
Sage leaves, for garnish

1. Preheat the oven to 275°F. Scatter the garlic and onions in the bottom of a shallow roasting pan just large enough to hold the beef and add the bay leaves.

2. In a small bowl, stir together the salt, peppercorns, and mustard. Generously brush this mixture onto the beef and place the beef on the onions and garlic in the roasting pan.

3. Pour the stock and the whiskey around the meat. Cover the pan tightly with a lid or with aluminum foil. Roast for 6 hours, or until the meat is very tender. When done, temporarily transfer the beef to a large plate or board. With a slotted spoon, remove the onions and garlic from the pan to a small bowl. Return the beef to the pan; cover and refrigerate overnight. Cover and refrigerate the garlic-onion mixture separately.

4. The next day remove the beef from the refrigerator. Remove and discard all the congealed fat on the meat and in the pan, leaving the gravy in the pan.

5. Heat the oil in a medium, heavy skillet; add the

carrots, potatoes, and mushrooms and sauté for 15 minutes. Add the garlic-onion mixture and sauté until very brown, about 15 minutes, then blend in the flour. Transfer the gravy from the pan to the skillet. Add the tomato paste and blend well. Continue cooking the sauce for about 5 minutes. Stir in the chopped sage, remove the skillet from the heat, and set aside.

6. Preheat the oven to 325°F. Carve the beef into ¼-inch slices. Arrange the beef in overlapping slices in the center of the roasting pan, spoon the vegetables around it, and pour on the sauce. (*Can be made ahead up to this point, covered, and refrigerated. Remove from the refrigerator about 2 hours before reheating.*) Cover the pan loosely with a lid or aluminum foil and roast for about 45 minutes, or until the vegetables are tender.

7. Remove the pan from the oven and allow to stand for about 10 minutes before serving. Serve directly from the roasting pan or transfer to a large platter, garnished with sage leaves.

CABBAGE, FENNEL, AND APPLE SALAD WITH WALNUT VINAIGRETTE
·
SERVES 8

Refreshing after a hearty main course, this salad is still flavorful enough to hold its own.

1 medium head red or green cabbage (or ½ of each), shredded
8 stalks fennel, thinly sliced crosswise
2 large, tart green apples (such as Granny Smith), unpeeled, cored, and julienned

DRESSING
¼ cup walnut oil
¼ cup vegetable oil
¼ cup red wine vinegar
1 teaspoon Dijon mustard
Few drops hot pepper sauce

In a serving bowl, combine the salad ingredients. Combine the dressing ingredients in a small bottle or jar, shake well to blend, and pour over the salad. Toss well and serve immediately.

GRANDMA WYNN'S LEMON PUDDING CAKE
·
SERVES 8

This is a comforting, old-fashioned dessert that my grandmother used to make. I'd watch her make it and was always amazed that even though she poured just one batter into the pan, the end result had two layers: a light, moist cake on top and a warm creamy pudding on the bottom. Grandma's explanation? "The gremlin in the oven made magic!" And now, years later, I don't have an explanation any better than that.

6 large eggs, separated
Juice and grated rind of 2 lemons
4 teaspoons butter, melted
2 cups granulated sugar
⅔ cup sifted all-purpose flour
½ teaspoon salt
2 cups milk

Confectioners' sugar, for decorating
Lemon slices, for garnish
½ pint raspberries, for garnish

1. Preheat the oven to 350°F. Generously butter a shallow 1½-quart casserole or ovenproof glass 9½-inch deep-dish pie pan.

2. Combine the egg yolks, lemon juice and rind, and butter in a medium mixing bowl. Beat until slightly thickened and lemon-colored. In a separate bowl, sift together the sugar, flour, and salt. Beat alternately with the milk into the yolk-lemon mixture.

3. In a separate bowl, beat the egg whites until stiff but not dry, then gently fold them into the batter.

4. Pour the batter into the prepared pan and set the pan in a larger baking pan. Fill the outer pan with hot water to about halfway up the sides of the casserole. Bake the cake for 40 to 45 minutes, or until the surface is golden brown and a knife inserted into the center of the cake comes out clean.

5. Remove the cake from the oven and cool on a wire rack for no longer than 45 minutes. (*Or cool completely, store in the refrigerator, and rewarm in a slow oven before serving.*) To decorate, place a paper doily onto the cake and sprinkle with confectioners' sugar. Carefully remove the doily and gently arrange a few lemon slices and berries on the cake.

6. Serve warm, cut into wedges, and garnish each serving with a spoonful of raspberries.

My Birthday Dinner

for 8

Menu

SAUSAGE BUNDLES

• • •

JOHN'S FAMOUS "AMEDITEROCCAN" CHICKEN

SAFFRON AND WILD RICE WITH PIGNOLI

ARUGULA AND VIDALIA ONION SALAD WITH
BALSAMIC VINAIGRETTE (PAGE 220)

• • •

LITTLE RHUBARB PIES WITH
ORANGE-ZEST ICE CREAM (PAGE 221)

Birthdays are pretty special, and they should be celebrated with our nearest and dearest, so every year on May 3, I hold my own annual 32nd birthday party (I'm not saying how many years this event has been going on!) with a menu featuring some of my favorite foods, served to some of my favorite people. Some people may think I'm crazy for throwing my own party, but by doing so I get to indulge myself by choosing the menu and guest list myself.

I always got to pick my favorite foods for my birthday dinner when I was growing up, too. My birthday dinner was always chicken and dumplings, followed by banana walnut cake (a version of Mom's recipe appears on page 109) topped with mounds of vanilla ice cream. My current birthday menu still features chicken, and two other favorites, sausage and arugula, make appearances as well. Mom always baked us kids big, gooey birthday cakes, but now that I make my own birthday dinner, rhubarb pie, another of my all-time favorites, stands in for the cake. After dinner, I might set out hunks of Stilton and Sage Derby cheeses and crackers to enjoy with some good Port or Ginger-Currant Wine (page 212).

GETTING READY This is an easy menu to prepare, and there isn't much last-minute work, so I can be with my guests most of the evening.

Up to a month in advance, make the pastry for the rhubarb pies and freeze it.

Up to a week in advance, make the ice cream.

The chicken is best when prepared a day in advance, refrigerated, and reheated before serving; or make it and freeze it up to a month ahead of time, then thaw it overnight in the refrigerator.

Early in the day, bake the pies; rewarm them in a moderate oven for about 15 minutes before serving.

Also early in the day, prepare the salad ingredients and the dressing. Dress the salad just before serving.

The sausage bundles are best when prepared just before serving (in which case enlisting the aid of a guest is helpful), but I generally make them a few hours ahead of time (they should be slightly under-baked) and reheat them in a moderate oven.

The rice can be prepared up to an hour ahead and kept warm—see the note at the end of the recipe.

BEVERAGES My favorite wine is a California Zinfandel, so I serve it before dinner with both the hors d'oeuvres and the main course. A Beaujolais would be another good choice with the chicken.

Phyllo-wrapped bundles of sweet Italian sausage.

ABOVE: **I like the relaxed informality created by serving dinner buffet-style on a low table and sitting on the pillowed floor.**

"Amediteroccan" chicken with saffron and wild rice.

Little rhubarb pies garnished with sprigs of mint.

Sausage Bundles

•

MAKES 40

I love sausages of just about any variety in just about any form, so my birthday dinner has to include them in one way or another.

These only take a few minutes to put together if you have the sausage ready ahead of time. If you've never worked with phyllo dough, don't be scared off; it's much easier than you'd think. The only trick is to keep the dough covered with a damp cloth at all times to prevent it from drying out.

1 pound sweet Italian sausage
6 sheets phyllo dough
¼ *½ cup (1 stick) butter, melted*
3 tablespoons Dijon mustard, approximately
¼ cup grated Parmesan, approximately
¼ cup snipped chives

1. Prick the sausages all over with a fork and cut them crosswise into ½-inch pieces. Place the pieces in a skillet with 3 tablespoons water over medium-high heat. Sauté the sausage pieces until they are well browned and just cooked through, 10 to 12 minutes. With a slotted spoon, transfer to absorbent paper to drain. (*Can be prepared in advance up to this point.*)

2. Preheat the oven to 350°F. Lightly butter two 20-cup miniature muffin tins. Spread out the sheets of phyllo dough and keep them covered with a damp cloth.

3. Quickly and carefully transfer one sheet of dough onto the work surface and brush completely with melted butter. Spread the second sheet of phyllo smoothly over the first sheet and brush with additional butter; repeat with the third sheet. Lightly brush the top sheet with mustard and sprinkle lightly with Parmesan and some of the chives.

4. Cut the layered phyllo into 20 squares and press each square into a muffin cup, allowing the corners to overhang. Place a piece of sausage into each square.

5. Repeat steps 3 and 4 using the other muffin tin, reserving 1 tablespoon chives. Place the tins in the oven and bake until the phyllo is nicely browned, about 10 minutes. Transfer the bundles to a platter, sprinkle with remaining chives, and serve.

"Pleasantest of all ties is the tie of host and guest." —Aeschylus

John's Famous "Amediteroccan" Chicken

•

SERVES 6

I've been making this chicken dish for years. It's based on a recipe I cut out of a newspaper (or was it a magazine?), and I've fiddled with it countless times to get it just right. The name of the dish reflects its origins: the original was Moroccan and I've added some Mediterranean influences here in America.

Anyway, this is a great party dish since it can be prepared well in advance and even frozen, if you want. If you're really pressed for time, it can be served with plain rice rather than the rice recipe that follows.

12 small or 8 large boneless (but not skinless)
* chicken breast halves*
Salt
All-purpose flour, for dredging
2 tablespoons butter
2 tablespoons extra-virgin olive oil
1 garlic clove, finely chopped
1 small onion, chopped
1 cup golden raisins
½ cup slivered black olives
½ cup slivered green olives
½ cup sun-dried tomatoes, cut into ⅛-inch strips
1 teaspoon curry powder
½ teaspoon ground cumin
¼ teaspoon ground ginger
Pinch of cayenne pepper, or more to taste
2 cups well-seasoned chicken stock
Parsley sprigs, for garnish

1. Season the chicken with salt and then lightly dredge it in the flour. Reserve.

2. In a large skillet over medium-high heat, melt the butter and stir in the olive oil. Add the garlic and onion and sauté for 5 minutes. Push the onion and garlic to the side of the pan. Add the chicken and quickly brown on both sides.

3. Scatter the raisins, olives, and sun-dried tomatoes over the chicken. In a small bowl, whisk the stock and spices together and pour over the chicken. Cover loosely and simmer for 15 to 20 minutes, or until the chicken is cooked through. (*Can be made up to a day in advance, covered, and refrigerated.*)

4. Arrange the chicken in a deep platter around a mound of rice (recipe follows) and garnish generously with sprigs of parsley. Spoon a bit of the sauce over the chicken and pass the rest separately.

Saffron and Wild Rice with Pignoli

•

SERVES 6 TO 8

2 cups water
¼ teaspoon salt
½ cup wild rice, well rinsed
2 tablespoons olive oil
1 large garlic clove, crushed
1½ cups long-grain white rice
¼ teaspoon crushed saffron
3 cups simmering chicken stock
3 tablespoons toasted pignoli

1. Bring the water to a boil and add the salt. Stir in the wild rice and reduce the heat to low. Cover the pan loosely and cook until the wild rice is tender, about 45 minutes.

2. While the wild rice is cooking, pour the oil into a small Dutch oven or large, heavy saucepan over medium heat. Add the garlic and the white rice and sauté until golden, about 10 minutes. Discard the garlic. Stir the saffron into the chicken stock and then add the stock to the saucepan. Reduce the heat and simmer for 15 to 20 minutes, or until the rice is fluffy and tender.

3. Add the cooked wild rice and 2 tablespoons of the pignoli to the white rice and toss until blended. Mound the rice onto the center of a serving platter and scatter the remaining pignoli over it. (The rice can be kept warm in a covered, lightly oiled casserole in a very low oven up to 1 hour.)

Arugula and Vidalia Onion Salad

•

SERVES 8

Vidalia onions from Georgia are becoming more readily available during and just after their month-long growing season in the late spring. According to legend, these onions, grown in the "sweetest soil in the South," are so sweet they can be eaten like apples. I don't know if I'd go that far, but they are so subtly flavored that thick slices of them can be eaten on sandwiches with great relish. Here, their delicate sweetness balances the sharp flavor of arugula.

If you can't find Vidalias, look for other sweet onion varieties, such as Maui, Bermuda, or Walla Walla.

4 cups arugula leaves, washed
2 large Vidalia or other sweet onions, sliced horizontally and separated into rings
Balsamic Vinaigrette (page 220)

Place the arugula in a salad bowl and top with the onion rings. Drizzle the vinaigrette over the salad and toss just before serving.

Little Rhubarb Pies

•

MAKES 6

Triple recipe Orange Pastry for 9-inch pie (page 220)
4 cups diced rhubarb
1 tablespoon all-purpose flour
3 tablespoons sugar
¼ teaspoon ground cinnamon
¼ teaspoon ground ginger
¼ teaspoon ground cloves
3 tablespoons butter
½ cup raspberry jam

1. Preheat the oven to 425°F. Have ready 6 individual baking dishes (I use 4½-inch round Pyrex casseroles).

2. Divide the dough into 2 pieces. Roll it out one piece at a time to a thickness of about ⅛ inch and cut out 3 circles approximately 7 inches in diameter. Place a dough circle in each pie pan, letting the excess hang over the sides.

3. Spoon about ⅔ cup rhubarb into each pan. In a small bowl, combine the flour, sugar, and spices and then sprinkle this mixture over the rhubarb. Dot the rhubarb with the butter.

4. Fold the pastry over the rhubarb, making overlapping folds and leaving an opening at the center of each pan (don't go crazy trying to do this too neatly; the pies should have a rather rustic look). Place the pans on a baking sheet and bake for 20 to 25 minutes, or until the rhubarb is tender and the crust is golden brown. Transfer to a wire rack.

5. Place the jam in a small, heavy saucepan over low heat, and heat until thin and syrupy. Strain the jam into a small bowl and with a pastry brush glaze the rhubarb. Serve the pies warm (or allow them to cool to room temperature) with a small scoop of Orange-Zest Ice Cream (page 221).

BLOSSOM TIME FINGER-FOODS PARTY

for 30

◆

Menu

RED AND WHITE WINE SPRITZERS

• • •

SKEWERED TORTELLINI WITH
BASIL-GINGER DRESSING

SESAME CHICKEN FINGERS WITH
ROASTED GARLIC MAYONNAISE

STEAMED SUGAR SNAP PEAS WITH
PINK RADISH AND CAVIAR DIPPING SAUCE

LEEK-WRAPPED CRAB MOUSSE

• • •

LAMB SPRING ROLLS WITH
CURRIED HONEY MUSTARD

ASPARAGUS TIP AND PROSCIUTTO PUFFS

SPICY PORK AND SCALLION STICKS WITH
PLUM KETCHUP

HERBED CHEESE ROULADES

• • •

MINIATURE ORANGE-COCONUT
UPSIDE-DOWN CUPCAKES

CHOCOLATE-GLAZED ALMOND BARS

LEMON MELTAWAYS

RIGHT: The hors d'oeuvres buffet is laid out on a linen-
clothed table under a spectacular blossoming cherry tree.

I, like most people, get a whopping case of spring fever every year. When I was growing up I used to go out along the back roads before spring officially arrived and cut pussy willow and dogwood branches, along with small branches from the apple and cherry trees in our orchard. I'd bring the branches inside and put them in warm water to force the blossoms, admittedly, to force the whole issue of spring itself.

Now I find other excuses, like the first bit of warm weather, to have my first outdoor party. A warm late-afternoon "cocktail hour" is the perfect excuse to move the party onto a petal-strewn lawn and let everyone enjoy the fresh-smelling spring air.

This menu was originally planned for a spring wedding reception, but I think the arrival of spring itself is cause enough for a big celebration.

GETTING READY There's a good bit of work to be done for this party, but a lot of preparation can be done in advance. Enlist an extra pair of hands for the last few hours before the party. Remember to plan what serving dishes are to be used: The only way I ever remember for a large party is to write them down.

Up to a month or two in advance, make the plum ketchup and the curried honey mustard.

Up to a week in advance make the lemon meltaways and the roasted garlic mayonnaise.

A day in advance, make the filling for the spring rolls and make the crab mousse and the radish and caviar sauce. Make the cheese roulades and the chicken fingers. Bake the almond bars and the cupcakes and store them in tightly covered containers in a cool place.

Early on the day of the party, make the spring rolls and prepare the pork sticks and the asparagus and prosciutto puffs; arrange on baking sheets (I use the disposable foil ones for large parties), cover tightly, and stack in the refrigerator. Cook and marinate the tortellini. Steam and chill the sugar snap peas.

A few hours before the party, skewer the tortellini. Arrange the desserts on their serving dishes. Allow a half-hour for arranging the rest of the food on serving dishes and on the buffet.

> *"Tis not the food but the content*
> *That makes the table's merriment."*
> Robert Herrick

Skewered Tortellini with Basil-Ginger Dressing

·

MAKES APPROXIMATELY 4 DOZEN

DRESSING
½ cup light sesame oil
½ cup white wine vinegar
½ cup chopped sun-dried tomatoes
½ teaspoon dried red pepper flakes
1 tablespoon finely chopped gingerroot
¼ cup finely chopped basil

3 pounds cheese- and meat-stuffed fresh or frozen tortellini, preferably both green and white (to alternate on skewers)

1. In a large bowl, combine all the dressing ingredients and whisk to blend. Reserve.

2. Cook the tortellini in boiling salted water until *al dente*. Drain the tortellini, add them to the bowl with the dressing, and toss well to coat. Cover and refrigerate at least 2 hours (but no more than 6 hours, or the pasta may become soggy).

3. No more than 2 to 3 hours before serving, skewer 2 tortellini—1 green and 1 white—onto each bamboo skewer. Arrange the skewers on a serving platter and cover with plastic wrap or foil until serving time. Serve at room temperature.

Sesame Chicken Fingers

·

MAKES ABOUT 6 DOZEN

These are delicious hot, but for a crowd of this size serve them at room temperature, so they can be made a day ahead.

10 skinless and boneless chicken breast halves (about 2¾ pounds)

MARINADE
¼ cup light soy sauce
¼ cup dry white wine
¼ cup light sesame oil or *peanut oil*
1 tablespoon finely chopped gingerroot
1 large garlic clove, finely chopped
1 teaspoon salt

½ cup sesame seeds, approximately

1. One at a time, place each chicken breast on a cutting board and pound it lightly with a mallet to flatten slightly. Cut the chicken diagonally into "fingers" approximately ½ inch wide by 2½ to 3 inches long.

2. In a large shallow dish, stir together the marinade ingredients. Add the chicken and toss with the marinade. Cover and refrigerate 6 hours or overnight, turning once or twice.

3. Preheat the broiler. Lightly grease a large baking sheet.

4. Spread the sesame seeds out in a small, shallow bowl. Lift a few chicken pieces from the marinade, toss them in sesame seeds until lightly coated, and place them on the baking sheet. Repeat until all the chicken fingers are used. Broil the fingers about 10 minutes, turning once, until cooked through and nicely browned. Transfer to wire racks to cool.

5. If made ahead, the chicken fingers should be covered tightly and refrigerated. Reheat them briefly in a moderate oven and then allow to cool to room temperature before serving. Serve with Roasted Garlic Mayonnaise (recipe follows).

ROASTED GARLIC MAYONNAISE

•

MAKES ABOUT 1 CUP

Aïoli is a classic Provencal sauce made by blending pressed garlic into a lemony mayonnaise. This version, equally simple to make, is a bit more subtle and complex because roasting the garlic gives it a mellow, almost nutty flavor.

1 large garlic head
1 cup Homemade Mayonnaise (page 221)
1 teaspoon lemon juice

1. Preheat the oven to 375°F. Peel away the papery outer skin of the garlic, but leave the unpeeled cloves intact as a head. Wrap the garlic in heavy-duty aluminum foil and roast it for 1 hour and 15 minutes. Remove from oven, and allow to cool to the touch.

2. Place a small sieve over a small mixing bowl. Separate the garlic head into cloves and, one at a time, squeeze each roasted clove into the sieve. Discard the skins. With the back of a spoon, press the roasted garlic through the sieve into the bowl. Add the

mayonnaise and lemon juice and whisk well to blend. Store in the refrigerator, tightly covered, up to 3 weeks.

STEAMED SUGAR SNAP PEAS

•

For this menu and number of suggested guests I use about 2 pounds of peas. First pinch the stringy ends from the peas. Then place them in a steamer over boiling water until crisp-tender, 3 to 5 minutes. Drain, rinse under cold running water, and drain again. Chill the peas for up to a day before serving. To serve, arrange the peas in a shallow basket around a small bowl of Pink Radish and Caviar Dipping Sauce (recipe follows) and decorate with a few small pink flowers.

PINK RADISH AND CAVIAR DIPPING SAUCE

•

MAKES APPROXIMATELY 3 CUPS

This sauce has a surprising color and flavor—guests sample it a few times before they realize what "that wonderful taste" is.

1 8-ounce package cream cheese, softened
1 cup (1 8-ounce container) sour cream
Juice of ½ lemon
1½ cups finely chopped red radishes
2 shallots, finely chopped
2 ounces small-grain red caviar
Salt and white pepper to taste
Radish slices, for garnish

1. In a medium mixing bowl, beat together the cream cheese, sour cream, and lemon juice until smooth. Stir in the radishes and shallots until well blended and then stir in the caviar.

2. Transfer the mixture to a small serving bowl, cover tightly, and refrigerate for at least 4 hours before serving to allow flavors to mellow. Taste before serving and add salt and white pepper to taste. Garnish with paper-thin radish slices.

"It is a beauteous evening, calm and free."
William Wordsworth

A crab mousse encased in silky leeks is served on a bed of lemon leaves and garnished with blossoms.

Leek-Wrapped Crab Mousse

·

MAKES ONE 4-CUP MOUSSE

This mousse is wrapped in silky leeks, making a beautiful presentation. The mousse can also be molded in the usual way; skip the first two steps and chill the mousse in an oiled 4-cup decorative mold.

3 medium leeks
1 tablespoon (1 envelope) unflavored gelatin
¼ cup cold water
⅓ cup boiling water
⅔ cup Homemade Mayonnaise (page 221)
1 small onion, finely chopped
½ cup very finely chopped celery
2 tablespoons snipped chives
1 tablespoon lemon juice
1 teaspoon salt
¼ teaspoon cayenne pepper
2 cups (about 1 pound) finely flaked crabmeat
1 cup heavy cream

1. Trim the ends from the leeks and wash carefully to remove all sandy particles. Place the leeks in a skillet with water to cover and place over medium-high heat. Bring the leeks to a simmer and cook until just tender, about 10 minutes. Remove from the heat, drain, and cool. Separate the leeks into individual leaves and reserve.

2. Oil a 4-cup loaf pan. Line the pan crosswise with the leek leaves, overlapping the leaves slightly and letting the ends hang over the sides of the pan. Set aside. Chop any leftover leek leaves and reserve.

3. In a large mixing bowl, soften the gelatin in cold water and let stand 2 or 3 minutes. Gradually whisk in the boiling water until the gelatin is dissolved. Refrigerate for 2 or 3 minutes, or until the mixture has cooled off.

4. Add all the remaining ingredients (including any leftover chopped leek from step 2) except the crabmeat and heavy cream and whisk until well blended. Return the bowl to the refrigerator and chill about 15 minutes, or until the mixture is slightly thickened. (If the mixture becomes too thick, whisk for a few seconds until smooth.)

5. Whip the cream in a separate chilled bowl until soft peaks form. When the gelatin mixture has chilled and thickened, fold in the crabmeat and then gently fold in the whipped cream.

6. Transfer the mousse mixture to the prepared pan and fold the overhanging ends of the leeks up over the mousse. Cover with plastic wrap and refrigerate until firm, at least 3 hours. To serve, unmold the mousse onto a platter and cut into the leek wrapping.

Hot hors d'oeuvres are passed on platters decorated with flowers
(clockwise from above left): pork and scallion sticks with plum ketchup;
asparagus tip and prosciutto puffs; lamb spring rolls with curried honey
mustard; and sesame chicken fingers with roasted garlic mayonnaise.

$\mathcal{L}$AMB SPRING ROLLS

·

MAKES 50

I've made these ahead and reheated them, and I've cooked them immediately before serving. Surprisingly, these spring rolls have a better texture when prepared ahead and reheated, making them a perfect party hors d'oeuvre. Ground lamb is used in the filling, but ground lean pork can be substituted. Crunchy iceberg lettuce gives the filling texture.

> 2 tablespoons peanut oil
> 2 large garlic cloves, finely chopped
> 1 pound ground lean lamb
> 6 scallions, white and green parts, finely julienned
> 1 large green pepper, finely julienned
> ½ pound bean sprouts, well drained
> 1 cup finely shredded iceberg lettuce
> 50 spring roll wrappers (see note)
> Vegetable oil, for frying

1. In a skillet over medium-high heat, heat the oil and garlic. Add the lamb and cook until lightly browned, and then add the scallions and green pepper. Sauté for 5 minutes and then stir in the bean sprouts and lettuce. Remove from the heat and allow to cool. (*Filling can be made up to a day in advance up to this point, covered tightly, and refrigerated. Return the mixture to room temperature before proceeding.*)

2. Have a small dish of water to one side. Place a spring roll wrapper on the work surface. Place a generous teaspoonful of the filling on the wrapper about ½ inch from the edge closest to you. Fold the sides (perpendicular to you) over the filling and then carefully roll the wrapper away from you to achieve a short cigarlike shape. Watch as you roll to make sure the filling is tucked in. Dip a finger into the water, wet the edge, and press gently to seal.

3. Repeat, using all the wrappers and filling. Place the assembled spring rolls in a single layer on a platter or baking sheet and keep them covered with a slightly damp cloth until ready to fry.

4. In a large skillet, pour the vegetable oil to a depth of 1 inch. Heat the oil until very hot, about 350°F. on a candy thermometer. Using tongs, place a few spring rolls at a time into the oil and fry until they are lightly browned on all sides, about 5 minutes. Transfer the rolls to absorbent paper to drain and cool.

5. After cooling, the spring rolls can be tightly covered and refrigerated for up to 24 hours or frozen for up to a month. Bring them to room temperature before reheating.

6. Preheat the oven to 375°F. Place the spring rolls on a baking sheet and bake them for 10 minutes, or until heated through and nicely browned. Serve hot with Curried Honey Mustard (recipe follows).

NOTE Spring roll wrappers are available in freezer or produce sections of supermarkets or at oriental or specialty food shops. The quantity in a package is not consistent from maker to maker; I buy them in Chinatown in New York in packages of 50.

$\mathcal{C}$URRIED HONEY MUSTARD

·

MAKES ABOUT 2 HALF-PINTS

In addition to serving this sweet and pungent mustard as a dipping sauce for spring rolls, I like it with simple grilled chicken or chops. Make the mustard at least a week before you want to serve it; it will keep for several months in the refrigerator.

> ¾ cup white wine vinegar
> ¾ cup dry mustard
> 2 tablespoons good-quality curry powder
> ⅔ cup honey
> 2 large egg yolks, at room temperature

1. Place the vinegar in a small saucepan and bring to a boil. Remove the pan from the heat and stir in the mustard and curry powder. Cover and let stand overnight at room temperature.

2. Beat in the honey and egg yolks. Place the pan over low heat, and cook, stirring constantly, until thickened. Pour the mustard into 2 half-pint jars or crocks, cover tightly, and store in the refrigerator.

· · · · · · · · · · · · · · · ·

$\mathcal{R}$ed and $\mathcal{W}$hite $\mathcal{W}$ine $\mathcal{S}$pritzers

Spritzers are light and convivial drinks to serve at cocktail parties. They're also easy to serve—each guest can make his or her own at the bar, mixing sparkling water with red and white wines over ice. I like using some of the flavored bottled waters now on the market. With red wine try orange or cherry flavors; try lemon, lime, or raspberry flavors with white, and add a squeeze of lemon or lime.

· · · · · · · · · · · · · · · ·

Asparagus Tip and Prosciutto Puffs

•

MAKES 60

It may seem extravagant to use only the tips of asparagus for these hors d'oeuvres, but the leftover stalks are perfectly edible later, cut into 1-inch pieces and steamed or stir-fried or used as the base for a soup.

½ pound prosciutto, cut into ½-inch strips
60 2-inch asparagus tips
2 sheets (approximately 1 pound) frozen puff
 pastry, thawed
Dijon mustard

1. Preheat the oven to 425°F.

2. Wrap each asparagus tip with a strip of prosciutto and reserve.

3. Lay one sheet of puff pastry flat on a work surface and brush it lightly with mustard. Cut the pastry into 2-inch squares and place an asparagus tip diagonally on each square. One side corner at a time, roll the pastry around the asparagus, leaving the ends of the asparagus uncovered. Moisten the corners with water to seal. Repeat with the other sheet of pastry and remaining ingredients.

4. Arrange the pastry rolls 1 inch apart on baking sheets. (*Can be prepared up to 24 hours in advance up to this point, covered tightly with plastic wrap, and refrigerated.*) Bake until puffed and nicely browned, 15 to 20 minutes. Transfer to a serving platter, garnish with spring flowers, and serve hot.

Spicy Pork and Scallion Sticks

•

MAKES ABOUT 4 DOZEN

MARINADE
¼ cup dark soy sauce
2 tablespoons molasses
2 tablespoons vegetable oil
¼ cup dry red wine
½ teaspoon cayenne pepper
½ teaspoon ground cumin
3 bunches (about 1 dozen) scallions, green parts
 only, finely chopped (reserve firm bulb parts)

2 pounds pork tenderloin, cut into ½-inch cubes
Firm white bulb parts from 3 bunches scallions
 (see above), cut into 1-inch lengths

1. In a medium bowl, combine the marinade ingredients, add the pork cubes, and toss to blend. Cover and refrigerate, tossing occasionally, for 6 hours or overnight.

2. Soak 4 dozen bamboo skewers in water for 1 hour. Remove the wooden skewers from water. Skewer the meat and white parts of the scallions, alternating 3 cubes of meat and 2 scallion pieces for each skewer. (*Can be made up to 6 hours in advance up to this point. Place skewers on baking sheets, brush with marinade, cover tightly, and refrigerate until 1 hour before serving.*)

3. Preheat the broiler. Loosely cover the bare ends of the skewers with aluminum foil to keep them from scorching. Place the baking sheet under the broiler and broil, turning once, for 5 to 6 minutes on each side, or until pork is browned and cooked through. Transfer to a serving platter decorated with flowers, and serve hot with Plum Ketchup (recipe follows) for dipping.

NOTE These can also be grilled over hot coals, but make sure the skewers have been thoroughly soaked to prevent scorching.

Plum Ketchup

•

MAKES ABOUT 2½ CUPS

2 garlic cloves, very finely chopped
Juice and grated rind of 1 lemon
Juice and grated rind of 1 orange
2 cups damson or beach plum jam
2 teaspoons dry mustard
¼ teaspoon ground cloves
¼ teaspoon ground allspice
¼ teaspoon ground ginger
⅛ teaspoon cayenne pepper
⅓ cup dry red wine

In a heavy saucepan, combine the garlic and juices and simmer over medium heat until the garlic is tender. Add the other ingredients, stir well to blend, and bring to a simmer. Continue cooking, uncovered, stirring occasionally, until the sauce has thickened. Allow to cool, transfer to a covered jar, and store in the refrigerator for up to 3 months.

LEFT: Herb- and scallion-coated cheese roulades are surrounded by blossoms.

LEFT: A basket of chocolate-glazed almond bars and lemon meltaways with strawberries.

OPPOSITE: Tiny upside-down orange-coconut cupcakes are as pretty as spring flowers.

HERBED CHEESE ROULADES

•

MAKES ONE 9-INCH ROULADE

Lying on a bed of lemon leaves and decorated with herbs and tiny flowers, an herbed-cheese roulade is a beautiful addition to any hors d'oeuvre buffet. Here's one place where I allow myself to go a bit overboard with the decoration.

The recipe lists mint for the filling, but other leafy herbs, such as sage or parsley, can be substituted, or try using pungent greens such as watercress or arugula. I've also used combinations of ingredients such as a mixture of chopped sun-dried tomatoes and basil or minced smoked salmon and dill. Make three roulades for this menu.

2 8-ounce packages cream cheese, at room
  temperature
Freshly ground black pepper
1 large bunch mint
3 scallions, white and green parts, finely chopped

1. Place a large square of wax paper on the work surface. Spread the cream cheese into an even layer 9 inches square. Sprinkle the cheese with a generous grinding of pepper. Lightly press a single layer of mint leaves onto the surface, reserving the remaining mint leaves. Cover loosely with another piece of wax paper and refrigerate until partly firm, about 30 minutes.

2. Remove the cheese from the refrigerator. Remove the top piece of wax paper and, using the bottom piece, roll up the cheese like a jelly roll. Chop 3 or 4 of the reserved mint leaves and combine with the scallions. Sprinkle the chopped mixture over the cheese and gently press the herbs into the cheese. Refrigerate the cheese for another 30 minutes, or until completely firm, and then wrap well in fresh wax paper or plastic wrap and store in the refrigerator.

3. To serve, cut the roulade into ¼-inch slices, arrange the slices in an overlapping pattern on a serving platter, and garnish generously with remaining mint. Serve with small thin slices of dark pumpernickel bread or crackers.

MINIATURE ORANGE-COCONUT UPSIDE-DOWN CUPCAKES

•

MAKES 3 DOZEN CUPCAKES

I've always been a sucker for any kind of upside-down cake; this version, in the form of bite-size cupcakes, is always a hit, with its bright and shiny glaze and intense flavor. An added bonus is that these cupcakes can be mixed up and baked in half an hour.

TOPPING
⅓ cup (⅔ stick) butter
⅔ cup orange marmalade
⅔ cup flaked coconut

BATTER
½ cup (1 stick) butter, softened
½ cup sugar
2 large eggs
½ teaspoon vanilla extract
Grated rind of 1 orange
Grated rind of 1 lime
1½ cups all-purpose flour
2 teaspoons baking powder
¼ teaspoon salt
½ cup milk

1. Preheat the oven to 375°F. Melt the butter in a small, heavy saucepan. Drop ½ teaspoonful of melted butter into each cup of a 1½-dozen miniature muffin pan; repeat with 1 teaspoonful marmalade. Sprinkle 1 teaspoon coconut into each cup over the marmalade.

2. To make the batter, cream the butter and sugar together, then beat in the eggs, vanilla, and grated rinds. In a separate bowl, sift together the flour, baking powder, and salt. Stir (do not beat) the dry ingredients into the wet mixture alternately with the milk, stirring until smooth with each addition.

3. Divide the batter evenly among the muffin cups. Bake the cupcakes for 20 to 25 minutes, or until the cake springs back when touched lightly with a finger. Remove the pan from the oven and cool for 5 minutes on a wire rack. Loosen each cupcake with a knife and invert the pan onto the wire rack to cool.

CHOCOLATE-GLAZED ALMOND BARS

•

MAKES 3 DOZEN COOKIES

CRUST
1/3 cup (2/3 stick) butter
2/3 cup sugar
3 large eggs
3 tablespoons all-purpose flour
2/3 cup ground almonds
1/2 teaspoon vanilla extract
1/2 teaspoon almond extract

TOPPING
1/3 cup (2/3 stick) butter
1/2 cup sugar
1/2 cup light corn syrup
2/3 cup sliced almonds

GLAZE
2 ounces semisweet chocolate
2 teaspoons vegetable shortening

1. To make the crust, combine the butter and sugar in a medium bowl and beat well until light and fluffy. Beat in the eggs one at a time and then gradually beat in the flour and ground almonds. Beat in the vanilla and almond extracts.

2. Preheat the oven to 350°F. Lightly butter a jelly-roll pan (approximately 10½ x 15 inches), line it with wax paper, and butter the wax paper. Spread the dough in an even layer in the pan. Bake until the dough is very lightly browned at the edges, about 7 minutes. Remove from the oven.

3. While the crust is baking, combine the topping ingredients in a saucepan over medium heat and cook, stirring constantly, until the sugar dissolves and the mixture comes to a boil. Boil the mixture for 4 more minutes. Spread this mixture over the crust while both are warm.

4. Return the pan to the oven and bake until the topping is golden, about 5 minutes. While the cookies are baking, melt the chocolate and shortening in a double boiler over simmering water.

5. Remove the pan to a wire rack to cool slightly. Using a very small spoon (I use a demitasse spoon for

this), drizzle chocolate over the surface of the cookies —flick your wrist quickly to achieve a spattered effect. While the cookies are still slightly warm, cut into bars approximately 1 x 3 inches. Place the cookies on wire racks to cool completely.

6. Briefly place the cookies in the refrigerator to chill and firm up the chocolate. Remove from the refrigerator and pack the cookies in tins with wax paper between each layer and store in a cool place for up to 1 week.

LEMON MELTAWAYS

•

MAKES ABOUT 6 DOZEN COOKIES

3/4 cup (1½ sticks) butter, softened
3/4 cup sugar
1/4 cup milk
1 large egg
1 tablespoon lemon juice
Grated rind of 1 large lemon
1/2 teaspoon vanilla extract
2 cups all-purpose flour
1 teaspoon baking powder
1/4 teaspoon baking soda
1/4 teaspoon salt
Additional sugar, for coating

1. In a large mixing bowl, cream the butter and sugar together until smooth and fluffy. Beat in the milk and the egg, and then beat in the lemon juice, lemon rind, and vanilla.

2. In a separate bowl, sift together the flour, baking powder, baking soda, and salt. Beat the dry mixture into the wet mixture a third at a time. Cover the bowl with plastic wrap and refrigerate the dough until firm, about 2 hours.

3. Preheat the oven to 350°F. Lightly grease baking sheets.

4. Roll the dough into balls about ½ inch in diameter and then roll each ball in sugar. Place the sugar-coated balls about 2 inches apart on the baking sheets and bake for about 8 minutes, or until the edges are lightly browned. Cool the cookies on wire racks and store in tightly covered containers in a cool place for up to 2 weeks.

First Dinner on the Porch

for 2

♦

Menu

Spring Greens Soup

· · ·

Sautéed Veal Medallions with Wild Mushrooms and Herbs

Scalloped New Potatoes with Stilton and Sage

Steamed Asparagus and Sugar Snap Peas with Lemon Butter

· · ·

Early Lettuce Salad with Shredded Scallions

· · ·

Warm Pineapple Bread Puddings

ABOVE: A light soup of pureed green spring vegetables is garnished with sliced radishes and mint leaves. BELOW: The main course is a celebration of spring ingredients.

There's nothing more relaxing than sitting outdoors on a warm spring evening, breathing in the cool, fresh, sweet-smelling air. Every year I look forward to that first evening when the weather's just warm enough for dinner to be served on the screened-in porch, even if sitting outdoors requires a sweater. To ward off any evening chill, this dinner starts with a warm soup and ends with a warm dessert; hurricane-shaded candles and romantic old Frank Sinatra recordings help add a cozy glow.

GETTING READY The soup can be prepared a day in advance and gently rewarmed just before serving.

Early in the day get the pineapple bread puddings ready for baking, cover tightly with plastic wrap, and refrigerate; return to room temperature before baking.

About two hours before serving, start the scalloped potatoes or, if necessary, make them early in the day and reheat them in a moderate oven for twenty minutes.

The veal sauté and the vegetables should be cooked just before serving, but neither dish requires much work. Start preparing the veal twenty to twenty-five minutes before serving. Steam the vegetables while cooking the veal.

When the potatoes come out of the oven, adjust the oven heat, and put in the pineapple bread puddings. Whip the cream right after they come out of the oven.

BEVERAGES A medium-bodied red wine, such as a Beaujolais or a Zinfandel, or try a full-bodied white. Serve small glasses of Port after dessert.

SPRING GREENS SOUP

•

SERVES 6

A combination of green spring vegetables—leaf lettuce, peas, cucumbers, and scallions—enriched by fresh herbs and yogurt—gives this pretty soup its delicate yet complex flavor. I always make a bigger batch of this soup than this menu requires; it's delicious served cold for lunch the next day.

  3 tablespoons butter
  3 scallions, white and green parts, coarsely
    chopped
  2 cups shredded leaf lettuce
  2 cups fresh peas or thawed frozen peas
  2 large cucumbers, peeled, seeded, and chopped
  4 cups chicken stock
  1 tablespoon finely chopped mint
  1 tablespoon finely chopped parsley
  1 tablespoon finely chopped basil
  1 cup plain yogurt
  Salt
  Hot pepper sauce
  Mint sprigs, for garnish
  Thinly sliced radishes, for garnish

1. In a large, heavy saucepan over low heat, melt the butter. Add the scallions and lettuce, and sauté until wilted, about 2 minutes. Add the peas, cucumbers, and chicken stock; turn up the heat and bring to a boil. Reduce the heat and simmer for 5 minutes, or until the vegetables are tender.

2. Remove the pan from the heat and stir in the herbs and yogurt. Puree the mixture in batches in the bowl of a food processor fitted with the steel chopping blade. Season to taste with salt and a few drops of hot pepper sauce. *(Can be made up to a day in advance, covered, and refrigerated.)*

3. Return the soup to the saucepan and reheat over medium-low heat to just below the simmering point. Or serve the soup chilled. Serve in soup plates, with each serving garnished with a few sprigs of mint and a radish slice or two.

SAUTÉED VEAL MEDALLIONS WITH WILD MUSHROOMS AND HERBS

•

SERVES 2

Veal, mushrooms, and herbs seem to have a natural affinity for one another, so I don't complicate things here in this simple sauté.

  2 shallots, finely chopped
  1 large garlic clove, crushed
  2 tablespoons olive oil
  4 veal loin medallions, 3 to 4 ounces each
  ¼ cup Chardonnay or other dry white wine
  2 tablespoons finely chopped parsley
  2 teaspoons fresh rosemary leaves or ½ teaspoon
    dried rosemary
  Freshly ground black pepper
  4 shiitake mushrooms or morels, thinly sliced (see
    note)

1. In a heavy skillet, sauté the shallots and garlic in the oil for 5 minutes over medium heat. Turn the heat to medium-high, add the veal medallions, and quickly brown them on both sides.

2. Pour the wine over the veal. Add the herbs and season the veal liberally with pepper. Turn the heat down to medium and add the mushrooms. For medium-rare veal, simmer for about 8 minutes, turning the medallions once, until most of the liquid in the pan has evaporated. For more well done veal, cook a minute or two more, depending on individual taste.

3. Place 2 veal medallions on each plate, spoon the mushrooms and pan juices over the veal, and serve immediately.

NOTE If fresh wild mushrooms are unavailable, substitute 1 ounce dried wild mushrooms soaked for 2 hours in the white wine; strain the wine before using.

Scalloped New Potatoes with Stilton and Sage

SERVES 2

Scalloped potatoes gone to heaven!

1 large garlic clove, crushed
2 tablespoons butter
½ pound small new potatoes, thinly sliced
  crosswise (do not peel)
1 tablespoon all-purpose flour, approximately
Salt and freshly ground black pepper
2 teaspoons finely chopped sage
¼ cup crumbled Stilton
⅔ cup half-and-half

1. Preheat the oven to 350°F. Rub the inside of a small, shallow casserole or gratin pan liberally with the garlic and then grease the pan with 1 tablespoon of the butter. Discard the garlic clove.

2. Layer about a third of the potato slices in the pan and sprinkle lightly with flour and salt, and generously with pepper. Add a third of the sage and Stilton and pour a third of the half-and-half over all. Repeat this procedure twice. Press the potatoes down into the cream with the back of a spoon. Dot with the remaining butter.

3. Put the pan on a small baking sheet and place in the oven. Bake until the potatoes are very tender and the surface is nicely browned, about 1½ hours.

NOTE This dish is great for serving a crowd as well. The quantities don't have to be multiplied precisely; follow the basic method here and make a big panful.

Steamed Asparagus and Sugar Snap Peas with Lemon Butter

SERVES 2

¼ pound thin asparagus, cut into 1-inch pieces
¼ pound sugar snap peas
1 tablespoon butter
Juice of ½ lemon

Place the vegetables in a vegetable steamer over simmering water, cover, and steam 5 minutes, or until crisp-tender and vivid green. Drain the vegetables and rinse briefly under cold running water to stop the cooking. Return the vegetables to the pan and add the butter and lemon juice. Toss well and serve.

Early Lettuce Salad with Shredded Scallions

SERVES 2

The early leaf lettuce that comes up at the first sign of spring is wonderfully tender. If the small leaves are broken off when picked, new leaves will sprout in just a few weeks. These leaves are delicate and flavorful as well, and I like to add just a bit of shredded scallion and a drizzle of a simple white wine vinaigrette.

If you plant your scallions on Saint Patrick's Day, following the tradition my father and all our neighbors followed when I was growing up, weather permitting, the first ones will be ready before the end of the April rains.

4 cups leaf lettuce, torn into bite-size pieces
4 scallions, green part only
Edible flowers such as pansies or nasturtiums, for
  garnish
White Wine Vinaigrette (page 220)

Divide the lettuce between two salad plates. Cut the scallion greens into 2-inch lengths and then shred them lengthwise. Scatter the scallions and flowers over the lettuce and serve. Pass a cruet of dressing so each guest can dress his or her own.

Fixing Fiddlehead Ferns

As an alternative vegetable, you might want to try fiddlehead ferns, one of spring's special treats. Fiddleheads have a short season in late spring, and they can be a bit difficult to find even then. When I'm able to get my hands on some, I tend not to fiddle with Mother Nature when I prepare them; I want to really taste their delicate, earthy flavor. Here's a simple way to fix them:

Trim the stem ends of the fiddleheads and pull away any bits of brown membrane, then wash the fiddleheads well under cold running water. Drop the fiddleheads into boiling water and cook for 1 minute—no more. Quickly drain the fiddleheads and rinse them briefly with cold running water to stop the cooking. Return the fiddleheads to the hot saucepan, then add a dab of butter and a squeeze of lemon juice.

$\mathcal{W}$ARM PINEAPPLE BREAD PUDDINGS

•

MAKES 2

Butter, softened
Granulated sugar
4 slices good-quality, firm white bread
2 tablespoons dark rum
2 tablespoons firmly packed dark brown sugar
¼ teaspoon ground cinnamon
Pinch of grated nutmeg
2 teaspoons lemon juice
1 cup cubed ripe pineapple
1 tablespoon butter, melted and cooled
Unsweetened whipped cream or Vanilla Bean Ice
    Cream (page 221)

1. Preheat the oven to 375°F. Generously butter two 8-ounce ovenproof glass pudding dishes or ceramic ramekins and sprinkle the bottom of the dishes lightly with granulated sugar. Butter the bread on both sides and then cut it into cubes. Using half the bread cubes, place a single layer in the bottom of each dish.

2. In a medium mixing bowl, combine the rum, brown sugar, spices, and lemon juice. Add the pineapple and melted butter and toss well to coat. Layer half the pineapple mixture into the dishes, followed by the remaining bread cubes and then the remaining pineapple. Sprinkle lightly with additional granulated sugar.

3. Place the dishes in a shallow baking pan and pour hot water into the pan about halfway up the sides of the dishes. Place the pan in the oven and bake about 30 minutes, or until the puddings are nicely browned. Serve warm with dabs of whipped cream or Vanilla Bean Ice Cream (page 221).

ABOVE LEFT: A spring salad garnished with tiny pansies looks wonderful on this flower-rimmed plate. LEFT: A warm, fragrant pineapple bread pudding ends the meal.

Dinner in the Harbor

for 6
◆
Menu

Cape Cod Sunsets   Beer

Linguiça and Cheddar Corn Sticks

• • •

Cape Cod Chili with Simple Guacamole

Romaine and Grapefruit Salad

• • •

Banana Chip Ice Cream

Tarheels

Above: Back in the harbor at sunset, we served linguiça and Cheddar corn sticks with dark beer on the deck.

A few years ago, Phil and Sally Drew, who dock their beautiful seventy-year-old motor yacht, the *Valjora*, on Cape Cod, invited me to join them for the first day trip of the season. The *Valjora* has a well-equipped, roomy galley, with the original bronze gas stove and all the original fittings, so when we returned to Rock Harbor, where she docks, I volunteered to cook the celebratory dinner.

Spring evenings can get pretty cool at the water's edge, so a hearty dinner was in order. I went "fishing" at the harbor fish market after we docked, and found the makings for a spicy seafood chili for the main course.

While the chili was cooking we enjoyed a spectacular Cape Cod sunset on the aft deck with corn sticks livened with Cheddar cheese and linguiça, a piquant sausage made popular years ago by Portuguese immigrants who settled on the Cape. (We washed the corn sticks down with dark beer, but on a balmier evening I might serve Cape Cod Sunsets, a tequila-cranberry-orange concoction; the recipe is also included.) Down in the *Valjora*'s cozy mahogany-trimmed dining sa-

loon we tackled the chili and the salad, and then in the main cabin we settled down with dessert and coffee as the cool salt-sea air settled over the peaceful harbor.

GETTING READY Bake the cookies up to a week in advance and store them in a tin in a cool dry place. The ice cream, too, can be made up to a week in advance; transfer it from the freezer to the refrigerator to allow it to soften slightly for about 15 minutes before serving.

The chili can be prepared up to step 2 a day in advance. Reheat the sauce about half an hour before serving and add the seafood.

The corn sticks should be prepared no more than a few hours ahead.

The salad ingredients can be prepared early in the day, wrapped well, and refrigerated until needed. The dressing, too, can be prepared in advance. Dress the salad just before serving.

BEVERAGES Serve beer (or Cape Cod Sunsets) with the corn sticks. With the main course, continue with beer or serve a Rioja or Chianti. I like strong black coffee or espresso with this dessert.

Cape Cod Sunsets

•

MAKES 1 DRINK

For each drink, pour 1 jigger (1½ ounces) tequila into an ice-filled highball glass. Fill halfway with cranberry juice cocktail, fill to three-fourths full with orange juice, and top with a splash of soda. Garnish with an orange slice and a swizzle stick and serve, allowing each guest to stir his or her own.

Linguiça and Cheddar Corn Sticks

•

MAKES APPROXIMATELY 2 DOZEN

Delicious with an icy beer or a cool drink as the sun goes over the yardarm. Linguiça, a highly seasoned Portuguese sausage, is a great favorite down on the Cape. If linguiça is unavailable, substitute chorizo or pepperoni.

¾ cup stone-ground yellow cornmeal
¼ cup all-purpose flour
1 tablespoon baking powder
1 teaspoon salt
3 dashes hot pepper sauce
1 cup sour cream
2 large eggs
⅔ cup vegetable shortening, melted and cooled
1¼ cups raw corn kernels or 1 10-ounce package frozen corn kernels, thawed
¼ pound sharp Cheddar, grated
½ cup diced green or red pepper
¾ cup diced cooked linguiça, chorizo, or pepperoni

1. Preheat the oven to 375°F. Lightly grease 2 corn stick pans (or one 1-dozen muffin pan).

2. In a mixing bowl, combine the cornmeal, flour, baking powder, and salt and stir together with a fork until well blended. Add the hot pepper sauce, sour cream, eggs, and shortening and beat until smooth. Fold in the corn, cheese, pepper, and sausage.

3. Fill the pans with the batter until almost full. Bake about 25 to 30 minutes or until the edges are well browned and a toothpick or cake tester inserted in the center comes out clean. Serve hot or at room temperature.

Cape Cod Chili with Simple Guacamole

•

SERVES 6

Growing up in Ohio, I rarely had fresh seafood, so when I moved to the East Coast, I went seafood crazy. Over the years, I've experimented with a lot of different seafood dishes, and this seafood chili stew is one of my favorites.

1½ cups cooked, dried, or canned black beans, rinsed and drained
¼ cup olive oil
3 large garlic cloves, finely chopped
1 medium onion, chopped
¼ cup finely chopped celery
1 large red pepper, seeded and chopped
2 large ripe tomatoes, seeded and chopped
1 cup tomato sauce
4 tablespoons tomato paste
1 cup dry red wine
1 cup clam juice
1 tablespoon fresh oregano leaves or ¾ teaspoon dried oregano
1 teaspoon fresh thyme leaves or ¼ teaspoon dried thyme
1 tablespoon ground dried mild chili (not mixed chili powder)
1 teaspoon ground cumin
¼ teaspoon cayenne pepper (or more to taste)
1 pound cod filets, cut into 1-inch chunks
1 pound large shrimp, peeled and deveined
1 pound bay scallops
1½ dozen little neck or cherrystone clams

Steamed long-grain white rice
Tortilla chips
Simple Guacamole (recipe follows)

1. Place the olive oil in the bottom of a Dutch oven or large, heavy saucepan and place over medium heat. Add the garlic, onion, celery, and red pepper and sauté until the vegetables are tender, about 12 minutes. Add the tomatoes, tomato sauce and paste, wine, clam juice, herbs, and spices.

2. Bring the mixture to a simmer and cook, uncovered, until slightly reduced and thickened, about 30 minutes. (*Can be prepared ahead up to this point, cooled, covered, and refrigerated; reheat before proceeding.*)

3. Add the cod, shrimp, and scallops and return to a simmer. Cover loosely and cook until the shrimp turn pink and the cod and scallops are opaque, about 15 minutes. Meanwhile, steam the clams in shallow simmering water in a separate pot until they open, about 10 minutes.

4. Stir the black beans into the chili and simmer 2 or 3 minutes longer to heat through. Serve the chili over steamed rice and garnish each serving with a few clams, tortilla chips, and generous dollops of Simple Guacamole.

VARIATION Any firm white fish can be substituted for the cod. Try different seafood combinations in this recipe; for example, stir in chunks of cooked lobster meat a few minutes before serving, or use mussels in addition to or instead of the clams.

SIMPLE GUACAMOLE
•
MAKES ABOUT 2 CUPS

2 soft ripe Haas avocados
1 large garlic clove, finely chopped
Juice of 1 lime
½ teaspoon salt
Dash of hot pepper sauce

Cut the avocados in half lengthwise and remove the pits. Scoop the flesh into a mixing bowl and mash coarsely. Add the remaining ingredients and mix well. Cover with plastic wrap pressed directly onto the guacamole and refrigerate until needed.

VARIATIONS When making guacamole to use as a dip, add any of the following: 2 seeded and chopped medium tomatoes; 1 finely chopped, small hot chili pepper; 1 tablespoon chopped coriander.

"Nobody of any real culture ever talks nowadays about the beauty of a sunset. Sunsets are quite old-fashioned. They belong to the time when Turner was the last note in art."
Oscar Wilde

ROMAINE AND GRAPEFRUIT SALAD
•
SERVES 6

This simple salad is especially refreshing after a spicy main course.

1 grapefruit, peeled
4 cups romaine, washed and cut into ¼-inch shreds
½ small red onion, thinly sliced and separated into rings
Balsamic Vinaigrette (page 220)
Freshly ground black pepper

Cut the grapefruit horizontally into ½-inch-thick slices and separate each slice into wedges along the sectional divisions. Place the romaine in a serving bowl and top with the grapefruit and onion. Just before serving, drizzle the dressing over the salad and add a grinding of black pepper.

BANANA CHIP ICE CREAM
•
MAKES ABOUT 1½ QUARTS

2 large eggs, separated
1 cup mashed ripe bananas (2 to 3 bananas)
2 teaspoons lemon juice
¼ cup firmly packed light brown sugar
¼ teaspoon salt
⅛ teaspoon ground cinnamon
⅓ cup milk
1 cup heavy cream
1 teaspoon vanilla extract
½ cup dried sliced bananas, crushed

1. Beat the egg yolks until thick and lemon-colored. Add the mashed bananas and lemon juice and beat until smooth. Add the brown sugar, salt, cinnamon, and milk and beat until smooth.

2. In a separate bowl, beat the egg whites until stiff but not dry. In a separate bowl, beat the cream until soft peaks form. Fold the egg whites and cream into the banana mixture. Fold in the dried bananas.

3. Freeze in an ice cream maker according to the manufacturer's instructions.

𝒯ARHEELS

MAKES ABOUT 2½ DOZEN COOKIES

Chewy and chocolaty, these also have a few surprises: coconut, rum-soaked raisins, and oatmeal. The recipe comes from my friend Ron Spainhour, who hails from Winston-Salem in the Tarheel state.

¾ *cup raisins*
¼ *cup rum or brandy*
¼ *cup (½ stick) butter, softened*
¼ *cup vegetable shortening*
1 *cup firmly packed light brown sugar*
1 *large egg, lightly beaten*
3 *ounces semisweet chocolate, melted and cooled*
1 *teaspoon vanilla extract*
1 *cup all-purpose flour*
½ *teaspoon baking powder*
½ *teaspoon baking soda*
½ *teaspoon salt*
1 *cup shredded coconut*
1½ *cups quick-cooking oats*

1. Preheat the oven to 325°F. Grease baking sheets. Place the raisins and rum in a small bowl and let stand while making the dough.

2. In a mixing bowl, cream the butter, shortening, and brown sugar together until light and fluffy. Beat in the egg and then beat in the chocolate and vanilla.

3. In a separate bowl, stir the flour, baking powder, baking soda, and salt with a fork until well blended. Gradually beat this mixture into the butter-sugar mixture until well blended. Stir in the coconut and oats. Drain the raisins and stir them into the dough.

4. Using your fingers, roll tablespoonfuls of dough into balls and place the balls about 2 inches apart on the baking sheets. Flatten each ball slightly with the back of a fork. Bake until the edges are browned and a toothpick or cake tester inserted comes out clean, 12 to 15 minutes. Remove to wire racks to cool and store in tightly covered containers in a cool place.

OPPOSITE: A spicy seafood chili stew is served on an appropriate old restaurant china plate with rice, tostadas, and a dollop of guacamole in a clam shell.

TOP RIGHT: The table is set for dinner in the cozy, lantern-lit saloon. ABOVE RIGHT: A salad of romaine and grapefruit with balsamic vinaigrette complements the main course. RIGHT: Tarheel cookies with banana chip ice cream, served in a sailboat-decorated jelly glass from the forties.

WEDDING REHEARSAL BUFFET DINNER

for 20

◆

Menu

SESAME-PARMESAN RIBBONS

· · ·

ZINFANDEL-AND-GINGER-GLAZED HAM

POTATO AND PEA SALAD WITH MINT PESTO

JULIENNED BEET AND CARROT SALAD

STEAMED GREEN BEANS IN TOMATO VINAIGRETTE

· · ·

STRAWBERRY SEASON TRIFLE

I always seem to get called into service when a friend or relation gets married; if it's not the wedding reception itself (when someone close to me gets married I like to be a guest sharing the wedding and the reception rather than the one who's busy masterminding the event), I'm the one who plans other events during the big weekend.

As far as I'm concerned, the most enjoyable part of a wedding weekend is the rehearsal dinner. The rehearsal itself is usually good for a few laughs, and the dinner allows the two families and the couple's close friends to relax and let their hair down before the well-plotted and emotionally charged wedding day. And there's always that wonderful sense of anticipation in the air, creating a magical mood.

This easy menu was planned for a wedding party of eight with a dozen relatives thrown in. (If you've got a larger crowd to feed, the ham will serve plenty, and the salads and dessert can easily be multiplied.)

GETTING READY Just about everything here can be done in advance. All that's required before serving is arranging the food on the buffet table.

Make the puff pastry ribbons up to a week in advance and store them in tightly covered containers in a cool, dry place.

The ham should be cooked a day in advance. It can even be glazed and baked a day ahead, or early on the day it is to be served; bring to room temperature or reheat it before serving.

The beet and carrot salad can also be made a day in advance.

Early in the day, make the custard for the trifle and refrigerate it.

The potato and pea salad and the green bean salad can be made early in the afternoon.

Assemble the trifle no more than four hours in advance and top with the whipped cream preferably just before serving but no more than two hours ahead.

BEVERAGES We started off with a Champagne toast to the parents of the bridal couple as well as to the bride and groom themselves. Offer a choice of a red such as Gamay Beaujolais or a Zinfandel or a fruity white such as a Johannisberg Riesling with the main course, and have another round of toasts and Champagne with dessert.

SESAME-PARMESAN RIBBONS

·

MAKES ABOUT 5 DOZEN

Here's an easy-to-make, fast-to-disappear cocktail hour nibble. I use frozen puff pastry more often than not; if you want to make your own, Julia Child's is the best recipe I've come across. Bake these the day you're serving them if you can.

2 pounds frozen puff pastry, thawed in the refrigerator
¼ cup grated Parmesan, approximately
¼ cup sesame seeds, approximately

1. Preheat the oven to 375°F. Very lightly grease baking sheets.

2. Unfold a sheet of puff pastry on a floured pastry

board or a wax paper–lined cutting board. Sprinkle the pastry dough with Parmesan and sesame seeds and gently pat them into the pastry. Turn the dough over and repeat.

3. Cut the dough into ¼-inch-wide strips about 1 foot long. Lift 1 strip at a time and twist it 3 or 4 times before placing on a baking sheet. (*Strips can be prepared well in advance up to this point, frozen on baking sheets, and then gathered together and wrapped tightly for storing in the freezer.*)

4. Bake until golden brown, about 15 minutes. Serve hot or transfer to wire racks to cool and serve at room temperature.

ONION AND PEPPER PUFF-PASTRY STRAWS— Eliminate the cheese and seeds and substitute finely chopped onion and coarsely ground black pepper.

OTHER VARIATIONS Use caraway or poppy seeds rather than sesame seeds. For a sweet version use finely chopped nuts, grated semisweet chocolate, and a sprinkling of cinnamon sugar; or try a combination of finely chopped nuts.

ZINFANDEL- AND GINGER-GLAZED HAM
·
SERVES 20, WITH LEFTOVERS

While Dorothy Parker may have described a ham and two people as eternity, I describe a ham and *twenty* people as good common sense. I've sung the praises of hams before and given basic instructions for cooking them, but just in case, this recipe includes the instructions again. Don't forget that if you're using an uncooked ham, you need to start it at least 24 hours before serving. If you're using a precooked ham, skip steps 1 and 2.

1 smoked ham, 12 to 14 pounds
1 cup Zinfandel or other dry red wine
1 teaspoon ground cloves

GLAZE
1 6-ounce grape juice concentrate, thawed
1 cup Zinfandel or other dry red wine
½ cup firmly packed dark brown sugar
½ cup finely chopped gingerroot

Small bunches of red grapes, for garnish

1. Using a stiff brush, scrub the ham, then place it in a large pot with just enough cold water to cover. Cover the pot and soak overnight at room temperature.

2. Drain the ham well and rinse it, then return it to the pot and cover with cold water again. Stir in the cup of Zinfandel and ground cloves. Place on the stove and bring the liquid to a simmer. Simmer, loosely covered, for 20 minutes a pound, or until the ham reaches an internal temperature of 150°F. Add water as needed to keep the ham covered during cooking.

3. When the ham is cooked, allow to cool enough to handle easily. Remove it from the water and, with a sharp knife, remove the tough rind and carve away almost all the outer fat, leaving only a ⅛-inch layer. (*The ham can be prepared ahead up to this point. When cooled completely, wrap in foil or plastic wrap and refrigerate. Bring to room temperature and unwrap before baking and glazing.*)

4. To make the glaze, stir the grape juice concentrate, Zinfandel, brown sugar, and gingerroot in a small heavy saucepan. Place over medium-high heat, bring to a simmer, and cook until thick and syrupy, about 10 minutes.

5. Preheat the oven to 350°F. Place the ham on a rack in a shallow roasting pan, flatter side down. Diagonally score the layer of fat, being careful not to cut into the meat itself. Brush the ham liberally with glaze.

6. Bake the ham, basting and brushing with additional glaze every 20 minutes or so, for about 10 minutes a pound, or until it is heated through and well glazed and browned. Serve the ham warm or at room temperature, cut into thin slices and garnished with bunches of red grapes.

*"There is no love sincerer
than the love of food."*
George Bernard Shaw

Chinese paper lanterns on the
porch and torches on the lawn
gave our party a happy glow.
The buffet is laid out on a pretty
violet- and ribbon-strewn printed
tablecloth from the late forties.

These vibrant salads are perfect for serving a crowd (top to bottom): Steamed green beans in tomato vinaigrette, julienned beet and carrot salad with an orange-flavored dressing, and potato and pea salad with mint pesto.

ABOVE: The plaster bride and groom from the groom's parents' own wedding cake and an heirloom Staffordshire anniversary bowl from the parents of the bride were surprise pre-wedding gifts after a Champagne toast.

RIGHT: A spectacular fresh strawberry trifle, mounded with whipped cream and topped with toasted almonds and huge whole berries, is a festive dessert.

Potato and Pea Salad with Mint Pesto

SERVES 20

Potato salad and ham are longtime partners, and I suppose I could eat good old all-American potato salad —the classic with mayo, celery, and onions—just about any time. But every once in a while I like a change of pace. This is a perfect warm-weather version; it has no mayonnaise to worry about spoiling.

5 pounds small red new potatoes
¼ cup red wine vinegar
1 cup arugula or watercress
½ cup basil leaves
½ cup mint leaves
2 garlic cloves
⅔ cup olive oil
2 10-ounce packages frozen peas, thawed (see note)
1 medium red onion, coarsely chopped
2 yellow peppers, cut into thin strips
½ cup coarsely chopped pecans

1. Put the potatoes in a large pot with salted water to cover and place over high heat. Boil the potatoes until tender but still firm, about 20 minutes. Drain the potatoes, and allow them to rest until they're just cool enough to handle.

2. Meanwhile, combine the vinegar, arugula, basil, mint, and garlic in the bowl of a food processor fitted with the steel chopping blade. Process until the mixture is well blended and the garlic is finely chopped, about 30 seconds. With the processor still running, slowly add the oil through the feed tube, continuing to process until all the oil is incorporated and the mixture is smooth.

3. Cut the still-warm potatoes into quarters and place them in a large bowl. Add the peas, onion, yellow peppers, and pecans. Spoon the dressing over the vegetables and toss well to blend. Cover and refrigerate up to a day in advance. Bring to room temperature before serving.

NOTE Frozen peas work perfectly well in this recipe, but if you want to be a purist, by all means go ahead and substitute 3 cups cooked fresh peas.

Julienned Beet and Carrot Salad

SERVES 20

This vibrant salad, with its orange-flavored dressing, goes especially well with ham.

⅓ cup walnut oil
⅓ cup vegetable oil
Juice and grated rind of 1 large orange
Salt and freshly ground black pepper
2 pounds beets, cooked, peeled, and julienned (see note)
2 pounds carrots, peeled, julienned, and steamed 10 minutes
5 or 6 scallions, green and white parts, cut into 2-inch lengths and julienned

1. Combine the oils, orange juice, and orange rind in a small jar, cover, and shake well. Season with salt and pepper to taste.

2. Place the beets, carrots, and scallions in a large bowl. Pour the dressing over the vegetables and toss. Cover and let stand 2 hours before serving. (*Can be made up to a day in advance, covered, and refrigerated; return to room temperature before serving.*)

NOTE The easiest and least messy way to cook the beets is to place them, unpeeled, in a shallow baking pan and roast at 325°F until tender, 45 minutes to 1 hour depending on their size.

"After a good dinner one can forgive anybody, even one's own relations."
Oscar Wilde

Steamed Green Beans in Tomato Vinaigrette

• SERVES 20

3 pounds green beans, trimmed
⅓ cup olive oil
1 medium onion, chopped
1 large garlic clove, finely chopped
3 plum tomatoes, seeded and coarsely chopped
4 bay leaves
1 teaspoon capers
1 tablespoon lemon juice
Salt and freshly ground black pepper

1. Steam the beans until just tender, but no longer crunchy, about 12 minutes.

2. Combine the oil, onion, and garlic in a medium skillet and sauté over medium heat until the vegetables are transparent, about 5 minutes. Stir in the tomatoes, bay leaves, capers, and lemon juice; bring to a simmer and cook 5 minutes longer. Season to taste with salt and pepper.

3. Pour the dressing over the green beans and toss. Cover and let stand for a few hours before serving. *(Can be made up to 2 days in advance and refrigerated; return to room temperature before serving.)*

Strawberry Season Trifle

• SERVES 20

Trifle is one of my favorite treats at Christmastime, but there's no reason why trifle can't be a treat in summertime, too, when fresh fruits are abundant. By cooking a fruit-flavored liqueur into a syrup, the alcohol evaporates, leaving only a subtle flavor, so you can serve this to the kids, too. There may be a lot of steps here, but 90 percent of the work can be done well in advance—and the results are well worth the effort.

CUSTARD
1¼ cups sugar
¾ cup all-purpose flour
½ teaspoon salt
4 cups milk
8 large egg yolks
2 teaspoons vanilla extract

BERRIES
5 pints strawberries
¾ cup Chambord liqueur
¾ cup sugar

1 loaf day-old pound cake cut into ¼-inch slices
2 cups heavy cream
½ cup sliced almonds, toasted

1. To prepare the custard, combine the sugar, flour, and salt in the top of a double boiler. Stir in the milk, place the mixture over simmering water, and bring to just below the simmering point.

2. While the milk mixture is heating, beat the egg yolks in a mixing bowl until they are thick and pale yellow in color. Gradually pour the hot milk mixture into the eggs, beating continuously.

3. Pour the mixture back into the top of the double boiler and cook, stirring continuously, until the custard has thickened and thickly coats the spoon. *Do not allow the custard to simmer at any point.*

4. Remove the top of the double boiler from the heat and dip it into a large bowl of cold water to stop the custard from cooking any further. Beat the custard briskly for 5 minutes to help it cool rapidly; then beat in the vanilla. Allow the custard to cool and then cover tightly and chill. *(Can be made up to a day ahead and stored in the refrigerator.)*

5. To prepare the berries, first reserve ½ cup for decorating the trifle. Hull and halve the remaining berries and place them in a bowl. Combine the liqueur and sugar in a small saucepan over medium-high heat and bring to a simmer. Continue simmering for a few minutes, until the mixture is thick and syrupy. Remove from the heat, allow to cool 5 minutes, and then pour the syrup over the berries. When the mixture is cool, cover and let stand in the refrigerator for a few hours or overnight.

6. To assemble the trifle, use a large, clear glass bowl. Arrange a single layer of cake slices in the bottom of the bowl, and then spoon about one-fourth of the berry mixture over the cake, followed by one-fourth of the custard. Repeat until all of the ingredients are used up, except the reserved berries. *(Can be assembled up to 4 hours before serving, covered tightly, and refrigerated.)*

7. No more than 2 hours before serving, whip the cream and mound it over the top of the trifle. Just before serving, arrange the reserved berries on the trifle and sprinkle the toasted almonds over all.

S U M M E R

A SIMPLE CAMPFIRE SUPPER

for 6

•

Menu

OHIO SWEET CORN GAZPACHO

PAN-GRILLED SMOKED MOZZARELLA AND
TOMATO SANDWICHES ON
HERB AND GARLIC BATTER BREAD

• • •

GRANDMA WYNN'S BLACKBERRY DUMPLINGS

S'MORES

Every summer I'm lucky enough to wangle a weekend invitation to an enchanting old lakeside camp hidden away up in the wilds of the Berkshire Mountains in western Massachusetts, where the loudest sounds heard are the squawking of geese flying overhead in the daytime and the chirping of crickets at night. The cabin itself is rustic; the perfect place to get away from all the craziness of everyday life. There's no electricity and no hot water, and the only bow to the twentieth century is a small gas stove and a tiny gas-operated refrigerator.

Despite the lack of modern conveniences, I always volunteer to take on some of the cooking chores. This easy-to-prepare menu, with what little cooking there is, is done over an open wood fire just outside the cabin. The main course is composed of a cold soup and simple pan-grilled sandwiches. Warm blackberry dumplings washed down with hot coffee follow after the sun disappears beyond the lake and the cool evening air settles in. And then, as the fire crackles and burns down, we start telling ghost stories.

GETTING READY The bread can be prepared a day in advance, since it is being used to make grilled sandwiches. Or make the bread well in advance and freeze it; it can be thawed a day ahead if need be.

The soup is best prepared a day or two ahead of time. For picnics, transport it in an insulated jug or a cooler.

The sandwiches should be grilled just before serving, but assembling and cooking them takes no more than fifteen minutes or so.

The blackberry dumplings should be freshly made, but they're quite simple to do: start them about forty minutes before serving.

BEVERAGES A decent dry red jug wine is just fine with the soup and sandwiches. Beer is a good alternative to the wine. With dessert, serve a pot of coffee cooked over an open fire.

OHIO SWEET CORN GAZPACHO

•

SERVES 6

This recipe came about when, on the spur of the moment, I invited my neighbors over for supper and had to make do with what was on hand. I didn't have quite enough of the ingredients that go into a traditional gazpacho, but I had a couple ears of just-picked local corn. I seasoned the soup much the same way Mom seasons her piquant corn relish, hence the name. I've been making this soup ever since.

1 cup chicken or beef stock
2 tablespoons cider vinegar
2 tablespoons vegetable oil
1 teaspoon sugar
1 large garlic clove
1 large onion, coarsely chopped
1 large green pepper, coarsely chopped
2 cucumbers, peeled, seeded, and coarsely
  chopped
4 large ripe tomatoes, peeled, seeded, and coarsely
  chopped
2 cups cooked corn kernels (3 to 4 ears)
¼ teaspoon celery seeds
Salt
Hot pepper sauce
Parsley, for garnish

1. Place all the ingredients except the corn, celery seeds, salt, and hot pepper sauce in the bowl of a food processor fitted with the steel chopping blade and process until coarsely pureed. There should still be some recognizable bits of vegetables.

2. Transfer the mixture to a bowl or large jar and stir in the corn and celery seeds. Season to taste with salt and a few generous dashes of hot pepper sauce. Cover the soup and chill for a few hours before serving to allow the flavors to blend. Serve in mugs and garnish each serving with a big sprig of parsley.

$\mathcal{H}$ERB AND GARLIC BATTER BREAD
•
MAKES ONE 9 X 5 X 3-INCH LOAF

This is a no-work bread for those days when you don't want to spend a lot of time kneading. Fresh herbs are what makes it special, so when they're not available, or on those days when I don't want to bother doing any work at all, I skip the whole thing and use a good store-bought white or wheat bread for sandwiches instead.

For making grilled sandwiches, the bread can be baked a day or two in advance.

4 to 4½ cups all-purpose flour
2 tablespoons sugar
1 teaspoon salt
¼ teaspoon freshly ground black pepper
2 packages active dry yeast
1 cup milk
½ cup water
3 tablespoons butter
2 large eggs, lightly beaten
2 tablespoons chopped basil
1 tablespoon oregano
3 tablespoons snipped chives
2 large garlic cloves, very finely chopped

1. In a large mixing bowl, sift together 1 cup of the flour, the sugar, salt, pepper, and yeast. Combine the milk, water, and butter in a small, heavy saucepan over low heat, and heat until the butter is melted. With an electric mixer, gradually beat the liquid mixture into the dry mixture for 2 minutes. Add the eggs, herbs, and garlic and beat just until incorporated.

2. Beat in 1 more cup of flour at low speed and then beat at high speed for 2 minutes; repeat until a total of 4 cups of flour have been used. Beat in just enough additional flour to form a very stiff batter.

3. Cover the bowl with a towel, place in a warm

place, and allow the batter to rise until doubled in bulk, about 1 hour.

4. Preheat the oven to 375°F. Generously butter a 9 x 5 x 3-inch loaf pan. With a heavy spoon, punch down the batter and beat it for 30 seconds. Transfer the batter to the pan and let it rise against until it reaches the top of the pan, about 20 minutes.

5. Bake the bread until the crust is well browned and the loaf sounds hollow when tapped with a finger, about 35 to 40 minutes. Cool on a wire rack.

$\mathcal{P}$AN-GRILLED SMOKED MOZZARELLA AND TOMATO SANDWICHES
•

For each sandwich, layer thick slices of ripe tomato and thin slices of smoked mozzarella between 2 slices of herb and garlic batter bread. Coat the bottom of a skillet with olive oil and place over medium heat. Cook the sandwiches until the cheese is melted and the bread is golden brown, turning to brown on both sides. Serve immediately.

. . . .
"$\mathcal{M}$ore S'mores!"

Long before there was blackened redfish, bluefish, and everything else that's blackened these days, there were plain old blackened marshmallows (we politely called them "toasted," but let's face it, they invariably turned out completely charred). And there were S'mores—those gooey treats from our childhood, consisting of hot, well-toasted marshmallows and melting squares of milk chocolate squooshed between two graham crackers. S'mores were a staple at campfires for Boy Scouts, Girl Scouts, and 4H-ers like me, but there's no reason we can't savor them as grown-ups, too. Here's how they're made, just in case you've forgotten.

Stick a big marshmallow on the end of a long skewer (we always used green twigs with sharply whittled points or unbent wire coat hangers) and grill it over hot coals.

When the marshmallow is good and blackened (there's no subtlety allowed here), place it, still skewered, on a graham cracker. Place half a milk chocolate bar on top of the marshmallow and top with another graham cracker.

Holding the sandwich firmly between your fingers, pull out the skewer, squoosh the sandwich together, allow about 2 seconds for the chocolate to melt, and eat it immediately. Then make s'more.

. . . .

GRANDMA WYNN'S BLACKBERRY DUMPLINGS

•

SERVES 6

When Mom came for a recent visit, she was browsing through Marcia Adams's wonderful *Cooking from Quilt Country*, when a recipe for maple syrup dumplings caught her eye. "This is how your Grandma used to make her blackberry dumplings," she said. "I'd forgotten all about them, but they used to be one of our favorite summer desserts." So here's a recipe for Grandma Wynn's blackberry dumplings, reconstructed by Mom from memory and with a little help.

DUMPLINGS
1 cup all-purpose flour
1½ teaspoons baking powder
1 tablespoon sugar
½ teaspoon salt
½ teaspoon ground cinnamon
1 tablespoon vegetable shortening, chilled
1 large egg
½ cup buttermilk

BERRIES
1 quart blackberries
½ cup sugar
½ cup honey
½ cup water
¼ cup (½ stick) butter, melted

1 pint heavy cream, whipped to soft peaks

1. To make the dumplings, combine the dry ingredients in a medium bowl. Cut in the shortening until the mixture resembles coarse meal. In a separate bowl, beat the egg and buttermilk until blended. Add the liquid mixture to the dry mixture and beat with a fork until the dry ingredients are just moistened and a soft dough forms. Set aside.

2. In a medium skillet, combine the berries, sugar, honey, water, and butter. Place over medium heat and cook until the liquid begins to simmer. Drop the dough by tablespoonfuls onto the berry mixture; there should be 6 mounds of dough. Cover the skillet tightly with a lid or aluminum foil and continue cooking for 20 minutes (*do not lift the lid*).

3. Serve the dumplings and berries warm and top with a generous dollop of whipped cream.

VARIATIONS Substitute raspberries or blueberries for the blackberries.

ABOVE: Colorful sweet corn gazpacho is a cross between a soup and a salad. BELOW: Steamed blackberry dumplings.

· · · · · · · · · · · · ·

Berry Picking

When I was growing up, wild berry patches would overflow with raspberries, dewberries, and blackberries at the edges of the woods and along the fences. We kids would be handed milk pails and sent out to gather berries with our black cocker spaniel, Cinder. We all hated being sent out on this thorny chore, but we always came back having eaten more berries than we put in our pails, evidenced by our purple hands and mouths and Cinder's very purple tongue.

· · · · · · · · · · · · ·

Simple tomato and cheese sandwiches are cooked in a cast-iron skillet over the campfire. Later the fire will be used to toast marshmallows for S'mores.

BARBECUE AT THE BEACH

for 12

•

Menu

GRILLED CHICKEN AND RIBS GLAZED WITH
RASPBERRY KETCHUP

GRILLED SKEWERED CORN AND ZUCCHINI

CUCUMBER AND SWEET ONION SALAD WITH
LIME-PEPPER DRESSING

BULGUR WHEAT SALAD

• • •

MINTED WATERMELON ICE

JENNIFER'S WILD BLUEBERRY COOKIES

Before I moved to New York, I thought all beach parties were like the ones in those silly movies of the sixties starring Frankie Avalon and Annette Funicello, so when I was invited to my first beach party on eastern Long Island I didn't know what to expect. Well, we didn't play "beach blanket bingo," but we had a fine time, anyway.

Beach parties can involve anything from simple charcoal-grilled hot dogs, to the elaborate ritual of the clambake, to no cooking at all. This menu includes some of my favorite barbecue foods: chicken and ribs (this time with a raspberry glaze), corn on the cob grilled with hunks of zucchini, and watermelon (ice) for dessert. When packing up, don't forget to take along a cassette player with Beach Boys and Jan and Dean tapes, and music from those old beach-party movies.

GETTING READY Just about everything can be prepared in advance, so all that needs to be done just before dinner is the grilling.

Up to two months in advance, make the raspberry ketchup for the glaze.

Up to a week in advance, make the watermelon ice. Pack the frozen solid ice in a cooler to transport it.

The day before, make the bulgur salad and the cookies.

A few hours in advance make the cucumber salad. Steam the zucchini and marinate it with the corn. Marinate the ribs.

Prepare a fire forty-five minutes to an hour before you want to start grilling.

BEVERAGES With this barbecue, I like an assortment of hearty American beers. Have a big thermos of iced tea available, too.

GRILLED CHICKEN AND RIBS GLAZED WITH RASPBERRY KETCHUP

•

SERVES 12

RIB MARINADE
2 cups cider vinegar
1 teaspoon salt
½ teaspoon cayenne pepper
3 large garlic cloves, finely chopped

6 pounds spareribs, separated into 2-rib sections
4 fryer or broiler chickens, cut into eighths
Vegetable oil
Raspberry Ketchup (recipe follows)

1. In a large mixing bowl, stir together the marinade ingredients. Add the ribs and toss them to coat with the marinade. Cover and refrigerate at least 2 hours.

2. Prepare a charcoal or hardwood fire; when the coals are ash-covered and glowing, the fire is ready. Have a spray bottle of water handy to douse any flare-ups that may occur once the meat starts rendering fat.

3. Remove the ribs from the marinade and place them on a grill about 4 inches above the fire. Cover the grill with the lid (or cover the ribs loosely with foil) and cook the ribs, turning frequently with long-handled tongs, until cooked through and well browned, about 1 hour.

4. About 20 minutes after the ribs go on the grill, brush the chicken lightly with peanut oil. Place the chicken on the grill, skin side down, and return the cover. Cook the chicken, turning frequently with the tongs, until almost cooked through, about 40 minutes for dark meat and 30 minutes for white meat (all timing will depend on the heat of the fire).

5. Baste the meat with the ketchup and cook for an additional 5 to 10 minutes on each side, until the meat is glazed but not charred. Serve immediately with a dish of additional ketchup as a condiment.

RASPBERRY KETCHUP

•

MAKES APPROXIMATELY 3 HALF-PINTS

The Cranberry-Walnut Ketchup in *Special Occasions* was such a hit that I thought I'd try making ketchup with raspberries this time around. This ketchup will keep for a month in the refrigerator and is delicious as a condiment with ham, pork, or grilled or roasted duck.

2 pints raspberries
½ cup firmly packed light brown sugar
2 tablespoons water
2 medium onions, finely chopped
1 large garlic clove, finely chopped
½ cup white wine vinegar
1 tablespoon ground ginger
½ teaspoon ground cinnamon
½ teaspoon ground cloves
⅛ teaspoon cayenne pepper

1. Place the raspberries in a small, heavy saucepan with half the brown sugar and the water. Place over medium heat and cook, stirring occasionally and mashing the berries against the side of the pan, until the mixture comes to a boil. Reduce the heat and simmer for 5 minutes.

2. Remove from the heat and strain the mixture through a fine sieve to remove the seeds. Return the strained berry mixture to the pan and place over medium heat.

3. Stir in the remaining sugar and all other remaining ingredients and bring to a simmer. Reduce the heat and simmer the mixture, stirring occasionally, until the onions are very tender and the mixture has thickened.

4. Transfer the mixture to the bowl of a food processor fitted with the steel chopping blade. Process to a smooth puree.

5. Spoon the ketchup into sterilized half-pint jars, cover tightly, and refrigerate.

GRILLED SKEWERED CORN AND ZUCCHINI

•

SERVES 12

6 medium zucchini
6 ears fresh corn, husked

MARINADE
¼ cup (½ stick) butter, melted and cooled
¼ cup olive oil
3 tablespoons red or white wine vinegar
1 garlic clove, finely chopped
1 teaspoon sugar
½ teaspoon salt
½ teaspoon freshly ground black pepper

1. With a vegetable peeler, peel away ¼-inch-wide lengthwise strips of the zucchini skin, leaving the zucchini green-and-white striped. Cut the corn and zucchini crosswise into 1½-inch lengths. Steam the zucchini over simmering water for 5 minutes.

2. Combine the marinade ingredients in a large plastic container or storage bag and mix well. Add the vegetables and toss them to coat with the marinade. Close the container tightly, refrigerate, and marinate at least 2 hours.

3. Prepare a charcoal fire. Place the vegetables alternately on metal skewers, starting and ending with corn. Grill the vegetables, turning frequently and brushing with leftover marinade, until tender and nicely browned, about 15 minutes. Serve hot.

. . . .

A Little Extra Sustenance

Trail mix is a good anytime snack that's easy to carry and store—and it's no work at all to mix up a batch. Combine equal amounts of any or all of the following ingredients: coarsely chopped dried apples, pears, pineapple, dates, peaches, or apricots; raisins, dried sliced bananas; coconut flakes; toasted slivered almonds or whole unsalted roasted peanuts or cashews; pumpkin seeds or sunflower seeds.

. . . .

ABOVE: Just before dusk the fire is ready for grilling.

RIGHT: Grilled raspberry-glazed chicken and ribs are served with skewers of sweet corn and zucchini, a vegetable-flecked bulgur wheat salad, and a cucumber and sweet onion salad with peppery lime dressing.

BELOW: Minted watermelon ice is served in a paper cup with a wooden spoon and topped with watermelon seeds. In the background is a plate of wild blueberry cookies.

Cucumber and Sweet Onion Salad with Lime-Pepper Dressing

SERVES 12

6 large cucumbers
2 large sweet onions, such as Vidalias
Juice of 2 limes
½ teaspoon salt
½ teaspoon sugar
½ teaspoon hot red pepper flakes, or more to taste
¼ cup olive oil
¼ cup white wine vinegar
¼ cup water

1. Run a fork lengthwise down the cucumbers, making slight indentations, and repeat on all sides. Cut the cucumbers in half lengthwise and scoop out the seeds with a small spoon. Cut the cucumber halves crosswise into ⅛-inch slices.

2. Peel the onions and cut them lengthwise into quarters. Slice the quarters crosswise into thin strips. Place the onions and cucumbers in a large jar or mixing bowl. Add the lime juice, salt, and sugar, and toss. Add the remaining ingredients and toss again. Cover and let stand for up to 24 hours in the refrigerator before serving.

"The Onion Man"

As he mentioned frequently in his writings, one of James Beard's favorite foods, if not *the* favorite, was the onion. As a small child, he would sneak to the vegetable bin, grab an onion, and eat it raw like an apple, "skin and all." Years later, when he began his food career as a caterer, one of his signature hors d'oeuvres was a finger sandwich of thinly sliced sweet onion and sweet butter on thin slices of white bread.

Bulgur Wheat Salad

SERVES 12

This is a version of the Middle Eastern salad, tabbouleh. The addition of balsamic vinegar with its smoky flavor makes this salad especially compatible with grilled foods.

3 cups bulgur wheat
3 quarts boiling water
6 scallions, white and green parts, thinly sliced
4 medium ripe tomatoes, coarsely chopped, with their juice
2 large carrots, peeled and diced
2 medium zucchini, unpeeled and diced
1 yellow or green pepper, seeded and diced
¼ cup coarsely chopped green olives

DRESSING
3 large garlic cloves, finely chopped
½ cup chopped parsley
⅓ cup chopped basil
⅓ cup chopped mint
¾ cup extra-virgin olive oil
Juice and grated rind of 1 small lemon
⅓ cup balsamic vinegar
Pinch of sugar

1. Place the bulgur in a large bowl or pan and pour the boiling water over it. Cover and let stand for 2 hours. Drain the bulgur well, removing as much liquid as possible and return the bulgur to the bowl. Add the scallions, tomatoes, carrots, zucchini, pepper, and olives. Toss well to combine.

2. Combine the dressing ingredients in a small jar and shake well to mix. Pour the dressing over the bulgur-vegetable mixture and toss well. Cover the bowl or transfer the salad to a large jar and refrigerate up to 24 hours. Toss the salad again before serving.

Minted Watermelon Ice

•

MAKES 2 QUARTS

Here's a "fancy" version of sliced watermelon, the classic barbecue dessert. I save a few watermelon seeds to use as a garnish, so everyone still gets to pick out a few, or use miniature chocolate chips.

1 cup sugar
1 cup water
1 cup fresh spearmint leaves, plus extra for
    garnish
2 tablespoons light rum (optional)
16 cups coarsely chopped watermelon, seeded,
    and handful of seeds reserved

1. Combine the sugar, water, and mint in a small, heavy saucepan, and place over medium heat. Bring the mixture to a simmer, turn down the heat, and simmer for 3 minutes. Stir in the rum and simmer 2 minutes more. Remove from the heat and cool. Remove the mint leaves and discard them.

2. In batches, puree the watermelon in the bowl of a food processor fitted with the steel chopping blade. Transfer the melon puree to a mixing bowl and blend in the mint syrup. Pour the mixture into an ice cream maker and follow the manufacturer's instructions for freezing, *or* continue with step 3.

3. Pour the mixture into a large shallow pan and place in the freezer. When ice crystals begin to form, in about 30 minutes, remove from the freezer and beat the mixture until smooth. Return the pan to the freezer and repeat this process 2 or 3 times, or until a smooth, firm, finely grained consistency has been reached. Cover tightly and store in the freezer.

4. Serve the ice scooped into paper cups, garnished with mint leaves and watermelon seeds or miniature chocolate chips.

"When one has tasted watermelons
one knows what angels eat."
Mark Twain

Jennifer's Wild Blueberry Cookies

•

MAKES APPROXIMATELY 4 DOZEN

Every summer, my friend Jennifer Trainer, coauthor of *The Yachting Cookbook*, gathers baskets and baskets of wild blueberries from Blueberry Island near her family cabin in the wilds of upstate New York. These cookies are named for her.

Wild blueberries tend to be smaller than cultivated ones, so if you have to substitute the cultivated variety, make slightly larger cookies.

2½ cups all-purpose flour
1½ teaspoons baking powder
¼ teaspoon salt
¼ teaspoon grated nutmeg
½ teaspoon ground cinnamon
½ cup (1 stick) butter
1 cup sugar
1 large egg, beaten
½ cup milk
2 cups wild blueberries

1. Preheat the oven to 375°F. Grease baking sheets well.

2. In a mixing bowl, sift together the flour, baking powder, salt, and spices. In a separate large bowl, cream together the butter and sugar, and then beat in the egg. Beat the dry ingredients into the butter mixture alternately with the milk and then gently fold in the blueberries.

3. Drop the dough by teaspoonfuls onto the baking sheets and bake for 10 to 12 minutes, or until golden brown. Remove to wire racks to cool and store in tightly covered containers in a cool place for up to 3 days.

FOURTH OF JULY DINNER ON THE LAWN

for 6

♦

Menu

SHRIMP AND CORN SALAD IN GRILLED TOMATOES

• • •

GRILLED PEPPERED SWORDFISH STEAKS WITH
ORANGE AND PEPPER RELISH

STEAMED GREEN AND YELLOW BEANS IN
BROWN BUTTER

CORN FRITTERS

• • •

APPLE-STRAWBERRY COBBLER

Even though I'm usually a traditionalist, I sometimes like to add an unexpected element to a traditional event. This time, even though this is a not-so-formal menu, I thought it would be fun to set a formal table outdoors, with real glasses, dishes, and silver—the works—out on the lawn (no paper plates or paper napkins!). After the sun set, glass-shaded hurricane lamps added a warm glow.

Barbecues and the Fourth of July go hand in hand, but the menu doesn't have to include the usual hamburgers and hot dogs. At various times I've barbecued brisket, Southern pulled pork barbecue, and chicken in a number of ways, so I decided to grill fish this time. The rest of the menu is also somewhat nontraditional, but I can't let the Fourth go by without keeping a few traditional elements. So I've included corn (twice!) and tomatoes, and the meal ends with an all-American apple and strawberry cobbler.

GETTING READY The orange and pepper relish can be made up to two days in advance, and the shrimp and corn salad can be made a day ahead.

Bake the cobbler early in the day and rewarm it in a slow oven before serving. To make last-minute preparation easier, the beans, too, can be cooked a few hours in advance and rewarmed by tossing with butter in a skillet. Also a few hours ahead, pare and cook the corn for the fritters.

RIGHT: A pretty first course of shrimp and corn salad stuffed into a grilled tomato and garnished with parsley.

OPPOSITE: A damask-draped lantern-lit table on the side lawn is the perfect setting for dinner just before sunset.

The fish and fritters are best when made just before serving. Keep the fritters warm in a slow oven while grilling the fish.

BEVERAGES I like a Chardonnay with the shrimp and corn salad and with the strongly flavored main course, a not-too-heavy red, such as a Merlot.

SHRIMP AND CORN SALAD IN GRILLED TOMATOES

·

SERVES 6

Look for white corn with small kernels for this pretty and simple salad. By the way, if you don't happen to have a grill going, the tomatoes can just be left uncooked.

DRESSING

2 tablespoons Homemade Mayonnaise (page 221)
¼ cup olive oil
¼ cup corn or vegetable oil
¼ cup white wine vinegar
1 tablespoon grainy mustard
⅛ teaspoon ground cumin
2 tablespoons chopped coriander or parsley
1 scallion, white and green parts, finely chopped
Salt and freshly ground black pepper

1 pound cooked medium shrimp, peeled and
  deveined
4 ears white sweet corn, cooked and cut from the
  cob (approximately 1¾ cups kernels)
6 ripe medium tomatoes, 2½ to 3 inches in
  diameter
Olive oil
Sprigs of coriander or parsley, for garnish

1. To make the dressing, whisk together the mayonnaise and oils in a medium mixing bowl and then whisk in the vinegar, mustard, and cumin. Stir in the coriander or parsley and the scallions. Season to taste with salt and pepper.

2. Add the shrimp and corn, toss to coat, cover, and refrigerate at least 2 hours.

3. About an hour before serving, core the tomatoes, scoop them out with a small spoon, and turn them upside down on a rack to drain. If they are to be grilled, brush them lightly with olive oil and place them on the grill about 4 inches above glowing, ash-covered coals. Grill the tomatoes just until they begin to brown, about 5 minutes.

4. Turn the tomatoes upright and stuff them with the shrimp mixture. Place a tomato on each plate and garnish with coriander or parsley.

GRILLED PEPPERED SWORDFISH STEAKS WITH ORANGE AND PEPPER RELISH

·

SERVES 6

This recipe works equally well with bluefish or tuna steaks; the same method can also be used for grilling thick beef steaks.

MARINADE

1 tablespoon black peppercorns, coarsely ground
1 teaspoon cayenne pepper
1 teaspoon paprika
1 teaspoon dried oregano, crumbled to a powder

6 ½-inch-thick swordfish steaks
Olive oil

1. Combine the marinade ingredients in a small bowl and set aside.

2. Brush the steaks lightly with the oil, then rub them all over with the marinade. Cover and let stand for 1 hour. (Refrigerate the steaks if they are to stand for a longer time.)

3. Prepare a charcoal fire. The fire is ready when the coals are glowing and ash covered. Place the swordfish steaks on a grill about 4 inches from the

· ·

Roasted Peppers

1. Preheat the broiler and place the peppers on a baking sheet. Broil as close to the heat source as possible until the skin is charred, turning occasionally to char all sides. Or, one at a time, spear the peppers onto a long-handled fork and hold over a charcoal fire or an open flame on top of the stove, turning to char evenly.

2. Place the hot peppers in a plastic bag, close tightly, and allow them to sweat for 5 minutes; then remove them from the bag and pull off the charred skin.

3. Cut the peppers open, seed them, and use as the recipe indicates.

· ·

coals. Cook 4 minutes per side for medium-rare steaks, brushing lightly with additional oil if necessary to prevent sticking; cook the steaks a minute or two longer for more well-done. Serve the steaks with Orange and Pepper Relish (recipe follows).

ORANGE AND PEPPER RELISH

⅓ cup olive oil
3 scallions, white and green parts, thinly sliced
1 garlic clove, minced
2 large red peppers, roasted, peeled, seeded, and chopped (page 64)
2 large yellow peppers, roasted, peeled, seeded, and chopped (page 64)
1 large tomato, peeled, seeded, and chopped
Grated zest and chopped flesh of 1 small orange
¼ cup dry white wine
½ cup chopped basil
Salt and freshly ground black pepper

1. Place the oil, scallions, and garlic in a large skillet over medium heat and sauté 5 minutes.

2. Transfer the skillet mixture to the bowl of a food processor fitted with the steel chopping blade and add the peppers, tomato, orange zest, and chopped orange. Process with a few short pulses to achieve a lumpy, very coarse puree.

3. Transfer the mixture back to the skillet, stir in the wine, and bring to a simmer. Simmer until the wine is reduced and the mixture thickens, about 7 minutes. *(Can be made up to 3 days in advance up to this point, covered, and refrigerated.)* Stir in the basil and season to taste with salt and pepper. Bring to room temperature before serving.

STEAMED GREEN AND YELLOW BEANS IN BROWN BUTTER

•

SERVES 6

This method, which takes only a few moments to do just before serving, is how restaurant chefs serve perfect vegetables every time.

¾ pound green beans, trimmed
¾ pound wax beans, trimmed
3 tablespoons butter

1. Steam the beans until crisp-tender. *(Can be prepared early in the day and refrigerated. Return to room temperature before proceeding.)*

2. Melt the butter in a skillet over medium heat and cook until the butter is lightly browned, 2 or 3 minutes. Add the beans and toss them to coat with the butter. Cook until the beans are heated through. Serve immediately.

CORN FRITTERS

•

MAKES ABOUT 2 DOZEN

The flavor of freshly picked corn shines through in this simple recipe. These fritters are delicious when dipped into the relish. I love these for a weekend breakfast, too, slathered with honey or maple syrup.

½ cup all-purpose flour
¼ cup stone-ground yellow cornmeal
1 teaspoon baking powder
½ teaspoon salt
¼ teaspoon cayenne pepper
4 cups freshly scraped corn kernels (approximately 8 ears)
4 large eggs, well beaten
½ cup corn oil

1. Combine the flour, cornmeal, baking powder, salt, and cayenne in a mixing bowl and stir until blended. Add the corn and eggs and stir until blended.

2. Heat the oil in a skillet until a few drops of water flung into the pan sizzle and "dance." Drop the batter by tablespoonfuls into the pan and cook until each fritter is browned on one side, 3 or 4 minutes. Turn the fritters and brown them on the other side. *(These are best when freshly made, but if need be, the fritters can be made a few hours in advance and reheated in a single layer on a baking sheet in a slow oven.)*

· · · · · · · · · · · · · · · · ·

Corn Lore

According to farm folklore, corn stalks should be knee high by the Fourth of July or the crop won't be successful. And yes, it does grow as high as an elephant's eye. Corn grows very quickly. In fact, corn makes one of the most magical sounds on a farm: Walking through the cornfield on a quiet night, you can hear a muffled crackling sound—the sound of the corn growing.

· · · · · · · · · · · · · · · · ·

Apple-Strawberry Cobbler

•

MAKES ONE 9-INCH COBBLER

I love strawberries in almost any kind of dessert, but they tend to be too juicy when cooked alone. Here they're combined with apples, which marry well with the texture and flavor of the berries.

Basic Pastry for a 10-inch pie (page 220)
¾ cup sugar
½ teaspoon ground cinnamon
2 tablespoons cornstarch
2 tablespoons all-purpose flour
4 cups sliced baking apples, such as Rome or
  Granny Smith
1 quart strawberries, hulled and sliced
1 tablespoon lemon juice
Milk
1 teaspoon sugar, for top

OPPOSITE: **The colorful main course is served on Sandwich-pattern depression glass plates.** ABOVE: **As the evening air cools, a warm cobbler is a welcome dessert.**

1. Preheat the oven to 425°F. Roll out the pastry into an 11-inch circle ⅛ inch thick. Trim and reserve excess pastry. Line a 9- or 9½-inch deep-dish pie pan with the pastry, letting the edges overhang.

2. In a large mixing bowl, combine the sugar, cinnamon, cornstarch, and flour. Add the apples and toss them well to coat. Add the strawberries and lemon juice and toss gently to combine.

3. Mound the fruit mixture in the pan and dot the fruit with the butter. Turn the edges of the crust over the fruit, making overlapping folds every few inches or so and leaving the center of the fruit uncovered.

4. Cut out small leaf shapes from the leftover pastry, moisten the backs of each leaf with water, and arrange them around the edges of the pastry shell, pressing lightly to adhere.

5. Brush the surface of the dough with milk and sprinkle it with sugar. Bake for 40 to 45 minutes, or until the crust is well browned and the apples are tender. (If, during baking, the crust begins to get too brown, cover the cobbler with a piece of aluminum foil vented in the center to allow steam to escape.)

6. Serve warm or at room temperature with whipped cream or Vanilla Bean Ice Cream (page 221).

A MIDSUMMER NIGHT'S FINGER-FOODS PARTY

for 30

◆

Menu

TROPICAL TEA PUNCH

• • •

POTTED SHRIMP, ISLAND STYLE

GRILLED SKEWERED SAUSAGES AND PEPPERS

GRILLED SKEWERED CHICKEN WITH PINEAPPLE

CHERRY TOMATOES STUFFED WITH
ROASTED EGGPLANT PUREE

FOCACCIA WITH TOMATOES, BASIL, AND THYME

FOCACCIA WITH SMOKED MOZZARELLA,
ROASTED RED PEPPERS, AND OLIVES

• • •

MOCHACCINO CHIP COOKIES

IVA MAE'S FROZEN SHERRY MOUSSE CUPS

SKEWERED SPICED SUMMER FRUITS

Aside from the fact that a crowd can more easily fit on my lawn than in my house, I have good reason for being partial to entertaining big groups in the summer. My worst entertaining disaster took place in the winter. Years ago, when I lived in Ohio, I once invited sixty or seventy guests over for a New Year's Eve party. I spent several days preparing for the event, and then at about noon on New Year's Eve day it began to snow. And snow. And snow. Well, about two feet of snow later, three guests arrived. And they were the first and only ones who ever made it. So now I figure that in the summer the worst thing that can happen is a little rain—and if that happens we can simply move the party indoors.

There are lots of different tastes here, with influences from a variety of summery climes, from the Mediterranean to the Caribbean. And to drink on a warm summer evening, there's a wonderfully refreshing punch that includes all the virtues of iced tea and fruit juice with just a dash of old demon rum.

GETTING READY There's a good amount of preparation involved here, but if you work in stages, it won't be too overwhelming.

Up to a week in advance, make the sherry mousse cups and the cookies. The crusts for the focaccia can also be prepared a week in advance, prebaked, and frozen.

A few days before the party, stage a dry run of the buffet table, organizing serving pieces and so on.

A day in advance, prepare the eggplant puree, make the potted shrimp, and marinate the chicken.

Early on the day of the party, brew the tea for the punch, assemble the chicken skewers and the sausages-and-peppers skewers, pare and marinate the fruit, and prepare the ingredients for the focaccia toppings.

A few hours ahead, grill the skewers and arrange them on baking sheets for reheating.

An hour or two before the party, skewer the fruit, stuff the cherry tomatoes, and assemble the focaccia.

About a half-hour into the party, start heating the hot hors d'ouevres; stagger the timing so something different's being passed every half-hour or so and you're not in the kitchen for more than a few minutes at a time.

Tropical Tea Punch

MAKES APPROXIMATELY
THIRTY-EIGHT 6-OUNCE SERVINGS
(MORE IF RUM IS ADDED)

1 teaspoon whole cloves
4 cups strongly brewed Earl Grey tea, cooled
4 cups strongly brewed mint tea, cooled
1 quart pineapple juice
1 quart orange juice
1 quart apple juice
Juice of 2 lemons
2 liters ginger ale
Orange and lime slices, for garnish
Sprigs of mint, for garnish
Light rum (optional)

Add the cloves to the hot tea and allow the tea to cool. Combine the tea and cloves with the juices in a punch bowl. Just before serving, stir in the ginger ale and garnish with orange and lime slices and mint. Serve in tall glasses over ice; add rum to individual tastes.

Potted Shrimp, Island Style

SERVES APPROXIMATELY 40

Potted shrimp is a classic English "starter." Here's a zestier version as I imagine it might be made somewhere in the British West Indies. Serve it with toasted thin slices of French bread.

3 pounds medium shrimp
6 scallions, white and green parts, finely chopped
1 tablespoon finely chopped coriander
2 tablespoons finely chopped flat-leaf parsley
Juice and grated rind of 1 lime
½ teaspoon red pepper flakes
2 cups (4 sticks) butter
Sprigs of coriander or flat-leaf parsley, for garnish

1. Cover the shrimp with water in a saucepan and bring to a boil. Cook the shrimp until they are just pink. Drain and cool.

2. Peel and devein the shrimp, reserving the shells. Chop the shrimp finely and combine in a mixing bowl with the scallions, coriander, parsley, lime juice and rind, and red pepper flakes.

3. Melt the butter in a skillet over low heat. Coarsely chop the shrimp shells and add them to the skillet. Sauté over low heat for about 10 minutes, watching so the butter does not brown. Strain the butter through cheesecloth into a spouted cup or bowl, leaving behind the milky residue, then pour the butter over the shrimp mixture to cover.

4. Cool to room temperature, then cover with aluminum foil or plastic wrap and chill until the butter is firm. To serve, bring to room temperature and stir well. Mound into a small serving bowl or crock and garnish with coriander or parsley.

Grilled Skewered Sausages and Peppers

MAKES APPROXIMATELY 3 DOZEN

A classic combination uniquely served and simply prepared. The results depend mainly on the sausages themselves. Scout around for an Italian market that makes homemade sausages.

2 pounds Italian sweet and/or hot sausage
2 or 3 large red and/or green peppers, cut into
1-inch pieces

1. Prepare a fire in a grill (or preheat a broiler about 15 minutes before cooking). Soak 3 dozen 6- or 8-inch bamboo skewers in water for at least 30 minutes.

2. Prick the sausages all over with a fork. Place them in a shallow pan or skillet with water to cover and place over medium-high heat. Bring to a slow boil and cook the sausages for 10 minutes. Drain the sausages and cut them into ¾-inch lengths.

3. Alternate 2 pieces of pepper and 1 piece of sausage on each skewer. Grill over glowing ash-covered coals until the sausage is well browned and peppers are charred, approximately 10 minutes. Serve immediately. (*Can be grilled in advance and reheated just before serving.*)

"Be bright and jovial
among your guests tonight."
William Shakespeare

Vibrantly flavored hors d'oeuvres for a warm summer night (top to bottom): focaccia with two toppings (smoked mozzarella, roasted red pepper, and black olives; and tomatoes, onions, and herbs), grilled skewered chicken with pineapple and grilled skewered sausage and peppers, and a spicy Caribbean-style potted shrimp with toasts.

The hors d'oeuvres buffet is set up on the porch while the guests enjoy a first glass of tea punch on the lawn.

GRILLED SKEWERED CHICKEN WITH PINEAPPLE

•

MAKES APPROXIMATELY 4 DOZEN

The marinade for the chicken has a delicate curry flavor, which is enhanced by the pineapple.

MARINADE
1 teaspoon ground cumin
1 teaspoon ground coriander
1 teaspoon ground turmeric
1 small onion, peeled and quartered
2 large garlic cloves
⅓ cup soy sauce
⅓ cup lemon juice
1 tablespoon dark brown sugar

8 boned and skinned medium chicken breast halves
1 large, ripe pineapple, cut into ½-inch cubes or
2 1-pound, 4-ounce cans cubed pineapple packed in juice, drained

1. Sprinkle the cumin, coriander, and turmeric in the bottom of a small skillet and place over medium-high heat, stirring constantly, for 1 minute. Remove from heat and transfer the spices to a blender or the bowl of a food processor fitted with the steel chopping blade. Add the remaining marinade ingredients and process until the mixture is smooth.

2. Using a wooden mallet, pound the chicken breasts to a thickness of slightly more than ⅛ inch. Cut the chicken into strips about 3 inches long and ¾ inch wide. Place the chicken strips in a heavy plastic bag or a shallow bowl, add the marinade, and toss. Secure the bag tightly or cover the bowl and marinate overnight in the refrigerator.

3. Prepare a fire in a grill (or preheat a broiler about 15 minutes before cooking). Soak 4 dozen 8-inch bamboo skewers in water for 30 minutes.

4. Skewer one chicken strip at a time back and forth onto a skewer. Push the chicken up about an inch from the end and then add a pineapple cube. (*Can be prepared a few hours ahead up to this point, placed on a baking sheet, covered with plastic wrap, and refrigerated.*)

5. Grill or broil until the chicken is just cooked, 5 to 7 minutes. Do not overcook. Transfer to a shallow basket or tray lined with lemon leaves and garnish with a few exotic flowers. Serve immediately.

CHERRY TOMATOES STUFFED WITH ROASTED EGGPLANT PUREE

•

MAKES APPROXIMATELY 6 DOZEN

The eggplant takes on a wonderful smoky flavor when roasted. It also makes a delicious spread when served with toasted triangles of pita bread or toasted thin slices of French bread. Or try it as an impromptu pasta sauce, tossed with spaghettini or linguine with a few chopped tomatoes and a sprinkling of toasted pignoli.

ROASTED EGGPLANT PUREE
2 medium eggplants, about 1 pound each
2 large garlic cloves, peeled and halved
Juice of 1 large lemon
¼ cup olive oil
¼ cup chopped parsley
¼ cup chopped basil or mint leaves
½ teaspoon salt
Dash of hot pepper sauce
Pinch of ground cumin

3 to 4 pints cherry tomatoes, depending on size
Parsley sprigs, for garnish
Toasted pignoli, for garnish

1. Preheat the oven to 400°F. Prick the eggplants all over with a fork, place them on the top rack of the oven, and bake them for 20 minutes. Turn the heat to broil and broil the eggplants for 7 to 10 minutes, turning frequently to char all sides. Remove the eggplants from the heat, cut them in half, and reserve.

2. With the motor running, drop the garlic through the tube of a food processor bowl fitted with steel chopping blade. Scoop out the eggplant flesh from its skin and add the flesh to the processor. Discard the skin. Add the remaining ingredients and process to a coarse puree. (*Can be made up to 2 days in advance up to this point, covered tightly, and refrigerated.*)

3. No more than 6 hours before serving, cut the tops from the cherry tomatoes and scoop out the seeds with a small spoon (a demitasse spoon works well for this). Turn the tomatoes upside down on a rack to drain for an hour or so.

4. Using the small spoon, fill each tomato with the eggplant puree. Garnish each tomato with a small sprig of parsley and a few pignoli. Arrange the tomatoes on a platter, cover loosely with plastic wrap, and refrigerate until about 30 minutes before serving.

Focaccia with Two Toppings

•

MAKES TWO 10 X 15-INCH
FLAT BREADS

The variety of toppings used on this rustic flat bread can be endless, but in Italy they're usually little more than a drizzle of olive oil and a sprinkling of fresh herbs and coarse salt. I've listed two favorite topping combinations, but feel free to experiment. For the most aromatic and tasty focaccia, use the best-quality, most flavorful olive oil available, and do try to use fresh herbs.

DOUGH
1 package active dry yeast
1 cup warm water
3½ cups all-purpose flour, approximately
1 teaspoon salt
⅓ cup extra-virgin olive oil

TOPPING 1
2 tablespoons extra-virgin olive oil
¼ cup freshly grated Parmesan
*1 small onion, very thinly sliced and separated
    into rings*
2 firm, ripe medium tomatoes, very thinly sliced
*1 tablespoon fresh thyme leaves or 1 teaspoon
    dried thyme*
*1 tablespoon chopped fresh basil leaves or
    1 teaspoon dried basil*
Freshly ground black pepper

TOPPING 2
2 tablespoons extra-virgin olive oil
½ pound smoked mozzarella, diced
*1 large red pepper, roasted, peeled, and cut into
    thin strips (page 64)*
½ cup coarsely chopped ripe black olives
2 large garlic cloves, finely chopped
1 teaspoon fennel seeds
*1 tablespoon chopped fresh sage leaves or
    1 teaspoon dried sage*
Freshly ground black pepper

1. In a small bowl, dissolve the yeast in the water and let stand for 10 minutes.

2. In a large mixing bowl, combine 3 cups flour and the salt. Make an indentation in the center and pour in the yeast mixture and the oil. With a wooden spoon, beat the ingredients together to form a dough. Turn the dough out onto a floured surface and knead until smooth and elastic, adding more flour if necessary.

3. Form the dough into a ball, place it in a lightly oiled bowl, and cover with a damp cloth. Place the dough in a warm place and allow it to double in bulk, about 2 hours.

4. Punch down the dough and knead it for 3 or 4 minutes. Divide the dough into 2 equal pieces. On the floured surface, shape each piece of dough into a flat 10 x 15-inch rectangle. Transfer the dough to 2 oiled 10½ x 15½-inch (or larger) baking sheets. With the tips of the fingers, push "dimples" into the surface of the dough. Cover the dough and let rise again until doubled in bulk, about 1 hour.

5. Preheat the oven to 400°F. Place the baking sheets in the oven and bake breads until the edges of the dough are lightly browned, about 15 minutes. *(Can be made a day in advance up to this point; slide the dough onto wire racks to cool, wrap tightly in plastic wrap, and refrigerate. Or make well in advance, wrap well, and freeze.)*

6. For topping 1, first brush the crust liberally with olive oil. Sprinkle 3 tablespoons Parmesan over the crust. Scatter about two-thirds of the onion rings over the crust, arrange the tomato slices in a single layer over the onion, and top with the remaining onion rings. Sprinkle the thyme and basil over the tomatoes, followed by the remaining Parmesan and a few gridings of black pepper.

7. For topping 2, first brush the crust liberally with olive oil. Scatter the mozzarella over the crust and then arrange the strips of red pepper on top. Scatter the olives, garlic, fennel, and sage and add a few grindings of black pepper.

8. Bake the assembled focaccia for about 15 minutes, or until the edges of the crusts are well browned. Serve warm or at room temperature. *(The focaccia can be baked 1 day in advance, wrapped tightly, and stored in a cool place—not refrigerated. Bake them in a hot oven for 5 minutes or so to refresh them.)* Cut into small rectangles to serve.

Mochaccino Chip Cookies

•

MAKES ABOUT 6 DOZEN

I once emphatically stated that the absolute best chocolate chip cookie recipe is the one for the original Toll House Cookie that appears on the back of the chocolate chip package. I still stand by that declaration, but here's the first runner up.

½ cup (1 stick) butter, softened
½ cup vegetable shortening
1¾ cups firmly packed light brown sugar
2 large eggs
½ cup strong-brewed coffee, preferably espresso
3½ cups sifted all-purpose flour
1 teaspoon baking soda
½ teaspoon salt
½ teaspoon ground cinnamon
½ teaspoon grated nutmeg
1½ cups semisweet chocolate chips

1. In a large bowl, cream the butter, shortening, and brown sugar together until light and fluffy, then beat in the eggs and the coffee.

2. In a separate bowl, sift together the flour, baking soda, salt, and spices. Gradually beat this mixture into the wet mixture until well blended. Stir in the chocolate chips. Cover and refrigerate the dough for 1 hour.

3. Preheat the oven to 400°F. Grease baking sheets.

4. Drop the chilled dough by teaspoonfuls about 2 inches apart onto the baking sheets. Bake until the edges of the cookies are lightly browned, 8 to 10 minutes. Remove to wire racks to cool and then store in tightly covered containers in a cool place.

Iva Mae's Frozen Sherry Mousse Cups

•

MAKES APPROXIMATELY 30

2 large eggs, separated
½ cup confectioners' sugar
2 tablespoons dry sherry
½ teaspoon vanilla extract
¾ cup crumbled amaretti cookies or macaroons
1 cup heavy cream
Small fresh red cherries, preferably with stems

1. Line miniature muffin tins with pleated paper muffin cups.

2. Beat the egg yolks until thick and lemon-colored and then beat in the confectioners' sugar. Beat in the sherry and vanilla and then stir in ¼ cup of the cookie crumbs.

3. In a separate clean bowl and with clean beaters, beat the egg whites until stiff but not dry. In another bowl, beat the cream until stiff peaks form.

4. Fold the egg whites into the egg yolk mixture and then fold in the whipped cream. Spoon the mixture into the prepared muffin tins slightly mounding each. Sprinkle the remaining cookie crumbs over the mousse and top each cup with a cherry. Freeze until firm, 3 or 4 hours. Serve frozen.

Skewered Spiced Summer Fruits

•

MAKES 3 TO 4 DOZEN SKEWERS

Just about any combination of firm ripe fruit can be used here, depending on what's available at the market; below is a list of suggestions. Keep in mind the color combination of fruits when making your selection. Roughly speaking, I allow about 1 pound of fruit for every 3 people; this marinade is enough for 10 or 12 pounds of fruit, the idea being to complement the flavor of the fruit rather than overwhelm it. Prepare this no more than four or five hours before serving.

MARINADE
1 bottle white Zinfandel
1 cup sugar
3 cinnamon sticks
2 teaspoons whole cloves
4 star anise
Juice of 2 limes

SUGGESTED FRUITS
Pineapple, cored, peeled, and cubed (save the top for decoration)
Nectarines and/or peaches, pitted and cut into 1-inch chunks
Strawberries, hulled
Mangos, peeled and cubed
Ripe figs, peeled and quartered
Plums, cut into 1-inch chunks
Melon, seeded and cut into 1-inch chunks
Large seedless grapes

A colorful variety of fruits are soaked in a spicy white Zinfandel marinade and then served on skewers.

1. In a heavy saucepan, combine the marinade ingredients and bring to a boil. Reduce the heat and simmer, uncovered, until the liquid is reduced by half, 20 to 30 minutes. Remove from the heat and allow to cool.

2. While the syrup is cooking, pare the fruit. Using 6- or 8-inch skewers, place 3 or 4 pieces of fruit on the end of each skewer. Stand the skewers in a straight-sided container (I use plastic food-storage containers) that is deep enough to allow immersion of the fruit;

the skewers should be packed snugly in the container so they stand up.

3. Pour the cooled marinade over the fruit to just cover it. Cover with foil or plastic wrap and chill until just before serving.

4. Stand the pineapple top in the center of a serving platter. Arrange the skewers around the pineapple top, with the fruit toward the center. Drizzle some of the marinade over the fruit to keep it moist.

Band Concert Picnic on the Green

for 12

◆

Menu

PEANUT-COATED FRIED CHICKEN

UNCLE JOHN'S "CRAZY" SALAD

LOBSTER AND NEW POTATO SALAD

BEET AND APPLE SLAW

ZUCCHINI-BASIL MUFFINS

· · ·

SHAKER SWEET AND SOUR CHERRY PIE

CHOCOLATE ANGEL FOOD CAKE
WITH RASPBERRIES

All across America, from the town-square bandstand gazebo where the high school band plays to the huge portable bandstand erected for the New York Philharmonic in Central Park, people gather every summer to listen to music under the stars. Even a light rain doesn't deter the crowds from showing up, as you can see in the photographs we took when we went to hear the Boston Pops at a park on Cape Cod; the lure of beautiful music and food enjoyed on the lawn on a cool summer evening was just too strong.

This is an all-American picnic with food that packs easily and travels well. Fried chicken is a picnic classic, and here a crunchy peanut coating gives it a new twist. Three salads, a fresh cherry pie, and an old-fashioned chocolate angel food cake round out the menu.

GETTING READY Obviously, since this is a picnic, everything should be prepared in advance and packed and ready to go when you are. The muffins can be made up to 2 days ahead. Everything else in this menu can be prepared a day in advance if need be, but it's best to do all the cooking early on the day of the picnic.

A few of the steps can be done a day in advance. Cook the beets and store them, unpeeled and covered, in the refrigerator. Cook the lobster for the lobster and potato salad (for convenience's sake, I splurge and buy lobster tails, since it's quicker and easier to extract the meat from tails than from whole lobsters).

Make the pie and cake early in the day. While baking, cook the potatoes, and then prepare the lobster and potato salad. Prepare the beet and apple slaw next. The chicken is best when made only a few hours in advance so it doesn't need to be refrigerated and maintains its crisp crust. (If the chicken must be made sooner, allow it to cool completely before refrigerating so the crunchy coating doesn't get soggy.)

BEVERAGES I like a light, fruity white wine for a picnic like this, one that can be sipped all through the evening, such as a French Colombard or a Johannisberg Riesling. Add a few bottles of lemon- or lime-flavored mineral water to the cooler as well. You might also want to take along a thermos of coffee, hot or iced, depending on the weather.

Peanut-Coated Fried Chicken

·

MAKES 16 PIECES

Old-fashioned fried chicken with extra flavor and extra crunch.

1¾ cups shelled, salted, roasted peanuts
1 cup fine dry bread crumbs
2 large garlic cloves
¼ teaspoon cayenne pepper
½ teaspoon paprika
½ teaspoon ground ginger

¾ cup milk
1 large egg
1 cup all-purpose flour, approximately
2 fryers, cut into eighths and skin removed
Peanut oil, for frying

1. Combine the peanuts, bread crumbs, garlic, and spices in the bowl of a food processor fitted with the steel chopping blade. Process, using short pulses, until the ingredients are combined and the nuts are very finely ground.

2. Transfer the peanut mixture to a shallow bowl. In a separate shallow bowl, beat the milk and egg together to blend well. Put the flour in a third shallow bowl.

3. Dip the chicken pieces into the egg-milk mixture and then roll in the flour. Quickly dip each piece in the egg-milk mixture again and then roll in the peanut mixture. Place the chicken on a wire rack and allow the coating to dry for about 20 minutes.

4. In a large skillet, heat about 1 inch of peanut oil to 370°F. Arrange a single layer of chicken skinned side down (dark meat first) in the pan and fry, turning occasionally with tongs, until the chicken is very well browned on all sides. The dark meat should cook in 12 to 15 minutes, and the white meat in 10 to 12 minutes, depending on size.

5. Transfer the chicken to racks lined with paper towels or brown paper. Allow the chicken to cool completely before wrapping and refrigerating so the coating remains crisp. Return to room temperature before serving.

$\mathcal{U}$NCLE JOHN'S "CRAZY" SALAD

• SERVES 12

My nephew named this salad of leaf lettuce, oranges, olives, onions, and blue cheese. When I take salad that is mostly greens to a picnic, I carry the dressing in a separate bottle or jar and dress the salad just before serving.

5 cups leaf lettuce, washed, dried, and torn into
    bite-size pieces
2 oranges, peeled and sectioned
½ cup pitted ripe black olives
1 small red onion, sliced and separated into rings
1 cup loosely packed basil leaves
¼ pound blue cheese, crumbled
¼ cup toasted pignoli
Red Wine Vinaigrette (page 220)

In a large, shallow serving bowl, mound the lettuce and scatter the remaining ingredients, except the dressing, over it. Just before serving, drizzle the dressing over the salad and toss.

$\mathcal{L}$OBSTER AND NEW POTATO SALAD

• SERVES 12

This is a variation of what used to be known, in polite ladies' luncheon circles, as a "lobster mayonnaise." Fancy as it sounds, this is a basic all-American recipe with no gimmicks, and it's garnished the way we've seen potato salads garnished at picnics for generations.

DRESSING
1½ cups Homemade Mayonnaise (page 221)
1 teaspoon brown mustard
1 tablespoon lemon juice
¼ cup chopped parsley
Pinch of cayenne pepper

2 pounds new potatoes
Salt
3 cups cooked lobster meat, in chunks
1 cup thinly sliced celery
1 medium onion, finely chopped
2 ripe medium tomatoes, cut into wedges, for
    garnish
1 hard-boiled egg, sliced, for garnish

1. Combine the dressing ingredients in a small bowl, cover, and refrigerate until needed.

2. Boil the potatoes until tender in salted water to cover, about 20 minutes. When they're cool enough to handle, peel them and cut them into ⅛-inch-thick slices.

3. In a large bowl, combine the potatoes, lobster, celery, and onion. Add the dressing and gently toss to combine. Mound the salad in a shallow bowl or on a platter, cover with plastic wrap, and refrigerate until serving. (Keep chilled in a cooler if it's being transported.)

4. To serve, arrange the tomato wedges around the salad and arrange a row of egg slices across it.

ABOVE: A late afternoon rain stopped at sunset, just in time for us to raise the flag and spread out our colorful buffet.

BELOW: Unusual flavor combinations make up the main course: peanut-coated fried chicken and an array of colorful salads.

ABOVE: An old-fashioned chocolate angel food cake with raspberries. BELOW: A spectacular sweet and sour cherry pie.

Beet and Apple Slaw

The deep red and shocking pink colors in this salad always surprise anyone who sees it for the first time.

DRESSING
½ cup Homemade Mayonnaise (page 221)
½ cup sour cream
2 teaspoons prepared horseradish

3 pounds medium beets, unpeeled, washed, and
  trimmed
2 pounds crisp tart apples, such as Granny Smith
  or Macintosh
2 tablespoons cider vinegar
3 or 4 scallions, white and green parts, finely
  julienned

1. In a small bowl, combine the dressing ingredients, cover, and set aside.

2. Preheat the oven to 350°F. Place the beets in a shallow roasting pan and roast until tender, about 45 minutes (or boil the beets in salted water to cover until tender, about 45 minutes, and drain). When the beets are cool enough to handle, peel off the skins. When the beets are completely cool, cut them into matchstick julienne.

3. Peel and core the apples and cut them into matchstick julienne. Place them in a small bowl and toss with the vinegar. Add the beets, scallions, and dressing to the bowl and toss well to combine. Cover and refrigerate until serving.

VARIATIONS Substitute 1 cup julienned raw turnip or jicama for 1 cup of the beets.

Zucchini-Basil Muffins

If you're like me, you're always looking for recipes to use up the abundance of zucchini from the vegetable patch. These muffins, an unusual variation of zucchini bread, keep and travel well, making them perfect for picnics. If fresh basil is unavailable, eliminate it rather than substituting dried.

¾ cup sugar
3 large eggs
1 cup vegetable oil
2 cups all-purpose flour
2 teaspoons baking powder
½ teaspoon salt
¼ teaspoon freshly ground black pepper
¼ teaspoon grated nutmeg
1 cup grated raw and unpeeled zucchini
½ cup chopped basil leaves
½ teaspoon grated lemon rind

1. Preheat the oven to 350°F. Lightly grease two 1-dozen muffin pans.

2. In a large mixing bowl, beat together the sugar, eggs, and oil. In a separate bowl, sift together the flour, baking powder, salt, pepper, and nutmeg. Stir the dry mixture into the wet mixture until just blended, then fold in the zucchini, basil, and lemon rind all at once.

3. Spoon the batter into the prepared pans, filling the muffin cups about two-thirds full. Place the pans in the oven and bake until a toothpick inserted in the center of a muffin comes out clean, 35 to 40 minutes.

4. Remove the pans to wire racks, cool 10 minutes, and then remove the muffins from the pan and cool them completely. The muffins will keep well, tightly wrapped, for 2 or 3 days.

"A slight sound at evening lifts me up by the ears, and makes life seem inexpressibly serene and grand. It may be in Uranus, or it may be in the shutter." —Henry David Thoreau

Shaker Sweet and Sour Cherry Pie

•

MAKES ONE 9 X 13-INCH PIE

Most recipes for cherry pies call for canned cherries, which turn out too gloppy as far as I'm concerned, so I usually wait until cherry season to bake Mr. Washington a belated birthday pie. This method of making a pie with fresh cherries is from an old recipe from the Shakers of Ohio.

FILLING
4 cups pitted fresh sweet cherries
4 cups pitted fresh sour cherries
2 cups sugar
6 tablespoons cornstarch
¼ teaspoon salt
¼ cup finely chopped almonds
½ teaspoon almond extract
Grated rind of 1 lemon
¼ cup (½ stick) butter

Double recipe Basic Pastry for a 10-inch pie (page 220)
1 large egg, beaten with 1 tablespoon milk

1. Combine the filling ingredients, except the butter, in a medium saucepan and toss to blend. Place over low heat and cook, stirring occasionally with a wooden spoon, until the sugar has melted and some liquid forms on the bottom of the pan. Add the butter. Raise the heat to medium and cook, stirring occasionally to prevent sticking, until the liquid thickens, 10 to 15 minutes. Remove from the heat and allow to cool for 15 to 20 minutes.

2. Preheat the oven to 400°F. Divide the pastry in half and roll one half into a 12 x 16-inch rectangle or oval. Line a 9 x 13-inch rectangular baking dish (or equivalent oval dish) with the pastry, letting the edges hang over the edges of the dish. Spoon the filling into the prepared pastry shell.

3. Roll out the remaining pastry and, using a fluted pastry wheel, cut it into 1-inch wide strips, then use strips to make a lattice top. Fold the overhanging edges of the bottom crust up over the edges and crimp.

4. Brush the pastry with the beaten egg mixture. Bake until pastry is a rich golden brown, about 40 to 45 minutes. Remove to a wire rack to cool.

Chocolate Angel Food Cake with Raspberries

•

MAKES ONE 10-INCH CAKE

¾ cup sifted cake flour
4 tablespoons sifted unsweetened cocoa
1¼ cups sifted sugar
1¼ cups egg whites (about 10 large egg whites), at room temperature
¼ teaspoon salt
1 teaspoon cream of tartar
1 teaspoon vanilla extract

1 pint raspberries
¼ cup sugar

1. In a mixing bowl, stir the flour, cocoa, and sugar together. Using a sifter or fine sieve, sift the mixture until completely and evenly blended (sift 4 or 5 times). Preheat the oven to 350°F.

2. In a separate clean and greasefree bowl, beat the egg whites until soft peaks form. Add the salt and cream of tartar and continue beating until stiff but not dry. Fold in the vanilla.

3. Using a few tablespoonfuls at a time, gently fold the dry mixture into the beaten egg whites. When all the whites have been incorporated, gently transfer the batter to an *ungreased* 2-piece 10-inch tube pan with a removable outer rim. Tap the pan twice on the work surface to break up any large air pockets.

4. Place the pan in the lower third of the oven and bake for 40 to 50 minutes, or until the cake is well browned. When done, invert the pan so that the cake hangs inside it above the work surface. If the pan has feet, the cake will be about an inch above the surface; if the pan has no feet, stand it on a weighted bottle through the tube. Allow the cake to cool completely, hanging in the pan.

5. To remove the cake from the pan, first remove the outer rim. Then invert the cake onto a cake plate and gently tap it once or twice to separate it from the bottom.

6. Toss the berries with the sugar, cover, and let stand a few hours in the refrigerator. Just before serving, place the berries in the center hole of the cake. To cut the cake, use an angel food cake cutter or 2 forks. Serve each slice of cake with a few berries.

ABOVE: The main course celebrates the summer's bounty.
BELOW: A spice-scented peach upside-down cake.

A FARMSTAND SUPPER

for 6

◆

Menu

CORN ON THE COB WITH SPICY BUTTER

HOME-FRIED POTATOES WITH GARLIC AND HERBS

ORANGE-ROASTED BEETS

STEAMED BEET GREENS WITH BACON AND
RED ONION

SLICED TOMATOES

• • •

GRANDMA STAPLETON'S PEACH
UPSIDE-DOWN CAKE

No matter how old we are, we all cling to childhood memories, and this menu is made up of foods I remember from my childhood on our farm in Willard, Ohio. These dishes are typical of those Mom used to serve for supper on a summer night, and everything's simply prepared to retain the fresh, just-picked flavor.

At the end of a summer's day, Mom would send one of us out to the vegetable garden to pull up a few beets or pick a couple of tomatoes. Now I do my picking at a local farmstand in the country or the farmer's market in the city.

GETTING READY Aside from the cake and the spicy butter for the corn, which can be made early in the day, everything should be prepared just before serving. Start roasting the beets first and then start the home fries. Heat the water for the corn; husk it and cook it at the last minute.

BEVERAGES Only two drinks go with this kind of supper: iced tea and not-too-sweet lemonade.

I like setting a bright and colorful table in the summertime. The printed tablecloth and napkins, flowered glasses, and bakelite-handled flatware are flea market finds and the ceramic chickens are from my collection of farm animal figures. The green Fireking plates are just like the ones we used in the kitchen when I was growing up.

Corn on the Cob with Spicy Butter

SERVES 6

This is the easiest method there is for fixing perfect fresh corn. The spicy butter is subtle enough to enhance rather than overpower the just-picked flavor.

½ cup (1 stick) butter, softened
½ teaspoon salt
¼ teaspoon cayenne pepper
½ teaspoon ground cumin

1 dozen ears freshly picked sweet corn

1. To make the cayenne butter, combine the butter, salt, cayenne, and cumin in a small mixing bowl. Transfer to a crock, cover with plastic wrap, and refrigerate. Return to room temperature before serving.

2. Place a large kettle of salted water over high heat and bring to a rolling boil. While the water is heating, husk the corn, reserving a few of the inner husks. One at a time, add the corn ears to the water and add the reserved husks. Cover the kettle and remove it from the heat; let stand 5 minutes. (The corn can stand for 20 minutes or so, staying hot and not overcooking.)

3. Remove the corn from the water with tongs. Serve immediately and pass the crock of butter.

Perfect Corn on the Cob

Much has been written about the various ways for preparing "perfect" corn, but the truth is that the perfection lies more in the corn itself than the method of cooking it. There are three key words to remember: fresh, fresh, and fresh.

On our farm, Mom would set a kettle on the stove, and when the water was boiling, one of us kids would be sent out to the vegetable patch to pick the corn and then husk it on the kitchen steps, then into the kettle it would go.

Obviously most of us can't get corn quite that fresh, but if you can track down corn that's truly just picked, no matter how far you have to drive, it's worth it. When selecting corn, look for plump small kernels; corn with huge or even slightly wrinkled kernels is often too old to be worth eating. Once you get the corn home, refrigerate it immediately and don't take it out until just before cooking.

If corn is less than perfect, here are a few remedies: Old and tough corn may need to be boiled for a few minutes to help tenderize it. If the corn was picked a day or so ago, the natural sugars have begun turning to starch; a tablespoon of sugar added to the water will help sweeten it a little, even though it will never taste fresh-picked again.

Home-Fried Potatoes with Garlic and Herbs

SERVES 6 TO 8

I recently began using olive oil as an alternative to saturated fats for home-frying potatoes. Add a little garlic and fresh herbs, and the results are heavenly.

⅓ cup olive oil
2 large garlic cloves, finely chopped
1 medium onion, chopped
3 pounds small waxy potatoes, unpeeled and
   thinly sliced
2 teaspoons crumbled rosemary leaves
2 tablespoons chopped sage
Salt and freshly ground black pepper

1. Place the oil, garlic, and onion in a large skillet and sauté over medium heat for 5 minutes. Add the potatoes and toss to coat them with oil.

2. Cover the skillet and cook, turning frequently, for 20 minutes. Add the herbs and continue cooking, turning frequently, until the potatoes are well browned and tender, another 10 minutes. Season to taste with salt and plenty of pepper.

Orange-Roasted Beets

SERVES 6

Roasting beets enhances their earthy flavor, and roasting is a less messy method of cooking than boiling them. They can be roasted whole and then peeled or cooked as described here. Be sure to select beets that are approximately the same size so they cook evenly.

2 tablespoons butter
2 pounds medium beets, trimmed, peeled, and
   quartered
1 tablespoon olive oil
Juice and grated rind of 1 small orange

1. Preheat the oven to 350°F. Using half the butter, generously grease a 1½-quart casserole. In a bowl, toss the beets with the olive oil, orange juice, and orange rind. Transfer this mixture to the casserole. Dot the beets with the remaining butter.

2. Cover the casserole with a lid or aluminum foil and roast for 40 to 50 minutes, or until the beets are tender. Serve hot.

Steamed Beet Greens with Bacon and Red Onion

SERVES 6

When I was growing up, I only ate beets so I could have the greens—strange kid, huh? This down-home method of fixing the greens is still one of my favorite summer dishes.

3 slices bacon, coarsely chopped
1 small red onion, coarsely chopped
Greens from 2 pounds beets, well washed but
   not dried
Freshly ground black pepper
Cider vinegar

1. In a Dutch oven over medium heat sauté the bacon and onion until the onion is transparent and the bacon is cooked, about 10 minutes.

2. Add the washed greens, with water still clinging to them, to the Dutch oven. Cover tightly and steam the greens until tender, 10 to 15 minutes. Toss and season to taste with black pepper and vinegar.

BEET GREENS WITH BALSAMIC VINAIGRETTE
By substituting 3 tablespoons olive oil for the bacon, this menu becomes vegetarian. Use balsamic vinegar rather than cider vinegar.

. . . .

Sliced Tomatoes

When it comes to big, juicy, bright red, in-season, fresh-from-the-farm tomatoes, I like them plain and simple. I don't see any need to tamper with perfection. Others may disagree. For instance, "Pop" Walters, who used to help Dad out on the farm, would go through an elaborate ritual almost every day during tomato season: first he'd arrange sliced tomatoes on a big plate, then he'd spread them with a thin layer of yellow mustard and add a sprinkling of sugar and a grinding of pepper. And that was lunch. I have to admit that I have never tried Pop Walters "recipe," but I do recommend the following:

Cut large ripe tomatoes into ¼-inch-thick slices and arrange them on a serving platter. If you feel compelled to do something to the tomatoes, do no more than add a few drops of olive oil, a bit of chopped basil or oregano, and a grinding of black pepper, or as my grandfather used to do, sprinkle a generous pinch each of salt and sugar over them.

. . . .

Grandma Stapleton's Peach Upside-Down Cake
•
MAKES ONE 9-INCH CAKE

Grandma Stapleton's kitchen looked out over the orchard and a big patch of wildflowers, and just outside the kitchen door stood four hardy peach trees. Early in her marriage, Grandma had started the trees from pits, so by the time I came along, the trees had long been producing delicious fruit. Every summer, Grandma canned jars and jars of peaches, peach jam, and peach chutney, and she baked pies, cobblers, and this simple cake, my favorite of all. I like it best when it is still warm from the oven and topped with a dab of unsweetened whipped cream.

⅓ cup (⅔ stick) butter
½ cup firmly packed light brown sugar
¼ teaspoon ground cinnamon
⅛ teaspoon grated nutmeg
¼ teaspoon ground ginger
2 cups firm ripe peaches, peeled, pitted, and
   thickly sliced

¼ cup (½ stick) butter
½ cup granulated sugar
1 large egg
1 cup all-purpose flour
¾ teaspoon baking soda
¼ teaspoon salt
½ cup milk

1. Preheat the oven to 350°F. Melt ⅓ cup butter in a 9-inch ovenproof skillet over low heat; stir in the brown sugar and spices. Stir until the sugar is dissolved. Remove the skillet from the heat and arrange the peach slices in a pattern in a single layer over the brown sugar mixture.

2. In a mixing bowl, cream together ¼ cup butter and granulated sugar. Beat in the egg. In a separate bowl, sift together the flour, baking soda, and salt and beat this mixture into the butter-and-sugar mixture alternately with the milk. Carefully spoon the batter into the pan over the peaches.

3. Bake for 25 to 30 minutes, or until a cake tester inserted in the center of the cake comes out clean. Cool the cake in the pan for 10 minutes, then invert it onto a cake plate or stand. Serve warm or at room temperature with unsweetened whipped cream.

Indian Summer Dinner at Sunset

for 2
♦
Menu

GRILLED PLUM TOMATOES WITH
GRILLED CHEESE-STUFFED PITA WEDGES

•   •   •

GRILLED TROUT WITH MUSHROOMS AND
WILD THYME

WILD RICE AND VEGETABLE SALAD

•   •   •

BLUEBERRY CRISP

I f you have a spectacular western vista, there's nothing more pleasant than sitting down to the dinner table as the day is ending and the sky dissolves into layers of fabulous colors. But, as I've learned, you've got to have your timing down to a science.

First, you need a *Farmer's Almanac*. Check the time that the sun will set, so you can time dinner accordingly. Once in the country, I planned dinner for eight o'clock but hadn't bothered to check the time; the sun set at a little after half-past seven. I was grilling salmon steaks, and as the sun sank behind the trees, the steaks were cooked on one side but raw on the other. Well, I

ABOVE RIGHT: Grilled mushroom- and herb-stuffed trout with a salad of wild rice and vegetables. RIGHT: Blueberry crisp is decorated with wild blueberries.

OPPOSITE: As the sun sets beyond the lake, the simple first course is set out on a lantern-lit table.

finished cooking the salmon with the help of a flashlight and quickly added a few more candles to the table, and no one was the wiser. But I learned my lesson and now try to leave nothing to chance.

GETTING READY This dinner requires little last-minute work except the not-unpleasant job of tending the grill.

Early in the day, prepare the salad and the stuffing for the fish. Also mix the oil and garlic for the first course.

The blueberry crisp can also be prepared early in the day, though it's best when it comes out of the oven about an hour before serving.

A few hours before dinner, stuff the fish and refrigerate them.

An hour before dinner, remove the salad from the refrigerator to bring it to room temperature.

Prepare the grill and light the fire about forty-five minutes before you want to start cooking. Have the pita wedges and tomatoes ready for grilling when the fire is ready.

BEVERAGES A full, dry white wine, such as a Sauvignon Blanc or Chenin Blanc, is delicious with dinner. I like strongly brewed black coffee or espresso with the fruity crisp.

GRILLED PLUM TOMATOES WITH GRILLED CHEESE-STUFFED PITA WEDGES

•

SERVES 2

When made with in-season tomatoes, this is utterly simple and utterly delicious.

2 whole wheat pitas
⅓ cup soft goat cheese or herb-flavored soft cheese such as Boursin
2 tablespoons extra-virgin olive oil
1 garlic clove, crushed
4 firm ripe plum tomatoes, cut into wedges
Freshly ground black pepper

1. In a small dish, combine the oil and garlic and let stand for a few hours.

2. Cut each pita in half. Using a blunt knife, spread the cheese inside the pita. Press the pitas closed and cut each half into 3 wedges.

3. Brush the tomatoes and pita with the mixture

and grill over hot coals until the tomatoes just begin to soften and brown and the pita is well browned.

4. Arrange the tomatoes on a serving plate and surround them with the pita. Sprinkle the tomatoes lavishly with fresh pepper.

GRILLED TROUT WITH MUSHROOMS AND WILD THYME

•

SERVES 2

Trout are now raised on farms and are more readily available in markets across the country, so if you're not an angler, you don't have to forgo the pleasures of eating this succulent fish. When we photographed this menu, we were lucky enough to find a patch of wild thyme nearby; fresh thyme from the market is a perfectly respectable substitute.

2 rainbow or brook trout, 12 ounces each, dressed
¼ cup olive oil
2 shallots, finely chopped
½ pound mushrooms (any variety)
¼ cup coarse fresh bread crumbs
1 tablespoon thyme leaves
Salt and freshly ground black pepper
1 lemon, cut into thin round slices
Sprigs of thyme

1. Prepare a charcoal or hardwood fire. When the coals are glowing and ash covered, the fire is ready for cooking.

2. Generously brush the trout inside and out with olive oil and reserve remaining oil.

3. To make the stuffing, combine the shallots, mushrooms, bread crumbs, and thyme leaves with the reserved olive oil in a small bowl. Season with salt and pepper to taste. Stuff the trout with this mixture. Place 2 or 3 lemon slices inside each trout (reserve the remaining lemon slices).

4. Place a sprig of thyme on each side of the trout and carefully tie the trout in 2 or 3 places to hold the stuffing in place.

5. Grill the trout about 5 inches above the fire for 5 to 8 minutes per side, depending on the heat of the fire, until the flesh flakes easily with a fork. Serve immediately, garnished with reserved lemon slices.

Wild Rice and Vegetable Salad

2 cups water
¼ teaspoon salt
½ cup wild rice, well rinsed
⅓ cup olive oil
1½ tablespoons red wine vinegar
1½ tablespoons soy sauce
2 scallions, white and green parts, thinly sliced
1 small cucumber, peeled, seeded, and diced
1 small carrot, peeled, cooked, and diced
1 small head radicchio, shredded (see note)
1 tablespoon chopped basil or mint
Salt and freshly ground black pepper
Basil or mint leaves, for garnish

1. In a small saucepan, bring the water to a boil and add the salt. Stir in the wild rice and reduce the heat to low. Cover the pan loosely and cook until the wild rice is tender, about 40 to 45 minutes.

2. Combine the oil, vinegar, and soy sauce in a small bowl and whisk to blend. Add the warm wild rice and the remaining ingredients and toss well to combine. Cover and let stand at room temperature for 2 hours to allow flavors to blend. (*If made earlier, refrigerate the salad and return to room temperature before serving.*)

3. Toss the salad again before serving and moisten with a bit more olive oil if necessary. Garnish with basil or mint.

NOTE If radicchio is unavailable, substitute ¾ cup shredded red cabbage.

Blueberry Crisp

This recipe makes more than two generous servings, but I like to make enough so I can have leftovers the next morning for breakfast.

½ cup all-purpose flour
¼ cup firmly packed light brown sugar
½ teaspoon ground cinnamon
¼ cup (½ stick) butter
½ cup quick-cooking oats
1 pint blueberries

1. Preheat the oven to 350°F. Generously butter a shallow 1-quart casserole or a 9-inch ceramic or ovenproof glass pie pan.

2. In a small mixing bowl, stir together the flour, sugar, and cinnamon to blend. Cut in the butter until the mixture resembles coarse crumbs. Mix in the oats.

3. Spread the blueberries in the prepared casserole and then spread the topping over the berries.

4. Bake until the topping is nicely browned and blueberries are bubbly and tender, 35 to 40 minutes. Serve warm, spooned into shallow dishes, with a drizzle of heavy cream or a small scoop of softened Vanilla Bean Ice Cream (page 221).

"The quicker a fresh water fish is on the fire after it is caught, the better it is."
Mark Twain

FALL

Dinner Away from It All

for 4

•

Menu

Yellow Pepper Soup

• • •

Grilled Marinated Duckling with
Peppery Plum-Mustard Glaze

Sautéed Watercress with Pecans

Skillet Corn with Sage

• • •

Apple Tartlets with Nutmeg-Scented
Orange Custard

When my friends Peter and Jennifer bought a large late-Victorian house in the Berkshires, they invited me for the grand tour. The house is a beauty, but the room that I liked the most was the attic, which is in pristine condition. In a corner under one of the gables, I discovered an enchanting spot, just perfect for a big party, a surprise birthday celebration, or an intimate dinner, away from sound systems, doorbells, and ringing telephones.

To usher in autumn, a quiet dinner was planned, when the temperature in the unheated, non-air-conditioned space would be just right. We carried a folding table upstairs along with Jennifer's grandmother's dining chairs, and then we set the table "to the nines." As a final touch, votive candles created a path that led from the top of the stairs to the table. To avoid endless trips upstairs, dinner was carried up from the kitchen on trays.

Obviously, we don't all have gabled Victorian attics, but take a look around your house—perhaps the end of a wide hallway, a sheltered corner of the yard, a nook or cranny under a staircase, or a romantic win-dow seat with a view would make the perfect hide-away.

GETTING READY Up to several weeks in advance, make the glaze for the duck and store it in the refrigerator. Up to two days in advance, make the custard sauce for the tartlets.

A day in advance, marinate the duck and prepare the soup up to the end of step 3.

A few hours in advance, scrape the corn and wash the watercress (both vegetables need to be cooked just before serving). The apple tartlets can be prepared a few hours ahead, if need be, but don't bake them until an hour or so before serving.

Light the fire in the grill at least an hour before you want to start cooking the duck. Once the duck (which requires close watching) is cooked, the vegetables take only a few minutes.

BEVERAGES Sauvignon Blanc with the soup; a dry, full-bodied red such as a Burgundy or a Cabernet Sauvignon with the duck.

Yellow Pepper Soup

•

SERVES 4

Rich in flavor and color, this soup starts dinner off with a bang, getting the palate ready for the flavors that follow.

  3 tablespoons olive oil
  1 small red onion, chopped
  2 shallots, chopped
  1 small garlic clove, crushed
  4 medium yellow peppers, seeded and coarsely
    chopped
  1 large carrot, peeled and coarsely chopped
  2 tablespoons all-purpose flour
  2 cups hot chicken stock
  ¼ teaspoon dried thyme
  1 teaspoon fennel seeds
  1 tablespoon chopped fresh basil leaves or 1
    teaspoon dried basil
  1 bay leaf
  Salt
  Red pepper sauce
  ½ cup heavy cream
  1 tablespoon Sambuca liqueur

1. In a large, heavy saucepan over medium heat, heat the oil to sizzling. Add the onion, shallots, garlic, yellow pepper, and carrot and sauté until the onion is transparent and softened, 10 to 12 minutes. Whisk in the flour and cook, stirring constantly, for 5 minutes.

2. Gradually whisk in the chicken stock and then add the thyme, fennel seeds, basil, and bay leaf. Bring the mixture to a simmer, cover loosely, and simmer until the vegetables are mushy and the mixture is fairly thick, 30 to 40 minutes.

3. Remove the bay leaf and transfer the soup to the bowl of a food processor fitted with the steel chopping blade. Process until smoothly pureed. *(The soup can be prepared 1 or 2 days in advance up to this point and refrigerated; reheat before proceeding.)*

4. Return the soup to the pan over low heat and bring to just below the simmering point. Stir in ¼ cup of the cream (reserve the remaining ¼ cup) and cook 5 minutes—do not allow the soup to simmer.

5. Just before serving, stir the reserved cream together with the liqueur to blend. Season to taste with salt and red pepper sauce. Ladle the soup into 4 shallow soup bowls. Drizzle a generous tablespoon of the cream mixture onto each serving of soup in a swirling pattern. Serve immediately.

*G*RILLED MARINATED DUCKLING WITH PEPPERY PLUM-MUSTARD GLAZE

•

SERVES 4

MARINADE
2 large garlic cloves, crushed
2 scallions, white and green parts, coarsely
  chopped
1 teaspoon coarse salt
1 teaspoon black peppercorns, crushed
1 teaspoon dry mustard
1 cup dry red wine or ½ cup dry red wine and
  ½ cup dry sherry

2 4½- to 5-pound ducklings, quartered and wings
  removed
Peppery Plum-Mustard Glaze (recipe follows)

1. Combine the marinade ingredients in a small jar. Cover tightly and shake well. Set aside.

2. Trim the ducks of all excess fat and prick the skins all over with a fork. Put the ducks in a strong, clean plastic bag. Pour the marinade into the bag, shake the bag to coat the ducks all over, and then tie

the bag shut. Refrigerate overnight. Shake and turn the bag occasionally to distribute the marinade.

3. Remove the ducks from the bag and discard the bag and marinade. Wipe the ducks with paper towels. Then grill or broil the duck as follows:

4. *Grilling Method:* Prepare a charcoal fire. Place the ducks on the grill about 5 inches above glowing, ash-covered coals. Have a spray bottle of water handy to extinguish flareups once the duck starts cooking and releasing fat. Grill the duck, turning and pricking the skin with a fork frequently to release additional fat, for about 45 minutes.

Broiling Method: Preheat the broiler. Place the ducks skin side down on a broiling pan (I use disposable foil pans) and place on a rack 4 to 5 inches below the heat. Broil for 10 minutes, remove the pans from the broiler, and carefully pour off all the fat. Turn the ducks over with tongs and prick the skin again to release the excess fat. Broil for an additional 20 minutes.

5. When the skin is nicely browned on all sides, brush the duck with the glaze. Continue cooking, turning frequently to avoid charring. The duck is done to medium-rare when the skin is crisp and well browned and the juices are slightly pink when the meat is pierced with a knife; cook the duck about 7 minutes longer for medium-well. Brush the duck lightly with additional glaze a minute or two before removing from the heat.

PEPPERY PLUM-MUSTARD GLAZE
½ cup beach plum or damson plum jam
2 tablespoons dry mustard
2 large garlic cloves, crushed
1 tablespoon finely chopped fresh ginger or
  1 teaspoon ground ginger
¼ cup sherry vinegar or red wine vinegar
1 tablespoon olive oil
1 teaspoon cracked black pepper
Salt

1. In a small, heavy saucepan, combine all the ingredients except the black pepper and salt. Bring to a simmer over medium heat, lower the heat, and simmer gently for 10 minutes.

2. Remove the glaze from the heat and strain through a double layer of cheesecloth. Stir in the pepper and season to taste with salt. Pour into a small jar or bowl and allow to cool. Cover and refrigerate overnight to allow the flavors to blend; the glaze will keep for several weeks in the refrigerator.

A yellow pepper soup is finished off with a swirl of cream.

The colorful main course on a simple gold-banded plate.

BELOW: An apple tartlet with a delicate puff pastry crust is served in a pool of nutmeg-scented orange custard.

SAUTÉED WATERCRESS WITH PECANS

•

SERVES 4

1 tablespoon olive oil
1 garlic clove, crushed
3 cups watercress leaves, stems removed and
   washed (do not dry)
¼ cup coarsely chopped pecans
Salt and freshly ground black pepper

1. Place the oil and garlic in a skillet over medium heat. Sauté the garlic for 1 minute and discard it.

2. Add the watercress and pecans to the pan and cover. Allow the watercress to steam for 2 or 3 minutes; when it is wilted remove the lid from the pan. Toss the mixture and sauté for 1 minute longer. Season to taste with salt and pepper and serve immediately.

VARIATION Substitute 2 or 3 tablespoons lightly toasted pignoli for the pecans.

Our hideaway dinner table is set up in a corner of the attic. Votive candles are placed all over the floor to add a warm, inviting glow.

Skillet Corn with Sage

SERVES 4

1 tablespoon butter
½ small onion or 3 scallions, white and green
    parts, finely chopped
½ red pepper, diced
5 medium ears very fresh corn
1 teaspoon chopped sage
¼ teaspoon salt
Freshly ground black pepper

1. Melt the butter in a small skillet over low heat and add the onion or scallions and the red pepper. Sauté until the onion is tender and translucent and the butter is lightly browned, about 10 minutes.

2. While the onion and pepper are cooking, use a sharp knife to scrape the corn kernels from the cobs, taking care to save all the milky juice. Add the corn, juice, sage, and salt to the pan. Turn up the heat and sauté quickly for 1 or 2 minutes, until the corn is just cooked. Season with fresh pepper and serve immediately.

Apple Tartlets with Nutmeg-Scented Orange Custard

MAKES 4

2 medium baking apples, such as Rhode Island
    Greening, Gravenstein, or Granny Smith
Juice of ½ lemon
3 teaspoons sugar
1 sheet (approximately ½ pound) frozen puff
    pastry, thawed
¼ cup (½ stick) butter, melted
Nutmeg-Scented Orange Custard (recipe follows)

1. Peel and core the apples and then cut them into very thin vertical slices. Place them in a small bowl and toss them with the lemon juice and 2 teaspoons sugar.

2. Lay the puff pastry out on a lightly floured pastry board. Using a small plate or bowl as a guide, cut out 4 disks approximately 5 inches in diameter. (Refreeze any leftover pastry for another use.)

3. Preheat the oven to 425°F. Sprinkle a baking sheet lightly with water and transfer the pastry disks to the baking sheet. Brush the disks lightly with butter and sprinkle them with the remaining sugar.

4. Arrange the apple slices on the pastry in an overlapping pinwheel pattern, leaving a ¼-inch border of pastry uncovered all around. Drizzle the remaining butter over the apples. (Tartlets can be prepared a few hours ahead, covered tightly with plastic wrap, and refrigerated.)

5. Bake the tarts for 10 to 12 minutes, or until the apples are caramelized and browned. To serve, spoon some custard sauce onto a large plate and place a warm tart in the center of each plate.

NUTMEG-SCENTED ORANGE CUSTARD
⅔ cup milk
2 large egg yolks, at room temperature
2 tablespoons sugar
½ teaspoon vanilla extract
Grated rind of 1 small orange
⅛ teaspoon grated nutmeg

1. In a small saucepan, scald the milk, remove from the heat, and set aside.

2. In the top of a double boiler, not yet over the heat, whisk (or beat with an electric hand mixer) the egg yolks and sugar until thick and lemon colored. Gradually whisk in the milk. Place over simmering water and cook, whisking constantly, until the custard is thick enough to coat a spoon, about 10 minutes.

3. Remove from the heat and stir in the vanilla, orange rind, and nutmeg. Serve the sauce warm or transfer it to a small bowl, place a piece of plastic wrap directly onto the surface of the sauce to prevent a skin from forming, cool, and chill thoroughly. (Can be made up to 2 days in advance.)

*"All human history attests
That happiness for man—the hungry sinner—
Since Eve ate apples, much depends on Dinner!"
Byron*

A "Back-to-the-Fifties" Cocktail Party

for 24

Okay, we're going to have a little fun here (all food snobs can skip right past this one —there's no radicchio or jicama here, the only Maytag in the kitchen is the dishwasher, and we'll be opening jars and cans like crazy). Though I admit to being only thirty-two, I have vivid memories of the fifties and early sixties. It was the age of Ike and Mamie, Uncle Miltie and Lucy, Elvis and Marilyn, Cape Canaveral and Disneyland, instant mashed potatoes and Polaroid pictures, *TV Guide* and TV dinners.

And it was the age of the blender and cream cheese. If it weren't for those two items, I doubt there would ever have been any cocktail parties in the fifties. It seems that no one needed a cookbook or a recipe file in order to entertain; you just used the recipes on the backs of boxes and cans.

Here are many of those quintessentially mid-century foods that I remember—the trendy foods of their day, the foods that America entertained with. As I began thinking about a lot of them, I realized I was remembering some of them with fondness. So, here they are for what they are, with no apologies: some of the greatest kitchen hits of the fifties and sixties.

Call up the Cleavers, the Stones, and the Nelsons on your Princess phone and invite them all over. Load up the fridge and plug in the can opener. Stack up some McGuire Sisters and Chuck Berry platters, put on your poodle skirt or your Perry Como sweater, and have a party.

GETTING READY Even though there's not a whole lot of work here, there is some preparation to be done on the day of the party.

A few days in advance, make the bacon-horseradish and black bean dips and the party mix. One day in advance, make the crabmeat dip, the meatballs, and all the sweets except the cupcakes.

Early on the day of the party, make the cupcakes and frost them. Set up the bar and the buffet table.

A few hours before the party, prepare the two canapes and the pigs-in-blankets; arrange them on baking sheets and stack them in the refrigerator (a lot of baking sheets are needed here, so either borrow some extras or carefully use foil ones). Bake and serve these alternately during the party, a tray or two at a time.

An hour or so before the party, prepare the toothpicked hors d'oeuvres and keep them covered until serving. Also take anything out of the refrigerator that's to be served at room temperature or heated.

Menu

JOE SANSONE'S BLENDER WHISKEY SOURS

FROZEN DAIQUIRIS

CHERRY CUBA LIBRES   MAI TAIS

. . .

CHIPS AND DIPS:

BACON-HORSERADISH DIP

IVA MAE'S HOT CRABMEAT DIP

BLACK BEAN DIP   HOT PIZZA DIP

. . .

PIGS-IN-BLANKETS

SWEET 'N' SOUR PORCUPINE MEATBALLS

ASSORTED "TOOTHPICKED" HORS D'OEUVRES

BACON, CHUTNEY, AND CHEESE CANAPES

TOASTED TUNA CANAPES

CLASSIC PARTY MIX

. . .

KEN'S CHOW MEIN NOODLE CANDY CLUSTERS

RICE KRISPIE SQUARES

COCA-COLA CUPCAKES WITH TUTTI-FRUTTI COCONUT FROSTING

FROZEN CHOCOLATE-COATED BANANAS

Mai Tais

MAKES 1 DRINK

When Hawaii gained statehood in 1959, the other forty-nine states went luau loony: pineapple turned up as an ingredient in everything from soup to nuts. Tropical drinks became all the rage, and Mai Tais topped the list of favorites. I'd guess another good reason for the Mai Tai's popularity was its voguish shade of pink. There are many different versions of the Mai Tai—this is fruitier and less alcoholic than most.

Combine 1½ ounces each of light rum, Rose's lime juice, and grenadine with 4 ounces pineapple juice, 2 drops almond extract, and ice in a cocktail shaker. Shake well and strain the mixture into an Old-Fashioned glass. Skewer a cube of pineapple, an orange slice, and a maraschino cherry onto a small paper umbrella and balance the umbrella on the rim of the glass.

Joe Sansone's Blender Whiskey Sours

MAKES 6 DRINKS

In the fifties and sixties, the blender became standard bar equipment in the American home. New drinks were born and old drinks were revised so they could be whirred up in a flash. Sets of whiskey sour glasses began appearing in many homes; the Sansones had two sets, one for "everyday" and one for "company."

4 cups crushed ice
1 6-ounce can frozen pink lemonade
½ to ⅔ cup whiskey (Scotch, Rye, Irish, Bourbon)
Maraschino cherries with stems, for garnish
Orange slices, for garnish

Place the ice, lemonade, and whiskey in a blender. Blend until smooth, 20 to 30 seconds. Pour into Whiskey Sour glasses and garnish each drink with cherries and orange slices.

FROZEN DAIQUIRIS Substitute limeade for the pink lemonade, substitute rum for the whiskey, and blend away. If you want to get fancy, throw in a very ripe banana or ½ cup very ripe strawberries or peach slices.

A whiskey sour is "in the pink" with the classic garnishes of an orange slice and a maraschino cherry.

Cherry Cuba Libres

MAKES 1 DRINK

The Andrews Sisters made Cuba Libres popular with their hit song, "Rum and Coca-Cola." In those days, when you could only get a cherry Coke at a soda fountain—a place where rum definitely wasn't served—a Cherry Cuba Libre would have been unheard of.

To make the drink, fill a tall glass with crushed ice, pour a jigger (1½ ounces) of dark rum over the ice, and pour in enough cherry cola to fill the glass. Skewer a maraschino cherry to a lime wedge with a toothpick or cocktail pick and perch this garnish on the top of the glass.

OPPOSITE: **A contemporary loft is the backdrop for our venture "back to the fifties." The pressed aluminum trays, stainless steel chafing dish, and the kitschy vases are all from the era.**

BACON-HORSERADISH DIP

•

One of those blender classics; everyone's mom had a recipe in her file. If you feel *compelled* to update this recipe, go right ahead and make it in a food processor.

1 small onion, coarsely chopped
½ pound bacon, cooked crisp and crumbled
2 tablespoons prepared horseradish
2 tablespoons chopped parsley
1 8-ounce package cream cheese, softened
1 cup sour cream
½ cup mayonnaise

Place all ingredients in a blender and blend until smooth, about 30 seconds.

CLAM DIP Substitute two 7-ounce cans drained chopped clams for the bacon.

IVA MAE'S HOT CRABMEAT DIP

•

MAKES ABOUT 3 CUPS

According to Iva Mae Montalbano's kids, this is one that always appeared front and center at extra-special occasions, served in a copper chafing dish—and it was always gobbled right up.

1 8-ounce package cream cheese, softened
½ pound lump crabmeat, flaked
⅓ cup mayonnaise
2 tablespoons lemon juice
1 tablespoon grated onion
1 teaspoon Worcestershire sauce
3 tablespoons chili sauce or ketchup

Mix all the ingredients in a small bowl and refrigerate overnight to allow flavors to blend. To serve hot, combine the ingredients in a 1-quart casserole, cover, and bake at 350°F. until melted and bubbly, 20 to 30 minutes. Serve directly from the casserole (or transfer to a chafing dish) with potato chips or melba toasts.

BLACK BEAN DIP

•

MAKES ABOUT 2½ CUPS

I'd guess that this dip was probably one of our first forays into the "exotic" cuisine from "south of the border." The original recipe was quite bland, so I've jazzed it up a bit. Please don't serve this with tortilla chips—Fritos are the only acceptable dippers.

1 16-ounce can black beans, drained and rinsed
2 8-ounce packages cream cheese, softened
1 large garlic clove, very finely chopped
2 tablespoons grated onion
¾ teaspoon dried oregano
¾ teaspoon chili powder
2 tablespoons Worcestershire sauce
A few dashes of Tabasco
¼ teaspoon salt

Combine all the ingredients in a blender and blend until the mixture is smooth. Store in a covered container in the refrigerator overnight to allow flavors to blend. Serve with corn chips.

HOT PIZZA DIP

•

MAKES ABOUT 4 CUPS

A classic open-the-can "convenience" recipe. It may not bear any resemblance to any pizza you've ever had, but I bet you'll have to admit it tastes pretty good.

2 8-ounce cans tomato sauce
1 6-ounce can tomato paste
1½ cups grated sharp American cheese
½ teaspoon dried oregano
2 or 3 dashes of Tabasco
Garlic melba toasts

Combine the sauce, cheese, and oregano in a heavy saucepan over low heat. Cook, stirring constantly, until the cheese is melted and the mixture is bubbly. Season to taste with Tabasco and serve hot with garlic melba toasts for dipping.

HOT MEXICAN DIP In the fifties, before anyone ever heard of Tex-Mex food, any dish made with beans, cheese, tomatoes, and a hint of spiciness was "Mexican." For a Mexican variation, reduce the quantity of cheese to 1 cup, stir in a can of refried beans, and heat until bubbly. Serve with corn chips.

Everyone's Favorite Onion Dip

You know the one—all you do is dump an envelope of dehydrated onion soup into a container of sour cream and stir. It's the one that causes everyone to turn up their noses at the mere mention of it. Well, anyplace I've ever been where it's been served (come on, admit it—you've been to those places, too) it always gets polished off. Anyway, *somebody's* got to be eating it or the onion soup people wouldn't still be printing the recipe on the box. (And don't forget the ruffled potato chips!)

Pigs-in-Blankets

MAKES 2 DOZEN

These were made with every kind of small sausage from Vienna sausages (those pasty little pinkish things that come in a can) to cocktail franks. I use fresh breakfast sausage links made by a neighborhood butcher.

2 cups all-purpose flour
1 tablespoon baking powder
½ teaspoon salt
¼ cup vegetable shortening, chilled
½ cup finely grated sharp Cheddar
¾ cup milk

¼ cup spicy brown mustard, approximately
*2 dozen small link breakfast sausages, cooked and
    cooled*

1. In a mixing bowl, stir the flour, baking powder, and salt together with a fork until completely blended. Cut in the shortening until the mixture resembles coarse meal. Blend in the grated cheese. Pour in the milk and stir quickly with a fork until all the dry ingredients are just moistened and a soft dough forms.

2. With floured hands and on a floured board, shape the dough into a rectangle about ¼ inch thick. Brush the dough lightly with mustard. With a floured knife, cut the dough into 1 × 2½-inch strips.

3. Preheat the oven to 450°F. Roll a sausage in each strip of dough and seal it by moistening the point with water. (*Can be prepared in advance up to this point and frozen, tightly wrapped. Thaw and return to room temperature before baking.*) Place on an ungreased baking sheet and bake for 12 to 15 minutes, or until golden brown. Serve hot.

Sweet 'n' Sour Porcupine Meatballs

MAKES ABOUT 5 DOZEN

There were Swedish Meatballs, Hawaiian Meatballs, Cocktail Meatballs, and every other variety of miniature meatballs one could think of, but strange as they seem, I like these best.

1½ cups coarse fresh bread crumbs
1½ cups milk
2 pounds ground beef round or chuck
2 medium onions, finely chopped
½ cup finely chopped celery
½ cup long-grain rice
½ teaspoon salt
¼ teaspoon freshly ground black pepper

SAUCE
2 cups tomato juice
1 8-ounce jar grape jelly
2 tablespoons cider vinegar

1. In a large mixing bowl, soak the bread crumbs in the milk for 10 minutes. Add the remaining ingredients and mix together with your hands. Shape the mixture into ¾-inch balls.

2. Preheat the oven to 350°F. Place the meatballs in a greased shallow baking dish. Combine the sauce ingredients in a small bowl and pour the sauce over the meatballs. Bake the meatballs for 1 hour and serve hot with toothpicks.

Assorted "Toothpicked" Hors d'Oeuvres

You remember these—they used to stand at attention in little rows like soldiers. Almost any combination goes, but here are a few ideas. For authenticity, use fancy plastic party picks or the wooden ones that have the colorful little cellophane frills.

Cubes of ham, pineapple, and Swiss cheese
*Stuffed olives, cocktail onions, and cubes of
    salami*
*Cubes of cucumber and provolone and rolled
    slices of pepperoni*
Cubes of liverwurst, gherkins, and cocktail onions
*Pitted dates, cubes of smoked turkey, and small
    balls of cream cheese*

ABOVE: Classic party mix and two trays of toothpicked hors d'oeuvres. ABOVE RIGHT: Little porcupine meatballs with sweet 'n' sour sauce, a tray of canapes, and pigs-in-blankets—all essential fifties party fare.

BACON, CHUTNEY, AND CHEESE CANAPES

•

MAKES ABOUT 4 DOZEN

These really are delicious. Don't knock 'em till you've tried 'em.

1 cup Major Grey's chutney, chopped
½ pound bacon, cooked crisp and finely crumbled
1 8-ounce package cream cheese, softened
¼ pound blue cheese, finely crumbled
Ritz crackers

1. In a small bowl, stir together the chutney and bacon. In a separate bowl, combine the cheeses and mix until smooth.

2. Spread a thin layer of the cheese mixture onto a cracker and spread a bit of chutney mixture over it. Place the crackers on a baking sheet. Cover with plastic wrap and refrigerate until needed.

3. Preheat the broiler. Place the crackers under the broiler and broil for 2 or 3 minutes, or until the cheese begins to melt. Serve hot.

TOASTED TUNA CANAPES

•

MAKES 2 DOZEN

These are like miniature tuna melts.

2 7-ounce cans tuna, drained and flaked
½ cup finely chopped celery
¼ cup finely chopped ripe black olives
2 scallions, white and green parts, finely chopped
2 teaspoons capers
⅛ teaspoon cayenne pepper
½ cup mayonnaise
1 1-pound square loaf German-style
   pumpernickel or rye bread, crusts removed
½ cup grated sharp Cheddar
Paprika

1. In a mixing bowl, combine the tuna, celery, olives, scallions, capers, cayenne, and mayonnaise and mix well.

2. Cut the bread slices diagonally into quarters. Spread the bread with a thin layer of the tuna mixture. Place the bread triangles closely together on baking sheets and sprinkle the cheese over the tuna mixture. Dust lightly with paprika. Cover tightly with plastic wrap and refrigerate until needed.

3. Preheat the broiler. Place the canapes under the broiler and broil until the cheese is melted and bubbly, 5 to 7 minutes. Serve immediately.

CLASSIC PARTY MIX

•

MAKES 8 CUPS

Thirty years ago, you just couldn't have a party without making a batch of Party Mix. The recipe's still on Chex boxes, but just in case, here's another variation.

½ cup (1 stick) butter
½ teaspoon salt
5 teaspoons Worcestershire sauce
¼ teaspoon paprika
⅛ teaspoon ground cumin
⅛ teaspoon cayenne pepper
2 cups Corn Chex cereal
2 cups Rice Chex cereal
2 cups Wheat Chex cereal
1 cup mixed nuts
1 cup thin pretzel sticks

1. Preheat the oven to 250°F. Melt the butter in a large shallow baking pan, and then stir in salt, Worcestershire sauce, and spices. Add the remaining ingredients and toss to coat everything with the butter mixture.

2. Place the pan in the oven and bake, stirring occasionally, for 45 minutes. Remove from the oven and spread the mixture out on brown paper or paper towels to cool. Store at room temperature in a tightly covered container.

KEN'S CHOW MEIN
NOODLE CANDY CLUSTERS

•

MAKES ABOUT 2 DOZEN CANDIES

When he was a kid, my friend Ken Daniels made these at Eastertime and used them as place cards. Each candy was made with an indentation in the center so it could be used as a "nest" to hold an egg decorated with someone's name. Pretty clever, huh?

1 12-ounce package butterscotch chips or
*   semisweet chocolate chips*
1 3-ounce can chow mein noodles
2 cups roasted peanuts

1. In the top of a double boiler over simmering water, melt the chocolate chips. Remove from the heat and quickly stir in the noodles and nuts to coat.

2. Lay wax paper on a work surface. Working quickly, drop tablespoon-size balls of the mixture onto the paper and allow to cool. Store in a tightly covered container at room temperature.

RICE KRISPIE SQUARES

•

MAKES 2 DOZEN COOKIES

The recipe's right there on the box, as it has been for years, but here it is anyway.

¼ cup (½ stick) butter
1 10-ounce bag marshmallows
5 cups Rice Krispies

1. Melt the butter in a large heavy saucepan over low heat. Add the marshmallows and continue stirring until they are melted and the mixture is smooth.

2. Butter a 9 x 13-inch baking pan. Pour the Rice Krispies into the saucepan and stir to completely coat them with the melted mixture. Quickly transfer the mixture to the baking pan and, using your fingers, press into an even layer.

3. Cool and cut into 1½-inch squares.

VARIATIONS Use Cocoa Krispies instead of Rice Krispies. Stir in 1 cup chunky peanut butter, 1 cup raisins, or 1 cup peanuts at the end of step 1.

An array of super-sweets—Rice Krispie squares, chocolatey chow mein noodle candy clusters, gooey Coca-Cola cupcakes, and frozen chocolate-coated bananas.

Coca-Cola Cupcakes with Tutti-Frutti Coconut Frosting

•

MAKES 3 DOZEN MINIATURE CUPCAKES

Here's one for anyone who's got a super sweet tooth. I remember Coca-Cola cake from years ago, but I never had a recipe for it. Recently, I discovered a recipe for a chocolate Coke cake in Bert Greene's *Honest American Fare*, one of my favorite cookbooks. It was a recipe passed on to him by a family in Indiana. The cake here is my adaptation of his recipe, but the way I remember it. The frosting is my own concoction, based on a traditional 7-minute frosting.

1 cup (2 sticks) butter, softened
½ cup miniature marshmallows
1 cup Coca-Cola
2 cups all-purpose flour
2 cups sugar
1 teaspoon baking soda
½ teaspoon salt
2 large eggs, lightly beaten
½ cup buttermilk
1 teaspoon vanilla extract

1. Preheat the oven to 350°F. Line three 1-dozen miniature muffin pans (or use nonstick pans) with miniature pleated paper cupcake cups.

2. In a medium saucepan over low heat, combine the butter and marshmallows. Cook, stirring constantly, until the ingredients are melted and the mixture is smooth. Remove from the heat and stir in the cola.

3. In a large mixing bowl, sift together the flour, sugar, baking soda, and salt. Gradually beat in the cola mixture and then beat in the eggs, buttermilk, and vanilla.

4. Fill the muffin pans about two-thirds full and bake until a toothpick or cake tester inserted in the middle comes out clean, 20 to 25 minutes. Remove the cupcakes to a wire rack and cool completely before frosting.

TUTTI-FRUTTI COCONUT FROSTING

2 large egg whites
1½ cups sugar
¼ teaspoon cream of tartar
⅓ cup water
1 teaspoon vanilla extract
½ cup chopped candied cherries
½ cup chopped dates
½ cup golden raisins
1 cup shredded coconut

In the top of a double boiler over simmering water, combine the egg whites, sugar, cream of tartar, and water. Beat until the mixture thickens and forms soft peaks, about 7 minutes. Remove from the heat, fold in the remaining ingredients, and frost the cooled cupcakes.

Frozen Chocolate-Coated Bananas

•

MAKES APPROXIMATELY 4 DOZEN

As far as I know, whole frozen chocolate-coated bananas on sticks are still sold in Disneyland. Here's the finger-food version.

8 ounces milk chocolate, coarsely chopped
2 tablespoons vegetable oil
1 cup chopped roasted peanuts
8 firm, ripe bananas

1. In the top of a double boiler over simmering water, combine the chocolate and oil and stir until melted. Keep warm.

2. Place the nuts in a shallow bowl next to the stove. Line a baking sheet with wax paper and place next to the bowl.

3. Peel the bananas and cut them diagonally into 1-inch pieces. Using a wooden skewer, dip each banana piece in the chocolate, turn it to coat on all sides, and let the excess chocolate drip off. Roll each banana piece in the nuts and place on the baking sheet.

4. Allow the bananas to cool. Place the baking sheet in the freezer for about 15 minutes to harden the chocolate. Pack the bananas in an airtight container and freeze until serving. Serve with bamboo skewers.

Sunday Supper

for 6

◆

Menu

Garlic-Stuffed Fried Chicken Breasts

Oven-Braised Carrots with Herbs

Grandma Stapleton's Mixed Greens

Sweet Potato–Apple Pancakes

• • •

Joe's "German" Banana Cake

Sunday has always been "the day of rest," a lazy day reserved for reading the paper, napping, spending a few hours in a museum, taking a long walk through the park or the woods, watching a game or a movie, or shopping. And on a Sunday evening I like having a few close friends over to relax together over a simple meal, to quiet down a bit after the busy weekend and calmly prepare for the inevitably crazy week ahead.

Sunday supper still means the same thing to me that it did years ago, even though the menu is different from those Mom used to make. Back then, the main meal of the day consisted of a big roast, loads of fresh vegetables, and a big cake or pie; nowadays it's a somewhat simpler, though still homey, affair.

The menu is an easy one that can be prepared in no particular hurry, perfect for someone like me who likes to cook on lazy afternoons. For the last-minute chores, I just invite someone into the kitchen to help and chat while I tend the stove.

GETTING READY The cake can be made early in the day. The garlic for the chicken can be roasted a day ahead if you'd like, and the chicken can be prepared a few hours ahead up to the end of step 2. Also a few hours in advance, steam the greens. Have the carrots ready to go into the oven about an hour before serving (or cook them a few hours in advance and reheat them in a moderate oven for 15 to 20 minutes). Just before suppertime, while frying the chicken, make the pancakes and sauté the greens.

BEVERAGES Beer, cider, or a light, dry red jug wine with supper. With the cake, coffee of course.

Garlic-Stuffed Fried Chicken Breasts

•

SERVES 6 TO 8

This variation of old-fashioned fried chicken is a nice surprise. A bit of pureed roasted garlic and herbs are stuffed under the skin, and then the chicken is fried in the traditional way.

Some people eat only one piece of chicken while some eat two; I've found that by multiplying the number of people by one and a half and then throwing in a couple of extra pieces I always have plenty (and maybe there'll even be a piece left over for the cook's lunch the next day!).

⅔ cup all-purpose flour
¼ teaspoon salt
¼ teaspoon paprika
¼ teaspoon cayenne pepper
½ teaspoon freshly ground black pepper
2 whole heads garlic, roasted (page 108)
¼ teaspoon rubbed sage
¼ teaspoon dried thyme
12 medium chicken breast halves
⅔ cup milk, approximately
Vegetable oil, for frying

1. Combine the flour, salt, paprika, and the cayenne and black pepper in a small, shallow bowl. Set aside.

2. Squeeze the pulp from the garlic cloves into a separate small bowl. Add the sage and thyme and mash with a fork until smooth. With a butter knife or other small blunt knife, carefully lift the skin away from the flesh of the chicken breasts and spread a scant teaspoonful of the garlic mixture over the flesh. Press the skin back down onto the chicken.

3. Pour the milk into a shallow bowl. Dip the chicken pieces into the milk and then roll them in the flour mixture. Place the chicken on a rack and allow the coating to dry for about 20 minutes. (*Can be prepared early in the day up to this point, covered, and refrigerated.*)

ABOVE: A homey old-fashioned Sunday supper is served family style on the candle-lit kitchen table.
BELOW: Garlic-stuffed fried chicken, sweet potato-apple pancakes, sautéed greens, and herb-roasted carrots.

A homey "German" banana cake has a crunchy and gooey frosting and filling.

4. In a large skillet, heat about 1½ inches of oil to 370°F. Arrange a single layer of chicken skin side down in the pan and fry, turning occasionally with tongs, until the chicken is well browned on all sides. The breasts should cook in about 10 to 12 minutes, depending on their size.

5. Transfer the chicken to a pan lined with paper towels or brown paper and hold them in a slow oven while cooking the remaining chicken.

OVEN-BRAISED CARROTS WITH HERBS

SERVES 6

Long, slow cooking with dried herbs and chicken stock gives these carrots a wonderful earthy flavor. Once the carrots are in the oven they require no attention whatsoever.

1½ pounds baby carrots, peeled
½ teaspoon dried basil
¼ teaspoon dried rosemary
⅛ teaspoon dried tarragon
¼ teaspoon salt
¼ teaspoon cracked black pepper
½ cup well-seasoned chicken stock
1 tablespoon lemon juice

1. Preheat the over to 325°F.

2. Place the carrots in a small shallow baking dish and sprinkle with the herbs, salt, and pepper. Pour the chicken stock and lemon juice over all and cover the pan tightly with its lid or with aluminum foil. Place in the oven and cook until the carrots are very tender, 45 minutes to an hour (timing will depend on thickness of the carrots). Serve hot.

. . . .

Roasted Garlic

To roast a whole head of garlic, preheat the oven to 375°F. Remove the outer papery layer of skin from a head (or heads) of garlic and wrap the garlic in heavy-duty aluminum foil. Roast the garlic for 1½ hours, remove from the oven, and cool for 10 minutes.

To make roasted garlic puree, as you pull the garlic cloves from the head, make a small incision in the skin of each clove and squeeze the roasted garlic into a small bowl. Mash the garlic with a fork.

. . . .

GRANDMA STAPLETON'S MIXED GREENS

SERVES 6 TO 8

My grandmother used to cook up all kinds of greens this way, either separately or in combination with other greens.

3 cups collard greens, well washed and coarsely shredded
3 cups kale, well washed and coarsely shredded
½ medium head green cabbage, cored and coarsely shredded
3 tablespoons butter
2 large garlic cloves, crushed
2 tablespoons sugar
2 tablespoons cider vinegar
Salt and freshly ground black pepper

1. Place the collard greens in a large kettle of boiling salted water and blanch for 5 minutes. Add the kale and blanch for 5 minutes longer. Remove the greens from the water, drain, and reserve. Add the cabbage to the water and blanch for about 7 minutes, until crisp-tender. Drain. *(Can be prepared several hours in advance, covered, and stored in the refrigerator. Return to room temperature before proceeding.)*

2. In a large skillet, melt the butter and add the garlic. Sauté the garlic for 3 or 4 minutes and discard. Add the sugar to the skillet and stir to dissolve. Add the greens and vinegar, toss well, and sauté until heated through, about 5 minutes. Season to taste with salt and plenty of pepper and serve.

"I love to eat, but even more, I love to sit and talk with friends around a table."
Federico Fellini

Sweet Potato–Apple Pancakes

SERVES 6

2 large eggs, lightly beaten
¼ cup all-purpose flour
¼ teaspoon salt
⅛ teaspoon grated nutmeg
3 large sweet potatoes
1 large tart baking apple
1 medium onion
Vegetable oil

1. In a mixing bowl, combine the eggs, flour, salt, and nutmeg. Set aside. Peel the sweet potatoes, apple, and onion and grate finely, using a hand grater or food processor fitted with the grating blade. Stir the grated ingredients into the batter.

2. Pour enough oil into a large skillet to cover the surface and place over medium heat. When the oil is sizzling, drop the batter by heaping tablespoonfuls into the skillet. Cook the pancakes until the bottoms are golden brown, about 5 minutes. Turn and brown the other sides, about 3 minutes.

3. Put the finished pancakes in a paper towel-lined pan and keep them warm in a slow oven while preparing the remaining pancakes. Serve immediately. *(These are best eaten immediately, but if they must be made in advance, they can be reheated in a single layer on a baking sheet in a 350°F. oven for 15 or 20 minutes.)*

Joe's "German" Banana Cake

MAKES ONE 2-LAYER 9-INCH CAKE

Whenever Mom comes to New York for a visit, I ask her to make only two things: apple dumplings and a banana cake. During one of her visits, she made the cake for dessert when I had a few friends over for dinner. My friend Joe Brescia loved the banana cake; he said it rivaled his all-time favorite, German Chocolate Cake (which, by the way, isn't German at all). Well, the next time Mom was in town, Joe dropped by with his newest creation. Here's the recipe, with thanks to both Mom and Joe.

CAKE
⅔ cup (1⅓ sticks) butter, softened
2½ cups sifted cake flour
1⅔ cups firmly packed brown sugar
1¼ teaspoons baking powder
1 teaspoon baking soda
1 teaspoon salt
1½ cups mashed very ripe bananas (2 or 3 bananas)
⅔ cup buttermilk
2 large eggs
1 teaspoon vanilla extract
⅔ cup chopped pecans

1. Preheat the oven to 350°F. Grease two 9-inch round cake pans.

2. In a large mixing bowl, combine the butter, flour, brown sugar, baking powder, baking soda, and salt and mix well. Add the bananas and half the buttermilk. Mix until the dry ingredients are moistened, then beat vigorously for 2 minutes.

3. Add the remaining buttermilk, the eggs, and the vanilla and beat for an additional 2 minutes. Fold in the nuts.

4. Pour the batter into the prepared pans and bake for 35 to 40 minutes, or until nicely browned and a toothpick or cake tester inserted in the center of the cake comes out clean. Cool for 10 minutes in the pan, then invert onto wire racks to cool completely.

FROSTING
⅔ cup evaporated milk
⅔ cup firmly packed dark brown sugar
2 large egg yolks
⅓ cup (⅔ stick) butter
1 teaspoon vanilla extract
1¼ cups shredded coconut
⅔ cup pecans

1. Combine the evaporated milk, brown sugar, egg yolks, and butter in a small heavy saucepan over medium heat. Cook, stirring constantly, until the mixture thickens, about 12 minutes. Remove from the heat and stir in the vanilla. Add the coconut and pecans and beat until the frosting is cool enough to spread.

2. To frost the cake, place one layer on a cake plate or cake stand. Spread the top with half the icing (don't worry if some of the icing oozes over the side—it's supposed to look like a big gooey cake). Top with the other layer and spread the remaining frosting over it. Cover and allow to stand a few hours before serving.

A HAYRIDE PICNIC SUPPER

for 16

♦

Menu

HARVEST MOON BREW

ASSORTED AMERICAN BEERS

RYE AND CARAWAY PRETZELS WITH MUSTARD

• • •

FENNEL- AND ORANGE-MARINATED ROASTED
PORK LOIN ON BLACK BREAD
WITH ROASTED PEPPERS

BAKED LIMAS AND HOMINY

CORINNE'S "GUESS AGAIN" SALAD

• • •

LITTLE SQUASH PIES IN PECAN CRUSTS

OATMEAL FIG BARS

APPLES AND PEARS

ABOVE AND RIGHT: After our moonlit ride on a tractor-
drawn hay wagon, we set up our picnic buffet on a
blanket-topped hay bale "table" in the lantern-lit barn.

One of the most memorable pleasures of growing up on a farm was the annual adventure of going on a hayride on a crisp fall night. We always had hayrides around Hallowe'en, planned to coincide with a harvest moon. A flatbed wagon was piled with straw and plenty of blankets, hitched to a tractor, and off we'd go down narrow back roads and rocky pasture paths. At the end of the bumpy ride, we'd come back to the lantern-lit hay barn for supper and square dancing.

Last fall I re-created one of those old-fashioned hayrides in the country. I borrowed a wagon and an old Ellis Chambers tractor (coincidentally just like one we had on our farm, so I didn't need any driving lessons!) from a neighbor and some hay and straw from a nearby riding stable. And I was in business. The menu was made up of food that's prepared ahead and can wait a while, once it's ready, making it really easy on the host. A great time was had by all, so I'm planning a repeat next year. Who knows? I might even add a square dance, caller, and all.

GETTING READY This is one of the easiest menus there is to serve, since there's absolutely no last-minute preparation.

A day in advance, make the pretzels, the squash pies, and the oatmeal fig squares. The pork and the limas and hominy can also be made in advance and put in a slow oven to rewarm about an hour before serving. The punch can be made a few hours in advance and rewarmed twenty minutes before serving.

Harvest Moon Brew

•

MAKES ABOUT THIRTY 6-OUNCE
DRINKS, MORE IF RUM IS ADDED

I serve this warming drink from October right on through the winter.

2 quarts fresh apple cider
2 quarts cranberry juice cocktail
1½ quarts orange juice
1 orange studded with whole cloves
4 cinnamon sticks
Orange slices, for garnish
Apple slices, for garnish
Light rum (optional)

Combine the cider, cranberry juice cocktail, orange juice, orange, and cinnamon sticks in a large kettle.

Place over low heat, bring to a low simmer, and simmer for 2 hours. Just before serving, add the orange and apple slices. To serve, ladle directly from the kettle into mugs or heavy glasses and stir in rum to taste.

Rye and Caraway Pretzels

•

MAKES ABOUT 4 DOZEN

2 envelopes active dry yeast
2 cups warm water
¼ cup (½ stick) butter, softened
½ teaspoon salt
2 tablespoons firmly packed dark brown sugar
3½ cups sifted all-purpose flour
2 cups rye flour
3 tablespoons caraway seeds
1 quart water
5 tablespoons baking powder
Coarse salt
Spicy mustard

1. In the bowl of an electric mixer or food processor fitted with the steel chopping blade, dissolve the yeast in the water. Add the butter, salt, brown sugar, and all-purpose flour and beat for 3 minutes.

2. Transfer the dough to a floured board and knead in the rye flour. Continue kneading until the dough is elastic and no longer sticky, and then knead in the caraway seeds. Place the dough in an oiled bowl, cover with a damp cloth, and let rise until doubled in bulk, about 1 hour.

3. Punch down the dough and knead for 2 or 3 minutes. Pinch off walnut-size pieces of dough and place them one at a time on the board. With lightly floured hands, roll them to form pencil-shaped sticks. Twist the sticks into a pretzel shape and lay them about 1½ inches apart on greased baking sheets. Cover again and let rise until doubled in bulk.

4. Preheat the oven to 450°F. Combine water and baking powder in a shallow saucepan and bring to a boil. Add a few pretzels at a time to the boiling water and cook until they float, about 30 seconds.

5. With a large slotted spoon, remove the pretzels and return them to the baking sheets. Sprinkle the pretzels generously with the coarse salt. Place in the oven and bake until very well browned, about 8 to 10 minutes. Remove the pretzels to wire racks to cool, and then store them up to 3 days in a tightly covered container. Serve with Cajun, deli-style, or other spicy mustard.

NOTE If you prefer a glazed finish, brush the pretzels with a mixture of 1 egg white beaten with 1 tablespoon water before baking.

𝒻ENNEL- AND ORANGE-MARINATED ROASTED PORK LOIN

•

SERVES 6 TO 8

MARINADE
1 cup cider vinegar
½ cup dry white wine
2 large garlic cloves, chopped
1 medium onion, coarsely chopped
½ teaspoon salt
1 teaspoon freshly ground black pepper
3 tablespoons fennel seeds, crushed
Juice and grated rind of 2 oranges

1 4- to 5-pound boned and tied pork loin roast

1. Combine the marinade ingredients in a heavy plastic bag and mix well. Add the pork roast, close the bag tightly, and shake the plastic bag to coat all sides of the pork. Place the bag in the refrigerator and marinate overnight, turning occasionally. (*Can also be marinated in a shallow nonaluminum pan covered with plastic wrap.*)

2. Preheat the oven to 350°F. Transfer the pork to a shallow roasting pan and spoon the marinade over it. Roast, basting frequently with the pan juices, until the internal temperature reaches 160°F., 1¾ to 2 hours.

3. Remove the pork from the pan and let stand for 10 or 15 minutes. (*The pork only benefits in flavor if made a day in advance and refrigerated overnight; rewarm in a 300°F. oven for about an hour.*)

4. Carve the roast into ¼-inch-thick slices and serve warm or at room temperature on black bread with strips of roasted red and green peppers (page 64).

ℬAKED LIMAS AND HOMINY

•

SERVES 16 TO 20

Hominy is one of those forgotten foods in many parts of the country, but it was standard fare on our table when I was growing up, cooked in a variety of ways. Here, I've combined it with lima beans, slowly baked in a spicy sauce.

¾ pound lean smoked bacon, diced
2 medium onions, chopped
2 garlic cloves, finely chopped
1 large green pepper, chopped
2 28-ounce cans tomatoes, crushed (do not use canned crushed tomatoes)
1 tablespoon grainy mustard
½ cup firmly packed dark brown sugar
1 teaspoon ground chili (not chili powder)
¾ cup dark rum
2 Granny Smith apples, pared and coarsely chopped
6 cups cooked lima beans or 4 10-ounce packages frozen lima beans, thawed
4 cups cooked hominy or 3 16-ounce cans (see note)

1. Place the bacon in a skillet over medium heat and sauté until it begins to render its fat, about 5 minutes. Add the onions, garlic, and green pepper and sauté 5 minutes longer. Transfer the mixture to a large mixing bowl. Add all the remaining ingredients except the lima beans and hominy and stir until blended.

2. Preheat the oven to 250°F. Stir in the beans and the hominy and transfer the mixture to a 6-quart Dutch oven or casserole. Bake for 3 or 4 hours, until the juices have thickened.

NOTE Hominy is available dried, but it's more easily found in cans, so that's how it's listed here. If you use dried, cook it according to the directions on the package before adding to the other ingredients and baking.

"Listen! the wind is rising,
and the air is wild with leaves.
We have had our summer evenings,
now for October eves!"
Humbert Wolfe

LEFT: For starters, rye and caraway pretzels are served with beers (on ice in a galvanized bucket). The warm, spice-scented fruit punch will be ladled from a canning kettle into half-pint mason jars for serving.

BELOW: Sliced pork loin, marinated and roasted in a heady mixture of orange juice, garlic, fennel, and pepper before roasting, is served surrounded by strips of roasted peppers.

Above: A sandwich of roasted pork with peppers on black bread, with "guess again" salad and baked limas and hominy.

Below: A salad of one vegetable "disguised" as another and a slow-baked spicy combination of lima beans and hominy.

Below: Little squash pies with crunchy pecan crusts and, in the basket, oatmeal fig bars, apples, and pears.

Corinne's "Guess Again" Salad

•

SERVES 16

As the story goes, Mom's old chum Corinne Coe took this salad to a potluck dinner once and everyone complimented her on her delicious potato salad. "Guess again," Corinne said, and that's how her cauliflower salad got its name.

2 medium (6-inch) heads cauliflower, trimmed
   and broken into large flowerets
Salt
1 medium onion, chopped
1 small green pepper, chopped
½ cup thinly diced celery

DRESSING
1 cup Homemade Mayonnaise (page 221)
1 cup sour cream
1 tablespoon Dijon mustard
1 tablespoon cider vinegar
¼ teaspoon sugar
¼ teaspoon salt
⅛ teaspoon cayenne pepper
1 tablespoon chopped dill
¼ cup chopped parsley

1. Blanch the cauliflower in a large kettle of boiling salted water for about 5 minutes; the cauliflower should be just tender, but not mushy. Drain and rinse with cold water to stop cooking. Drain well.

2. Cut the cauliflower into pieces about ¼ inch thick, as for potato salad. Place the cauliflower in a large bowl and add the onion, pepper, and celery.

3. Combine the dressing ingredients and whisk to blend. Pour the dressing over the cauliflower and toss to coat. Cover and refrigerate for no more than 4 hours before serving.

• • • • • • • • • • • • • • •

Straw and Hay

Let me clear up a misconception about hayrides. Most of the time they're really *straw* rides. Hay is composed of dried alfalfa, sweetgrass, clover, and other roughage which, when dried, are rough and chaffy. Straw is made from the residue left from combining grains such as oats, rye, barley, and wheat. Hay is for feeding livestock and straw is for bedding them down, so straw is much more comfortable for a ride.

• • • • • • • • • • • • • • •

Little Squash Pies in Pecan Crusts

•

MAKES 2 DOZEN TARTLETS

When it comes to fall desserts, these are right up there at the top of my list. The smooth spicy squash filling and the crunchy crust are perfect foils for one another.

CRUST
1 cup (2 sticks) butter, softened
3 cups all-purpose flour
⅓ cup sugar
1 teaspoon vanilla extract
¾ cup finely chopped pecans
1 tablespoon cold water

FILLING
1 cup firmly packed light brown sugar
¼ cup granulated sugar
¼ cup all-purpose flour
¼ teaspoon salt
1 teaspoon ground cinnamon
½ teaspoon ground ginger
½ teaspoon grated nutmeg
2 cups half-and-half
3 cups cooked and pureed butternut or acorn
   squash or pumpkin
¼ cup light rum
6 large eggs
1 teaspoon vanilla extract
24 pecan halves

1. To make the crust, combine the butter, flour, sugar, and vanilla in a large mixing bowl and knead until evenly blended, then blend in the pecans. Add the water and knead until smooth. Press walnut-size pieces of dough into 2-inch muffin cups, lining the bottom and sides.

2. To make the filling, combine the sugars, flour, salt, and spices in the top of a double boiler. Gradually whisk in the half-and-half and then blend in the squash. Place the mixture over simmering water, and bring to just below the simmering point.

3. While the squash mixture is heating, beat the eggs in a mixing bowl until they are thick and pale in color. Gradually pour the hot squash mixture into the eggs, whisking constantly. Then add the rum and blend well.

4. Pour the mixture back into the top of the double

boiler and cook, stirring constantly with a spoon, until the custard has thickened enough to coat the spoon, about 10 minutes. *Do not allow the custard to simmer at any point.*

5. Remove the top of the double boiler from the heat and dip it into a large bowl of ice water to stop the custard from cooking any further. Beat the custard briskly for 5 minutes to help cool it off rapidly, then beat in the vanilla. Allow the filling to cool. (*Can be made up to a day ahead and stored in the refrigerator, tightly covered; return to room temperature before baking.*)

6. Preheat the oven to 350°F. Spoon the filling into the crusts and top each with a pecan half. Bake the tartlets for 20 to 25 minutes, or until the crust is nicely browned. Remove to wire racks to cool. Store the tarts, covered, in the refrigerator until serving.

OATMEAL FIG BARS

•

MAKES ABOUT 4 DOZEN BAR COOKIES

Here's a chewy old-fashioned cookie that keeps and travels well.

FILLING
1 pound dried figs, chopped
1 cup sugar
½ cup orange juice

DOUGH
¾ cup (1½ sticks) butter, softened
⅔ cup firmly packed dark brown sugar
2¼ cups sifted all-purpose flour
2 teaspoons baking powder
½ teaspoon salt
½ teaspoon ground cinnamon
2½ cups quick-cooking oats
½ cup milk

1. Combine filling ingredients in a heavy saucepan and bring to a simmer. Cook, stirring frequently to prevent sticking, until the mixture forms a thick paste, about 20 minutes. Cool and reserve.

2. In a mixing bowl, cream together the butter and brown sugar. In a separate bowl, mix together the flour, baking powder, salt, cinnamon, and oats. Stir the dry mixture into the butter-sugar mixture alternately with the milk to form a dough.

3. Preheat the oven to 350°F. Grease a 9 x 13-inch cake pan. Press half the dough into the pan in an even layer. Spread the filling evenly over the dough and then spread the remaining dough over the filling.

4. Bake until nicely browned, 20 to 25 minutes. Cut into 1½-inch squares and cool in pan on a wire rack. Store, tightly wrapped, in a cool place.

. . . .

"Good Enough to Eat" Fall Apples and Pears

Most of the apples in supermarkets throughout the year are there for their looks more than their taste. A Red Delicious may be picture perfect, but it doesn't do much for me flavorwise, and I'm not that crazy about Mcintoshes, except in pies or cobblers. As far as munching goes, the Granny Smith is the only "supermarket" apple that has any character.

But apple lovers, don't despair! In the fall, farmstands and farmer's markets abound with an evergrowing number of old-fashioned varieties—now known as "antique" apples—that make great eating. There are hundreds of varieties, but most of them are grown in small quantities. Keep an eye out for them. Here are some of the tastiest of the most available fall varieties:

◆ *Gravenstein* (midsummer through early fall) Juicy and tart, and variegated in color; makes delicious applesauce, too.

◆ *Jonathan* (early fall through midwinter) A dark red apple with a nice tart flavor. Another good apple for both eating and cooking.

◆ *Northern Spy* (fall through winter) A pretty yellow apple with red markings; crisp, aromatic, and delicious for eating, cooking, and baking.

◆ *Rhode Island Greening* (fall through winter) Green or yellow; crisp, tart, and aromatic; a real apple-lover's apple, perfect for eating and baking the best apple pie.

And here are some good fall pears for eating:

◆ *Anjou* (fall through winter) Large, greenish yellow, with a winey flavor; good for cooking, too.

◆ *Bosc* (fall through early midwinter) Large and narrow, yellow to russet, with a tart flavor; good eating and excellent for cooking and baking.

◆ *Comice* (fall through midwinter) Large and plump, yellow; good for eating only.

◆ *Seckel* (fall) Small and brownish, with a delicious, spicy flavor; mainly an eating pear.

. . . .

"You have to eat oatmeal or you'll dry up. Anybody knows that."
Eloise (Kay Thompson)

A Theatre Party Dinner

for 8

•

Menu

GOLDEN SANGRIA

SARDINE AND OLIVE TAPENADE

POTTED HERBED GOAT CHEESE

TOASTS AND CRUDITES

· · ·

NEW WORLD PAELLA

HEARTS OF PALM AND AVOCADOS
WITH LIME VINAIGRETTE

· · ·

CLASSIC CHOCOLATE FONDUE

A quintessential New York evening spent with friends often means going to a play or a concert, and then eating dinner in a restaurant afterwards, but I also like to organize a group to come over on a Friday or Saturday night for a pre-theatre supper, go to the theatre, and then come back after the show for dessert, coffee, and after-dinner drinks. Obviously the event doesn't have to be centered around Broadway; anything goes, from a concert by a visiting philharmonic orchestra to the musical comedy at the high school.

This party was planned around food that's easy to serve and requires as little fuss as possible at the last minute. The first course is ready ahead of time and can be served while the paella is finishing up in the oven. And the dessert can be readied in just a few minutes after returning home.

GETTING READY Up to three days in advance, make the tapenade. Prepare the herb cheese up to two days in advance.

A day in advance, make the toasts for the tapenade and cheese; prepare the paella up to the end of step 3; prepare the fondue mixture.

Early in the day, prepare the salad ingredients and the dressing. Chill the sangria ingredients.

Rewarm the paella base and then put the paella into the oven about a half-hour before serving. Just before the paella comes out of the oven, assemble the salad.

Prepare the dippers for the fondue and rewarm the fondue itself just before serving.

BEVERAGES The sangria can be served with both the first and main courses, but if you'd prefer wine with the paella, serve a California Barbera or a Spanish Rioja. After dessert offer a selection of after-dinner wines or cordials (see pages 212 to 214).

GOLDEN SANGRIA

•

MAKES TWENTY-FOUR 8-OUNCE
SERVINGS

The name is actually a contradiction since *sangria* means "bloody," but this lighter version of the classic wine punch is delicious just the same.

> 2 cups pear nectar
> 1 quart white grape juice
> ⅓ cup superfine sugar
> ¼ cup cognac
> 3 liters dry white wine
> 1 yellow apple, cored and sliced
> 1 yellow pear, cored and sliced
> 2 oranges, sliced
> 1 lemon, sliced
> 2 liters club soda or seltzer

Combine the pear nectar, white grape juice, sugar, and cognac in the bottom of a punch bowl or a pitcher and stir until sugar is dissolved. Add the wine and fruit, cover the bowl, and let stand 1 hour. Just before serving, stir in the club soda. To serve, ladle the sangria into tall glasses over ice.

OPPOSITE ABOVE: Starters and golden sangria are
served in the living room before the theatre.
OPPOSITE BELOW: Sardine and olive tapenade and potted
herbed goat cheese are surrounded with an array of
crudités, toasts, and hard-boiled eggs.

Sardine and Olive Tapenade

•

MAKES ABOUT 3 CUPS

Sardines are one of those foods you either love or hate. I love them, whether in a sandwich on black bread with mustard and sweet onions or in this pungent and nontraditional version of tapenade.

2 3¾-ounce cans sardines packed in olive oil
Extra-virgin olive oil
2 large garlic cloves
3 scallions, white and green parts, coarsely chopped
½ cup drained and pitted oil-cured black olives (see note)
½ cup drained and pitted oil-cured green olives
1 teaspoon fresh thyme leaves or ¼ teaspoon dried
½ cup loosely packed flat-leaf parsley
Juice of 1 medium lemon
3 tablespoons drained capers
Freshly ground black pepper
Sprigs of flat-leaf parsley, for garnish
Drained capers, for garnish

ACCOMPANIMENTS
Toasted slices of baguette
Raw broccoli flowerets
Raw cauliflower flowerets
Cherry tomatoes
Halved hard-boiled medium eggs
Strips of green, yellow, and red pepper

1. Drain the oil from the sardines into a liquid measuring cup. Add enough olive oil to make 1 cup. Reserve.

2. With the motor running, drop the garlic cloves into the bowl of a food processor fitted with the steel chopping blade and process until the garlic is chopped fine. Turn off the processor and add the sardines, oil, and remaining ingredients except pepper. Process until smooth. Season to taste with plenty of black pepper.

3. Transfer the tapenade to a small serving bowl, cover with plastic wrap, and refrigerate for at least 6 hours to allow flavors to blend, or up to 3 days. To serve, garnish with parsley and capers. Place the bowl on a platter surrounded by an assortment of the listed accompaniments.

NOTE Pitted olives packed in brine are too bland for tapenade. Look for oil-cured olives in the deli department of large supermarkets or in specialty or ethnic food shops. Pit the olives with a cherry pitter or a narrow paring knife.

Potted Herbed Goat Cheese

•

MAKES ABOUT 2 CUPS

The herbs can be varied here; they just need to be assertive enough to stand up to the strongly flavored goat cheese.

½ pound soft goat cheese
1 8-ounce package cream cheese, softened
2 tablespoons milk
¼ cup chopped parsley
1 tablespoon chopped tarragon
1 tablespoon chopped chervil
1 tablespoon chopped dill
2 shallots, finely chopped
¼ teaspoon cracked black pepper
Herb sprigs, such as tarragon, parsley, or rosemary

Combine all the ingredients except herb sprigs in a bowl and blend well. Cover with plastic wrap and refrigerate overnight to allow the flavors to blend. (*Can be made up to 3 days in advance, covered tightly with plastic wrap, and refrigerated.*) To serve, bring to room temperature, garnish with herb sprigs, and serve with an assortment of tapenade accompaniments (see preceding recipe).

New World Paella

•

SERVES 10

Paella became immensely popular fifteen or twenty years ago, when Americans first discovered it, and then it seemed to disappear. I'm getting on a one-man bandwagon for a paella revival—it's easy to make ahead and to serve, and just about everyone loves it. I use boneless chicken and have eliminated the traditional lobster, making this an easy-to-serve and easy-to-eat buffet dish. Another modification of the more traditional method of making paella is that I bake it in the oven, which is a lot easier on the cook.

⅓ cup extra-virgin olive oil
1 large garlic clove
1 ounce salt pork or smoked bacon, diced
1 medium onion, coarsely chopped
1 large red pepper, coarsely chopped
*6 boneless and skinless medium chicken breast
    halves, cut into 2 × ½-inch strips*
*2 chorizo sausages (about ¼ pound), cut
    diagonally into ⅛-inch slices*
¼ pound smoked ham, diced
*1 tablespoon fresh oregano leaves or 1 teaspoon
    dried*
2 bay leaves
¼ teaspoon salt
½ teaspoon cayenne pepper
½ teaspoon ground coriander
2 teaspoons capers
3 tablespoons tomato paste
2¼ cups long-grain rice, rinsed and drained
2 pounds large shrimp, peeled and deveined
1 pound bay scallops
1½ dozen cherrystone clams, scrubbed
1½ dozen mussels, scrubbed and debearded
4 cups chicken stock, heated
1 teaspoon crushed saffron
*½ pound snow peas, trimmed and diagonally cut
    in half (see note)*
*1½ cups cooked dried black beans or 1 16-ounce
    can black beans, drained*

1. Preheat the oven to 350°F.

2. Pour the olive oil into a Dutch oven or a paella pan and place over medium-high heat. (Or use a large, heavy skillet and transfer the mixture to a large baking dish at the beginning of step 4.) Add the garlic, salt pork, onion, and red pepper, and sauté 5 minutes. Add the chicken and sauté until lightly browned.

3. Turn the heat down to medium, add the chorizo and ham, and sauté for 5 minutes. Stir in the oregano, bay leaves, salt, cayenne, coriander, capers, tomato paste, and rice; mix well. (*Can be prepared up to a day ahead up to this point, transferred to a covered container, and refrigerated; reheat before proceeding.*)

4. Add the seafood, hot stock, and saffron to the pan. Mix well, cover the pan loosely with a lid or aluminum foil, and place in the oven. Bake until the rice is just tender and all the liquid is absorbed, about 30 minutes. Using a large, heavy spoon, gently stir in the snow peas and beans and cook 5 minutes longer. Serve immediately.

NOTE If snow peas are unavailable, substitute one 10-ounce package frozen peas, thawed.

Hearts of Palm and Avocados with Lime Vinaigrette

•

SERVES 8

LIME VINAIGRETTE
⅓ cup olive oil
⅓ cup vegetable oil
Juice of 2 limes
¼ cup white wine vinegar
1 large garlic clove, crushed
Pinch of salt·
Crushed red pepper flakes to taste

*6 hearts of palm (see note), cut into matchstick
    julienne*
*2 ripe Haas avocados, sliced and tossed with the
    juice of 1 lime*
*1 large head romaine lettuce, torn into bite-size
    pieces*
1 head Boston lettuce, torn into bite-size pieces
*1 medium red onion, thinly sliced and separated
    into rings*
½ cup pitted green olives

1. Combine the dressing ingredients in a jar, shake well, and let stand at room temperature for a few hours. Before serving, discard the garlic clove and shake the dressing again.

2. Combine the salad ingredients in a large serving bowl. Pour the dressing over the salad and toss. Serve immediately.

NOTE Hearts of palm are available in cans in large supermarkets or in specialty or ethnic food shops.

*"My dinner parties are always great because
I have the right formula—eight people,
eleven bottles of wine."*
Ed Koch

A colorful paella, served in a large terra-cotta baking dish, is chock full of chicken, sausage, and shellfish.

CLASSIC CHOCOLATE FONDUE
•
MAKES ABOUT 5 CUPS

12 ounces semisweet chocolate, coarsely chopped
3 cups heavy cream
2 tablespoons instant coffee granules
⅔ cup brandy
1½ teaspoons vanilla extract
½ teaspoon ground cinnamon

ACCOMPANIMENTS
1-inch cubes of pound cake, sponge cake, or
    chocolate cake
Thickly sliced pears, apples, or banana, tossed
    with lemon juice to prevent browning
Cubes of pineapple
Whole strawberries
Sectioned tangerines or small oranges
Bamboo skewers

1. In the top of a double boiler over simmering water, combine the chocolate and cream and stir constantly until the mixture is smooth. Stir in the remaining ingredients. *(Can be prepared ahead, covered, and refrigerated; reheat before serving.)*

2. To serve, transfer the mixture to a fondue pot or chafing dish positioned above a low heat source to keep warm. Arrange the foods to be dipped on a large serving platter with bamboo skewers.

ABOVE: Chocolate fondue with fruits and cake for dipping.

An Old-Fashioned Waffle Supper

for 12

◆

Menu

CHARLESTON RICE WAFFLES

SOUR CREAM–BUTTERMILK WAFFLES

PECAN WAFFLES

WHOLE WHEAT GINGERBREAD WAFFLES

• • •

SAVORY TOPPINGS:

CREAMED DEVILED CRAB

CREAMED CHICKEN AND MUSHROOMS
WITH TARRAGON

HAM AND EGGS IN CHEDDAR SAUCE

• • •

SWEET TOPPINGS:

APPLES AND CURRANTS IN CINNAMON SAUCE

SLICED PEARS IN BRANDY SAUCE

BANANAS IN ORANGE-RUM SAUCE

Throughout the Midwest, waffle or pancake suppers have been held as popular fundraisers for years. And they're always a lot of fun—all the waffles you can eat at a good price and for a good cause. I remember waffle suppers a different way. Mom and one or two neighbors used to have big waffle suppers just for fun. All the kids would take part in unofficial waffle-eating contests (my brother Larry always won), so I'm not quite sure how much fun our mothers had; we managed to keep them on duty at the waffle irons through most of the evening.

Waffle parties are nothing new in this country. Thomas Jefferson brought a waffle iron home to Monticello from a trip abroad, and waffle parties were all the rage during the latter 1700s.

This menu offers alternatives. If you decide to serve savory toppings over the waffles, serve a simple dessert of fruit and cheese. Waffles with any of the sweet toppings make a meal in themselves. And, of course, there's no reason why a choice of waffles and toppings can't be offered.

GETTING READY All the toppings can be prepared in advance and rewarmed in heavy pans over very low heat. The batters, too, can be prepared an hour or two ahead and stored in pitchers or batter bowls in the refrigerator. The trickiest part of this supper is having the waffles ready. When there's a good-sized crowd, I borrow an extra iron rather than cook the waffles a little ahead of time and try to keep them warm. The waffles take only a few minutes to bake, so it doesn't take very long to have a couple of waffles on everyone's plate. It gets a little hectic at times, but that's part of the fun.

BEVERAGES Fresh apple cider is my choice, but you might prefer a sparkling hard cider. And a big pot of coffee.

Charleston Rice Waffles

◆

MAKES 6 TO 10, DEPENDING ON IRON SIZE

2¼ cups sifted all-purpose flour
4 teaspoons baking powder
1 teaspoon salt
1 cup cooked rice, cooled
¼ cup (½ stick) butter, melted
2 large eggs, lightly beaten
2 cups milk

1. In a mixing bowl, sift together the flour, baking powder, and salt. Stir in the rice. Add the remaining ingredients and stir until the dry ingredients are just moistened.

2. Bake the waffles in a seasoned electric waffle iron according to the manufacturer's directions.

SOUR CREAM–BUTTERMILK WAFFLES

·

MAKES 6 TO 10,
DEPENDING ON IRON SIZE

These are just about the best waffles I've ever eaten, and they're great with both sweet and savory toppings.

3 cups all-purpose flour
4 teaspoons baking powder
1 teaspoon baking soda
½ teaspoon salt
1 tablespoon sugar
6 large eggs, separated
1 cup sour cream
2 cups buttermilk
½ cup (1 stick) butter, melted and cooled
½ cup vegetable shortening, melted and cooled

1. In a large mixing bowl, stir the dry ingredients together with a fork until completely blended. In a separate bowl, beat the egg yolks, sour cream, and buttermilk together until completely blended. Pour this mixture and the butter and shortening over the dry ingredients and stir until a smooth batter is formed.

2. In a clean, separate bowl, beat the egg whites until stiff but not dry, and gently fold them into the batter. Bake the waffles in a seasoned electric waffle iron according to the manufacturer's directions.

PECAN WAFFLES Stir ½ cup finely chopped lightly toasted pecans into the batter.

WHOLE WHEAT GINGERBREAD WAFFLES

·

MAKES 6 TO 10,
DEPENDING ON IRON SIZE

Definitely a dessert waffle.

¾ cup whole wheat flour
1½ cups all-purpose flour
2 teaspoons baking powder
½ teaspoon baking soda
½ teaspoon salt
1 tablespoon ground ginger
1½ teaspoons ground cinnamon
½ teaspoon ground cloves
½ teaspoon grated nutmeg
⅔ cup firmly packed dark brown sugar
1 cup dark molasses
⅔ cup vegetable shortening, melted
1 cup milk
2 large eggs, separated

1. Combine the flours, baking powder, soda, salt, and spices in a mixing bowl and stir with a fork or whisk until completely blended. Add the brown sugar, molasses, shortening, milk, and egg yolks. Beat until smooth.

2. In a separate, clean bowl, beat the egg whites until stiff but not dry. Gently fold into the batter. Bake the waffles in a seasoned electric waffle iron according to the manufacturer's directions.

CREAMED DEVILED CRAB

·

SERVES 6 TO 8, OVER WAFFLES

This goes especially well with the rice waffles.

¼ cup (½ stick) butter
4 scallions, white and green parts, finely chopped
2 shallots, finely chopped
½ cup finely diced celery
¼ cup chopped parsley
3 tablespoons all-purpose flour
1 teaspoon dry mustard
⅛ teaspoon cayenne pepper
1½ cups half-and-half
1 cup clam broth
2 tablespoons dry sherry
1½ pounds lump crabmeat, picked over to remove
    any bits of shell and cartilage and flaked
Salt and hot pepper sauce

1. Melt the butter in a large, heavy saucepan or Dutch oven over medium heat and add the scallions, shallots, and celery. Sauté until the vegetables are very tender, about 15 minutes. Stir in the parsley.

2. Stir in the flour, mustard, and cayenne, and cook for 3 minutes. Slowly add the half-and-half, clam broth, and sherry, stirring constantly. Bring to a simmer and cook, stirring constantly, until the sauce thickens, about 10 minutes. Stir in the crabmeat. Season to taste with salt and hot pepper sauce. Cook 5 minutes longer and serve.

A "mix and match" waffle supper includes (clockwise) ham and eggs in Cheddar sauce and creamed chicken and mushrooms, both on sour cream-buttermilk waffles; creamed devilled crab on rice waffles; and bananas in orange-rum sauce on gingerbread waffles.

CREAMED CHICKEN AND MUSHROOMS WITH TARRAGON

•

SERVES 6 TO 8, OVER WAFFLES

Here's my family's much-told creamed chicken and waffles story: When I was a kid, the six members of my immediate family, along with a few other relatives, were invited by one of my aunts (who shall remain nameless) for Thanksgiving dinner. When we were all seated, my aunt proudly brought dinner to the table. Dinner for sixteen consisted of one chicken, creamed, and six small waffles. Needless to say, Dad stopped the car at a diner on the way home.

Well, despite that memorable Thanksgiving dinner, waffles with creamed chicken remain one of our favorite Sunday suppers.

¼ cup (½ stick) butter
1 pound mushrooms, thinly sliced
1 small onion, chopped
1 garlic clove, crushed
¼ cup thinly sliced celery
3 tablespoons all-purpose flour
1 cup half-and-half
1½ cups well-seasoned chicken stock
8 large chicken breast halves, cooked, skinned,
  boned, and cut into chunks
1 10-ounce package frozen peas, thawed
1 tablespoon chopped fresh tarragon leaves or 1
  teaspoon dried tarragon
Salt and freshly ground black pepper

1. Melt the butter in a large, heavy saucepan or Dutch oven over medium heat and add the mushrooms, onion, garlic, and celery. Sauté until the onion and celery are tender and most of the liquid released by the mushrooms has evaporated, about 15 minutes. Remove and discard the garlic.

2. Stir in the flour and cook 3 minutes. Slowly add the half-and-half and the chicken stock, stirring constantly. Bring to a simmer and cook, stirring constantly, until the sauce thickens, about 10 minutes. Stir in the chicken and tarragon and season with salt and pepper to taste. Cook 5 minutes longer and serve.

CREAMED OYSTERS AND MUSHROOMS Substitute 2 pints shucked oysters for the chicken. Substitute the liquor from the oysters, plus enough clam broth or water to make 1½ cups, for the chicken stock.

HAM AND EGGS IN CHEDDAR SAUCE

•

SERVES 6 TO 8, OVER WAFFLES

¼ cup (½ stick) butter
1 small onion, chopped
3 tablespoons all-purpose flour
1 cup half-and-half
1½ cups well-seasoned chicken stock
1 cup grated sharp yellow Cheddar
3 cups diced cooked ham
4 hard-boiled large eggs, coarsely chopped
Salt and hot pepper sauce

1. Melt the butter in a large, heavy saucepan or Dutch oven over medium heat and add the onion. Sauté until the onion is very soft, about 15 minutes.

2. Stir in the flour and cook for 3 minutes. Slowly add the half-and-half and the chicken stock, stirring constantly. Bring to a simmer and cook, stirring constantly, until the sauce thickens, about 10 minutes. Add the cheese and stir until melted and smooth. Stir in the ham and eggs and season to taste with salt and hot pepper sauce. Cook 5 minutes longer and serve.

• •

Waffle-Making Tips

◆ For waffles to bake perfectly, a traditional waffle iron needs to be well seasoned before it is used, just like a skillet. Nonstick waffle irons usually require no seasoning—in either case, the manufacturer's instructions will tell you how to treat your iron.
◆ Once a waffle iron has been seasoned, it should not be washed with soap and water. Wipe it with a paper towel to remove any bits of cooked-on batter or crumbs.
◆ Preheat the waffle iron thoroughly before using. For most irons, the iron is ready when the light goes out.
◆ If you have a batter bowl with a pouring spout, use it to make the batter. If not, transfer the batter to a pitcher so it can be easily poured onto the iron.
◆ When pouring the batter onto the iron, cover only about three-fourths of the surface with batter; the batter will spread out when the iron is closed. After one or two tries, you'll know just how much batter to pour onto your iron.
◆ When steam stops escaping from the edges of the iron, the waffle should be done, usually four or five minutes.
◆ Leftover batter can be stored tightly covered for a day or two in the refrigerator. To refresh the batter, blend together ½ teaspoon baking powder and 1 tablespoon milk and stir this into the batter. Stir in a little more milk, if necessary, to return the batter to its original consistency.

• •

Apples and Currants in Cinnamon Sauce

·

MAKES 5 CUPS

This is delicious over ice cream-topped pecan waffles.

3 cups peeled diced tart baking apples
4 cups dried currants
½ cup sugar
1½ teaspoons ground cinnamon
Grated rind of 1 orange
1 tablespoon cornstarch
1 cup apple juice or water

1. Combine the apples, currants, sugar, cinnamon, and orange rind in a medium heavy saucepan. Place the pan over medium heat, stir until the sugar is dissolved, and bring the mixture to a simmer. Simmer until the apples are crisp-tender, 5 to 7 minutes.

2. In a small bowl, combine the cornstarch and apple juice or water and stir until smooth. Stir in a few tablespoons of liquid from the currant mixture until smooth and then stir this mixture back into the saucepan. Simmer the mixture until thickened, 3 or 4 minutes. Serve warm or chilled.

Sliced Pears in Brandy Sauce

·

MAKES ABOUT 4 CUPS

To be truly decadent, serve this over waffles and ice cream. To be a bit more restrained, simply double the fruit for the amount of sauce here, and serve the fruit spooned into goblets.

1 cup water
1 cup sugar
⅓ cup light corn syrup
1 cinnamon stick
2 pounds firm ripe pears, peeled and sliced
½ cup cognac

1. Combine the water, sugar, corn syrup, and cinnamon stick in a small, heavy saucepan and place over medium-high heat. Bring to a boil and boil until thick and syrupy, about 7 minutes. Add the pears and stir to coat them with the syrup. Bring the syrup to a boil again for 1 minute.

2. Remove the pan from the heat, stir in the cognac, and allow the mixture to cool. Transfer the mixture to a jar, cover tightly, and store in the refrigerator for up to 2 weeks. Rewarm in a heavy pan over low heat before serving.

VARIATIONS In season, substitute peaches, nectarines, or firm ripe plums for the pears.

Bananas in Orange-Rum Sauce

·

SERVES 6

Almost any firm fruit in season would be good with this sauce: sliced peaches, pears, and apples are good alternatives.

½ cup (1 stick) butter
½ cup firmly packed dark brown sugar
½ teaspoon ground cinnamon
6 firm ripe bananas, cut into diagonal slices
¼ cup Grand Marnier
¼ cup dark rum
Juice and grated rind of 2 oranges

1. Melt the butter in a skillet over medium heat. Stir in the brown sugar and cinnamon and stir until the sugar is melted. Add the bananas and sauté for 2 or 3 minutes, or until well glazed.

2. Turn up the heat to medium-high and add the Grand Marnier, rum, and orange juice and rind. Bring to a boil and cook, stirring constantly, until it reduces slightly and thickens, about 7 minutes. Serve hot over waffles with a scoop of vanilla ice cream.

· · · · · · · · · · · · · · · ·

More Waffle Toppers

Any combination of seasonal fruit, such as a mixture of fresh summer berries or a mixture of sliced peaches and plums, is delicious served over Gingerbread Waffles with a big dollop of plain yogurt. Firm fall fruits such as apples or pears should be poached in a little fruit juice to soften.

For à la mode waffles, top waffles and ice cream with crushed sweetened strawberries, maple syrup and broken walnuts and pecans, or hot fudge sauce.

· · · · · · · · · · · · · · · ·

A
NATIVE FEAST
OF
THANKSGIVING

for 12

◆

Menu

CORN AND OYSTER CHOWDER

CORNMEAL CRACKERS

· · ·

CRANBERRY-GLAZED TURKEY
WITH PAN GRAVY

WILD RICE–CRANBERRY DRESSING

GRATIN OF BUTTERNUT SQUASH AND YAMS

STEAMED ROOT VEGETABLES AND BRUSSELS
SPROUTS WITH WILD MUSHROOM BUTTER

HOT POPOVERS

· · ·

PUMPKIN-RUM CUSTARDS
BAKED IN MINIATURE PUMPKINS

GRAPE-WALNUT PIE   APPLE CIDER PIE

Thanksgiving is the oldest American celebration, and it's the holiday most closely associated with food and feasting. When I think of Thanksgiving, I realize how very fortunate I am to have all the necessities of life, and a few of the luxuries as well. To me, the most important of those luxuries are friends and family and the reassur-

ing sense of tradition that days like Thanksgiving celebrate.

Just before dusk, at the end of a lazy day (well, a semi-lazy day for the cook), we all sit down at a candlelit table for a leisurely dinner that extends to a few happy hours. Serving this big dinner as a buffet prevents the table from getting overloaded and lets everyone stretch between courses. We usually wait an hour or so after finishing the main course before serving dessert—sort of a seventh-inning stretch.

When planning this menu, I decided the dinner would be more meaningful if I used as the main ingredients only those that were available to the Pilgrims in Massachusetts. I've taken quite a bit of "artistic license" here and there, and used a few ingredients and cooking ideas the Pilgrims or their Native American friends never knew, and the way this dinner looks is admittedly total fantasy. But the essentials of this dinner are how I imagine that first grateful dinner might have been.

GETTING READY This is a big dinner to prepare alone, but on holidays there's always enough volunteer help for the last-minute kitchen chores. Much of the work can be done in advance, but a lot of it can be done at a leisurely pace.

The crusts for the apple pie can be prepared well in advance and frozen. (The nut crust for the grape pie doesn't freeze well, so I make it no more than a day in advance and refrigerate it.) The cornmeal crackers can be made up to two weeks ahead.

One or two days before Thanksgiving, make the cranberry glaze and the filling for the pies. Make the soup no more than a day in advance. Also bake the custards.

Early on Thanksgiving day, make the stuffing; don't stuff it into the bird until just before roasting, or bacteria can start to grow. Also early in the day, the gratin can be assembled, covered, and refrigerated. Assemble and bake the two pies early so there's room in the oven for the turkey later.

Up to a few hours before dinner, pare the root vegetables and make the mushroom butter. Put the gratin into the oven about half an hour before the turkey is done. Have the batter for the popovers ready, and when the turkey comes out of the oven, turn the oven up to bake them. Meanwhile, steam the root vegetables and make the gravy.

BEVERAGES I always serve American wines with Thanksgiving dinner, no matter what the menu. With the first course, I like a light dry white, such as a California Sémillon or a Sauvignon Blanc; with the glazed turkey, a dry, light bodied red, such as a dry Grenache (rosé), or a fruity Gamay.

Thanksgiving dinner begins with a delicious corn and oyster chowder and crisp cornmeal crackers.

CORN AND OYSTER CHOWDER

•

SERVES 12, AS A FIRST COURSE

Nowadays, we think of oysters as a luxury food, but a few centuries ago they were in such bountiful and accessible supply that people actually complained of having to eat too many. Too many oysters—can you imagine?

⅓ cup (⅔ stick) butter
6 slices bacon, coarsely chopped
2 medium onions, coarsely chopped
1 cup diced celery
1 large green pepper, coarsely chopped
1 large garlic clove, crushed
3 pints shucked oysters, with their liquor
¼ teaspoon white pepper
¼ teaspoon salt
Pinch of ground allspice
4 cups corn kernels, fresh or frozen
½ cup chopped parsley
3 tablespoons brandy (optional)
4 cups half-and-half
Cayenne pepper (optional)

1. In a large, heavy saucepan over medium heat, melt the butter and add the bacon, onion, celery, green pepper, and garlic clove. Sauté until the vegetables are soft and the bacon is crisp, 10 to 12 minutes. Remove and discard the garlic. With a slotted spoon, transfer the bacon and vegetables to the bowl of a food processor fitted with the steel chopping blade.

2. Add the oysters to the pan and sauté them until the edges begin to curl, about 5 minutes. With a slotted spoon, remove the oysters to the food processor. Add the salt, pepper, and allspice to the food processor bowl and process until the mixture is coarsely chopped.

3. Return the mixture to the pan and stir in the oyster liquor. Place over medium heat and bring to the simmering point. Stir in the corn and the parsley (reserve 1 tablespoon for garnish); stir in the brandy if it's being used. Simmer for 5 minutes.

4. Stir in the half-and-half and continue heating to just below the simmering point—do not allow to boil. *(The soup can be made completely up to a day in advance and gently reheated over low heat.)* Serve hot, garnished with a sprinkling of the reserved chopped parsley and perhaps a dash of cayenne pepper.

An opulent combination of fall leaves and flowers, branches of bittersweet, dried corn and gourds, and beeswax candles takes center stage on a table set with unmatched plates decorated in earthy fall colors.

CORNMEAL CRACKERS

•

MAKES ABOUT 4 DOZEN

A tasty, crunchy accompaniment to the creamy soup.

1 cup stone-ground yellow cornmeal
½ teaspoon salt
⅛ teaspoon cayenne pepper
1¼ cups boiling water
2½ tablespoons butter, softened
1 large egg, lightly beaten

1. Preheat the oven to 425°F. Grease 2 baking sheets.

2. In a small mixing bowl, stir together the cornmeal, salt, and cayenne. Gradually stir in the boiling water, keeping the mixture smooth. Stir in the butter until smooth, then stir in the egg.

3. Drop the batter onto the prepared baking sheets by scant tablespoonfuls, about 3 inches apart. Bake until the edges are brown, about 20 minutes. Remove to wire racks to cool and store in a tightly covered container in a cool place for up to 3 weeks.

CRANBERRY-GLAZED TURKEY WITH PAN GRAVY

•

SERVES 12, WITH PLENTY OF LEFTOVERS

1 18- to 20- pound turkey
Salt and freshly ground black pepper
Wild Rice–Cranberry Dressing (recipe follows)
¼ cup (½ stick) butter, softened
Cranberry Glaze (recipe follows)

1. Preheat the oven to 325°F. Rinse the turkey well, inside and out, and pat dry with paper towels. Rub salt and pepper into both the neck and body cavities.

2. Stuff both cavities loosely with the stuffing (see note) and close both ends with trussing skewers and string. Place the turkey breast side up on a rack in a large roasting pan. Rub the skin lightly with softened butter. Insert a meat thermometer into the thickest part of the thigh without touching the bone.

3. Place the turkey in the oven and roast for 15 minutes per pound (20 minutes per pound if the tur-

key weighs less than 15 pounds), basting every 30 minutes with the pan juices. During the last 45 minutes or so of roasting, brush the turkey every 10 minutes with the Cranberry Glaze.

4. The turkey is done when the meat thermometer registers 180°F. or when the juices run clear when the thigh is pricked with a meat fork. Remove the turkey to a warm platter, cover loosely with aluminum foil, and let it rest for about 30 minutes before carving while you make the gravy.

NOTE Any stuffing that does not fit into the turkey can be packed into a buttered heavy-duty aluminum-foil packet and roasted for about 45 minutes.

PAN GRAVY
¼ cup (½ stick) butter
¼ cup all-purpose flour
½ cup Cranberry Glaze (recipe follows)
Pan drippings, skimmed of fat
Turkey or chicken stock, or water
Salt and freshly ground black pepper

1. Melt the butter in a heavy saucepan over medium heat and stir in the flour until incorporated. Gradually stir in the glaze to form a smooth paste and cook 5 minutes, stirring constantly.

2. When the turkey comes out of the roasting pan, skim the fat from the pan juices and discard. Scrape the bottom of the pan to remove any browned bits, stir them into the juices, and pour the juices into the saucepan.

3. Stir the contents of the saucepan until smooth. Add stock or water to thin the gravy if necessary. Bring to a boil, reduce the heat, and simmer 5 minutes longer. Season with salt and pepper to taste, pour into a gravy boat, and serve.

"My folks didn't come over on the Mayflower, but they were there to meet the boat."
Will Rogers

WILD RICE–CRANBERRY DRESSING

·

MAKES 10 CUPS

This is a heady combination, a far cry from the traditional white bread, onions, and sage.

3 cups (1 12-ounce bag) cranberries
1 cup Ruby Port
1 cup sugar
6 cups water
½ teaspoon salt
1½ cups wild rice
½ cup (1 stick) butter
1½ cups long-grain white rice
2 medium onions, finely chopped
¾ cup chopped celery
3 cups well-seasoned chicken or turkey stock
½ cup chopped parsley
¼ cup chopped celery leaves
½ teaspoon dried thyme
½ teaspoon dried marjoram
½ teaspoon dried rubbed sage
Salt and freshly ground black pepper

1. Place the cranberries, Port, and sugar in a saucepan over medium-high heat. Bring to a simmer and cook until the berries begin to pop, about 7 minutes. Drain off all the liquid and set aside the cranberries (reserve the liquid for cranberry glaze—recipe follows).

2. Bring the water to a boil and add the salt. Stir in the wild rice and reduce the heat to low. Cover the pan loosely and cook until the wild rice is tender, about 45 minutes.

3. Meanwhile, melt the butter in a large, heavy saucepan over medium heat. Add the long-grain rice, onions, and celery, and sauté until the rice is golden and the vegetables are crisp-tender, 7 to 10 minutes.

4. Add the stock to the vegetable-rice mixture, turn up the heat, and bring to a boil. Reduce heat, cover, and simmer until rice has absorbed almost all the liquid, 15 to 20 minutes. Remove from the heat.

5. In a mixing bowl, combine the drained cranberries, cooked wild rice, and cooked white rice mixture. Add the parsley, celery leaves, and dried herbs and toss to combine all ingredients. Then add salt and freshly ground black pepper to taste.

6. Stuff the dressing into the turkey just before roasting. Or, to bake separately, transfer to a greased casserole, cover with buttered foil, and bake at 350°F. for 1 hour.

CRANBERRY GLAZE

·

MAKES ABOUT 1½ CUPS

This ruby glaze turns the bird a deep, rich mahogany color as it roasts. The glaze is also excellent on a whole baked ham.

Drained liquid from cranberries for Cranberry–
Wild Rice Dressing (preceding recipe; also see
note below)
1 cup cranberries
Grated rind of 1 large orange
⅛ teaspoon ground cloves
⅛ teaspoon freshly ground black pepper

Combine the ingredients in a small saucepan over medium heat and simmer until cranberries all pop, about 10 minutes. Press the mixture through a sieve to remove cranberry skins. Transfer to a jar, cover, and refrigerate until needed.

NOTE To make the glaze without making the wild rice–cranberry dressing, simply combine a 12-ounce bag cranberries, 1 cup Ruby Port, and 1 cup sugar with the orange zest, cloves, and pepper and simmer until berries all pop, about 10 minutes. Sieve and store as above.

"There is one day that is ours. There is one day when all we Americans who are not self-made go back to the old home to eat saleratus biscuits and marvel how much nearer to the porch the old pump looks than it used to . . . Thanksgiving day is one day that is purely American."
O. Henry

GRATIN OF BUTTERNUT SQUASH AND YAMS

·

SERVES 10 TO 12

With the inclusion of sausage and Cheddar, some may think this is pretty substantial to be a side dish, but I know one family who wouldn't think of having Thanksgiving without it. And anyway, Thanksgiving is an occasion that allows us a little excess, isn't it? The recipe comes from my friend Nolan Drummond.

1 pound bulk sausage
4 scallions, white and green parts, chopped
1½ pounds yams, peeled and cut into chunks
1½ pounds butternut squash, peeled and cut into chunks
2 tablespoons butter
¼ teaspoon grated nutmeg
Salt and freshly ground black pepper
¼ pound sharp Cheddar, grated
¼ cup finely chopped walnuts or pecans

1. Place the sausage in a skillet over medium heat and break it up into small bits with the back of a spatula or spoon. When the sausage begins to release its fat, add the scallions. Sauté until the sausage is cooked through, about 10 minutes. Remove from the heat, pour off the excess fat, and reserve.

2. Steam the yams and squash over simmering water until tender but not mushy, about 20 minutes. Remove from the heat and transfer the vegetables to a mixing bowl. Mash the vegetables with the back of a spoon—they should remain rather lumpy. Add the butter and nutmeg, then season lightly with salt and generously with pepper.

3. Preheat the oven to 350°F. Generously butter a shallow 2-quart baking dish.

4. Spread half the yam and squash mixture in an even layer in the baking dish, scatter half of the sausage mixture over the vegetables, and top with half of the cheese. Repeat and sprinkle on the nuts. (Can be prepared up to this point a few hours in advance, covered tightly, and refrigerated; or freeze up to a month in advance. Return to room temperature before proceeding.)

5. Bake for 30 minutes or until heated through and the cheese is bubbly and browned, then serve.

STEAMED ROOT VEGETABLES AND BRUSSELS SPROUTS WITH WILD MUSHROOM BUTTER

·

SERVES 12

Any combination of vegetables from those listed below will work here; 4 pounds of vegetables will serve 12 people generously. The vegetables should be cut into similar sizes; the steaming times suggested here are guidelines; actual cooking times will depend on the age, freshness, and size of the vegetables. If you select small, young vegetables, they can be left unpeeled and steamed whole.

WILD MUSHROOM BUTTER
3 tablespoons finely chopped dried wild mushrooms, such as morels, shiitake, or porcini
⅓ cup boiling stock or water
⅓ cup (⅔ stick) butter
1 shallot, finely chopped

SUGGESTED VEGETABLES
White turnips, 2 inches in diameter, halved and steamed 15 to 20 minutes
Rutabagas, cut into 1-inch chunks and steamed 15 to 20 minutes
Parsnips, cut into 1-inch chunks and steamed 10 minutes
Salsify (oyster plant), cut into 2-inch lengths and steamed 10 to 12 minutes
Carrots, cut into 2-inch lengths and steamed 15 to 20 minutes
Brussels sprouts, steamed 6 to 8 minutes

1. Combine the mushrooms and stock or water in a small bowl. Let stand for 30 minutes to reconstitute the mushrooms. Melt the butter in the bottom of a large, heavy saucepan over medium-low heat and add the mushrooms and shallot. Sauté until the shallot is tender, 3 to 5 minutes.

2. Add the steamed vegetables to the saucepan and toss with the butter to coat. Serve. (If need be, the vegetables can be prepared a few hours in advance, covered tightly, and stored at room temperature; reheat in a covered shallow baking dish in a 350°F. oven.)

ABOVE: The abundant main course, served from the sideboard, stars a magnificent cranberry-glazed turkey. The "fixings" include hot popovers, steamed autumn vegetables with wild mushroom butter, wild rice-cranberry dressing, and a squash and yam gratin.

LEFT: For dessert, a platter of pumpkin-rum custards baked in miniature pumpkins, a grape walnut pie with a walnut crust, and a lattice-topped apple cider pie.

Hot Popovers
·
MAKES 2 DOZEN

I usually don't serve bread with meals except on special occasions. Old-fashioned popovers take only a few seconds to mix and always make a meal seem more festive.

6 large eggs
3 cups milk
3 cups sifted all-purpose flour
3 tablespoons butter, melted
¼ teaspoon salt

1. Preheat the oven to 450°F. Grease 2 popover pans or heavy, deep muffin pans very well and place the pans in the oven to preheat. (Do not use thin aluminum pans; if you don't have a popover pan or heavy muffin pan, use custard cups set on a baking sheet.)

2. In a mixing bowl, preferably one with a pouring spout, beat the eggs until completely blended, then beat in the milk. Add the other ingredients and beat just until smooth—do not overmix.

3. Remove the hot pans from the oven and immediately pour the batter into the cups until they are about two-thirds full. Return the pans to the oven and bake for 20 minutes.

4. Lower the oven temperature to 350°F. *but do not open the oven.* Bake for an additional 10 to 15 minutes, or until the popovers are firm and golden brown (it's okay to open the oven to check for doneness after 30 minutes total baking time). Serve hot with sweet butter.

VARIATIONS Add a few tablespoons of grated sharp cheese or a tablespoon of chopped chives to the batter before baking.

Pumpkin-Rum Custards Baked in Miniature Pumpkins
·
SERVES 8

Even though this spicy custard is just as delicious baked in custard cups, it tastes better when baked in little pumpkins.

8 miniature pumpkins, approximately 4 inches in diameter
3 cups half-and-half
3 tablespoons cornstarch
2 cups pumpkin puree (recipe follows)
6 large egg yolks
½ cup firmly packed dark brown sugar
½ cup granulated sugar
¼ cup dark rum
1 teaspoon vanilla extract
¼ teaspoon salt
½ teaspoon ground cinnamon
¼ teaspoon ground ginger
¼ teaspoon grated nutmeg, plus extra for tops

1. Preheat the oven to 325°F. Carefully cut the tops from the pumpkins and scoop out the seeds. Reserve.

2. Combine all remaining ingredients in a mixing bowl (use a spouted batter bowl if you have one) and beat until smooth.

3. Ladle or pour the pumpkin mixture into the pumpkins and dust the top with a little grated nutmeg if you'd like. Place the pumpkins in a shallow roasting pan.

4. Bake until the custard is set and very lightly browned at the edges, 30 to 40 minutes. Remove the pumpkins to wire racks to cool, cover with plastic wrap, and refrigerate 6 hours or overnight. Serve cold.

Pureed Pumpkin

Preparing pureed pumpkin isn't at all difficult, and the flavor is fresher than that of canned pumpkin. At the market, be sure to select an "eating" pumpkin, such as a sugar pumpkin or cheese pumpkin, rather than one of the big field pumpkins grown for Jack o'Lanterns. Here's how:

1. Cut open a pumpkin and remove seeds. Cut into quarters and wrap the pieces tightly in foil. Place on a baking sheet and bake at 325°F. for an hour or so, or until the pumpkin is quite tender and falling apart. Or cut raw pumpkin into big chunks and steam until tender but not mushy. When the pumpkin is cool enough to handle, scrape the pulp from the skin.

2. Puree the pumpkin pulp in the bowl of a food processor fitted with the steel chopping blade. Store the puree in a tightly covered container for no more than two days.

GRAPE-WALNUT PIE

·

MAKES ONE 9-INCH PIE

8 cups (about 3 pounds) Ribier grapes or other
   large black grapes
1¼ cups sugar
4 tablespoons all-purpose flour
Juice and grated rind of 1 small lemon
⅛ teaspoon salt
2 tablespoons butter
1 cup lightly toasted finely chopped walnuts
Double recipe Walnut Pastry for a 9-inch pie
   (page 220)

1. Over a shallow bowl to catch the juices, halve and seed the grapes. Reserve.

2. Combine the grape juice, sugar, flour, lemon juice and rind, and salt in a small nonreactive saucepan and whisk to blend well. Place over medium heat and bring to a boil, stirring constantly. Reduce the heat and simmer for about 5 minutes, or until the mixture thickens slightly. Stir in the butter, the reserved grapes, and the walnuts. Remove from the heat and allow to cool. *(Filling can be prepared a day in advance and refrigerated, tightly covered.)*

3. Preheat the oven to 425°F.

4. Divide the pastry into 2 equal parts and roll out one half. Use to line a 9-inch pie shell, then spoon the cooled filling into the lined shell. Roll out the other half of the pastry and cut out decorative shapes—tur-

keys or grapes and grape leaves. Place the decorative shape onto a greased baking sheet.

5. Place the pie pan and the baking sheet in the oven and bake until the pastry is well browned and the juices are thick and bubbly. Transfer the pie and pastry shapes to a wire rack and cool. Arrange the pastry shapes on the pie before serving.

APPLE CIDER PIE

·

MAKES ONE 9-INCH PIE

This old-fashioned pie is especially apple-y, with the concentrated flavor of dried apples intensified by freshly pressed cider. This is the best apple pie I know of for serving with a sliver of good sharp Cheddar.

3 cups fresh apple cider
½ pound dried sliced apples
½ cup firmly packed light brown sugar
1 teaspoon ground cinnamon
¼ teaspoon grated nutmeg
¼ teaspoon ground cloves
3 tablespoons butter
Double recipe Basic Pastry for a 9-inch pie
   (page 220)
1 large egg beaten with 1 tablespoon milk

1. In a medium, heavy saucepan over medium heat, bring the cider to a simmer. Add the dried apples and simmer until the apples are softened and plump, about 10 minutes.

2. Stir in the brown sugar, spices, and butter and continue cooking until most of the liquid has been absorbed and the remaining liquid is quite thick, about 10 minutes longer. Remove from the heat and allow to cool. *(Filling can be prepared a day in advance and stored in the refrigerator; return to room temperature before proceeding.)*

3. Preheat the oven to 400°F.

4. Line a 9-inch pie pan, preferably ceramic or ovenproof glass, with half the pastry and fill the lined pan with the apple mixture. Roll the remaining pastry dough to make a lattice top for the pie and crimp the edges.

5. Brush the surface of the pastry with the beaten egg mixture. Bake the pie until the pastry is golden brown, 35 to 40 minutes. Serve warm or at room temperature.

W
I
N
T
E
R

"Puttin' on the Ritz" Cocktail Party

for 20 to 24

◆

When it comes to entertaining, I tend to be more down-home than uptown, but once a year it's fun to "gussy up" and throw a "ritzy" party. I send out calligraphed invitations well in advance and ask my guests to dress to the nines.

This time I decided to have a *real* cocktail party, featuring drinks from the days when cocktails were *cocktails*—not highballs or wine spritzers, but those fabulous concoctions sometimes smooth, sometimes frothy, sometimes shaken, sometimes stirred.

The first thing I did was to assemble my cocktail menu, picking a variety of drinks from the past, both the popular classics and others with names that caught my fancy. Next, I hired an experienced bartender. And I planned a written cocktail menu (including brief descriptions) to be available at the bar during the party so my guests could select from the special drinks. I also spent a few evenings making cassettes of some of my favorite cocktail pianists playing the music of the cocktail's golden era: the music of Porter, the Gershwins, Kern, Berlin, Rodgers and Hart, Arlen, and Coward. And on the day of the party, out came the silver cocktail shaker, the crystal ice bucket, and the silver trays (from tag sales rather than Tiffany).

GETTING READY There are some hosts who enjoy being the bartender, but I'm not one of them, so for this kind of party I splurge and hire one. The choice is yours. In either case, make sure you have all the bar equipment and drink ingredients you'll need for the drinks you intend to serve, from the liquors to the lemons and limes.

Menu

CLASSIC COCKTAILS:

AMERICANOS   BRONX COCKTAILS

CHAMPAGNE COCKTAILS   KIR ROYALES

MANHATTANS   CLASSIC MARTINIS

MISSISSIPPI MULES   MOSCOW MULES

NEGRONIS   OLD-FASHIONEDS

POLO COCKTAILS   RITZ COCKTAILS

ROB ROYS   RUSTY NAILS   SAZERACS

SIDECARS   STINGERS   TUXEDO COCKTAILS

• • •

DUCK PÂTÉ WITH CRANBERRIES

BLACK AND RED CAVIAR TORTE

PROSCIUTTO-STUFFED MUSHROOMS

SALMON AND RED PEPPER MOUSSE

BLACK AND WHITE MELBA TOASTS

JUMBO SHRIMP WITH THREE DIPPING SAUCES

CRAB AND GOAT CHEESE KISSES

MUSTARD-DEVILED PECANS

• • •

RUM-DOUSED LEMON POPPY-SEED CAKE

STRAWBERRIES WITH HAZELNUT CREAM

COCONUT LACE WAFERS

MOCHA MACADAMIA TRUFFLES

CHAMPAGNE GRAPES

The preparation and cooking of the food can be done over a few days. Several days in advance, make the melba toasts, deviled pecans, coconut wafers, and truffles.

The day before the party (and this is the big work day), make the pâté, the caviar torte, the sauces for the shrimp and strawberries, the mousse, and the lemon cake.

Early on the day of the party, prepare and cook the shrimp. A few hours ahead, make the goat cheese kisses; reheat them just before serving. Prepare the stuffed mushrooms.

Allow a half-hour or more before the party for assembling the buffet.

CLASSIC COCKTAILS

·

EACH MAKES 1 DRINK

Half a century ago, every host worth his salt (and, sometimes secretly in those days, quite a few hostesses) could mix a Martini practically blindfolded. Nowadays, most of us don't know how to mix any drink more complicated than a gin and tonic, or, at most, our own versions of a Bloody Mary. You've probably got a bartender's guide stashed away somewhere, but just in case, here are some of the most popular classics, along with a few of my favorite off-the-beaten-track cocktails, that can help make anyone's reputation as a bartender. The directions here are for somewhat lighter drinks than the traditional recipes, but even so, some of these drinks are pretty potent, so don't encourage your guests to drink up too quickly or too much.

AMERICANO Fill a highball glass with crushed ice. Pour 1½ ounces Campari and 1½ ounces sweet vermouth over the ice and fill with club soda or seltzer. Garnish with a slice of lime.

BRONX COCKTAIL Combine 1 ounce gin, ½ ounce sweet vermouth, ½ ounce dry vermouth, and 2 ounces orange juice in a cocktail shaker with ice. Shake well and strain into a cocktail glass. Garnish with an orange slice.

CHAMPAGNE COCKTAIL Place a small lump of sugar in the bottom of a Champagne glass and add 2 dashes bitters. Fill the glass with chilled Champagne, add a twist of lemon, and garnish with an orange slice.

KIR ROYALE Place a teaspoon of crème de cassis in a champagne flute and fill the flute to two-thirds full with chilled Champagne. To make a regular kir, use a dry white wine rather than Champagne and serve the drink in a wine goblet over ice, garnished with a twist of lemon.

· ·

The Well-Equipped Bar

Here's a list of basic equipment for drink making:

• *Jigger measures* Have several on hand, glass ones marked with ¼-ounce calibrations or the standard double one that measures 1 ounce on one end and 1½ ounces at the other. Old sterling bar measures are not hard to find and add a nice touch to the bar.

• *Cocktail shakers* Having one is essential; having two is even better. A wide variety are available, both new and old, made from glass, silver-topped crystal, stainless steel, silver-plate, and sterling.

• *Glass pitchers* A large, tall one for mixing Martinis and other stirred drinks and a smaller one for water.

◆ A *wire bar strainer*
◆ A *long bar stirrer*, made of glass, stainless steel, or silver
◆ *Measuring spoons*
◆ A *small paring knife*, for cutting fruit
◆ A *small cutting board*

• *Ice buckets* It's best to have a standard-size insulated one and a smaller one when there are only a few for drinks. For larger parties a cooler or Styrofoam chest should be stashed under the bar.

◆ *Ice tongs*
◆ An *ice crusher*, either manual or electric
◆ A *corkscrew, bottle opener, and can opener*
◆ An *electric blender*, for making frozen drinks
◆ A *citrus juicer*, either hand or electric
◆ A *citrus peeler*

• *Glasses* Have a good number of each of the following varieties: Old-Fashioned, highball, stemmed cocktail, wine, Champagne, and cordial. If you have the space or budget for only one type of glass, buy extra-large all-purpose wine glasses; just about any drink can be served in them.

◆ *Other bar equipment* It's nice to have a wooden muddler, a crystal siphon for making sparkling water, bar towels, a small sink, and a handcarved turn-of-the-century bar!

· ·

MANHATTAN Stir 1½ ounces blended whiskey and ¾ ounce sweet vermouth with ice and strain into a cocktail glass. (To make a dry Manhattan substitute dry vermouth for the sweet vermouth.) Garnish with a maraschino cherry.

CLASSIC MARTINI Stir 1½ ounces 80-proof gin and ½ ounce dry vermouth together with ice and strain into a Martini glass. Garnish with 1 or 2 small pitted green olives. For a drier Martini increase the quantity of gin and decrease the quantity of vermouth to taste.

MISSISSIPPI MULE Combine 1½ ounces gin, ½ ounce crème de cassis, and the juice of ¼ lemon with ice in a cocktail shaker. Shake well and strain into a small cocktail glass.

The Perfect Martini

Do I even dare bring up this subject? Endless words have been said or written about making the perfect Martini. The most controversy seems to be in the proportions. While the original recipe called for equal quantities of gin and dry vermouth, there are some who feel that by merely passing the closed vermouth bottle over the glass containing the gin, the vermouth has made sufficient contribution.

All I can offer is the classic proportions (three parts gin to one part vermouth) and a few tips I've picked up here and there; you'll have to decide for yourself whether you want more or less vermouth or whether you want to replace the olive with a twist of lemon peel or even an onion (which, incidentally, makes the drink not a Martini at all, but a Gibson).

The gin and vermouth are best chilled before mixing; in fact, once it's been opened, vermouth should be stored in the refrigerator to preserve its flavor.

The old saw tells us that Martinis should be shaken, not stirred, so the gin doesn't get bruised. Okay, but do stir the Martini vigorously with the ice so the gin and vermouth are well blended and a bit of the ice melts into the drink, making it smooth and palatable.

Martinis can be served either straight up or on the rocks, but the classic way is up, in a stemmed conical glass designed specifically for the purpose.

Vodka Martinis, though not really Martinis at all in the truest sense, are very popular these days. They're made by simply replacing the gin with vodka, plain or flavored. Other Martini variations can be made with white rum or tequila.

MOSCOW MULE Fill a highball glass halfway with crushed ice. Add 1½ ounces gin and a squeeze of lime. Fill the glass with ginger beer (or ginger ale if ginger beer is unavailable), stir, and serve.

NEGRONI Fill an Old-Fashioned glass with ice cubes. Pour ¾ ounce gin, ¾ ounce Campari, and ¾ ounce sweet or dry vermouth over the ice and add a splash of club soda or seltzer and a twist of lemon.

OLD-FASHIONED Combine ½ teaspoon superfine sugar, a dash bitters, and 1 teaspoon water in an Old-Fashioned glass and stir well. Stir in 2 ounces blended whiskey and fill the glass with ice cubes. Garnish with a maraschino cherry and an orange slice.

POLO COCKTAIL Combine 1 ounce gin, ½ ounce dry vermouth, ½ ounce sweet vermouth, and the juice of ½ lime in a cocktail shaker with ice. Shake well and strain into a cocktail glass.

RITZ COCKTAIL Combine ½ ounce brandy and ½ ounce Cointreau in a Champagne glass, fill the glass with chilled Champagne, and stir. Add a twist of lemon.

ROB ROY Stir 1½ ounces Scotch whiskey, ¾ ounce sweet vermouth, and 1 dash bitters together and strain into a cocktail glass. Garnish with a maraschino cherry.

RUSTY NAIL Fill an Old-Fashioned glass with ice cubes. Pour ¾ ounce Scotch whiskey and ¾ ounce Drambuie over the ice and stir to blend.

SAZERAC Stir 2 ounces blended whiskey or bourbon, ½ teaspoon Pernod, a dash bitters (preferably Peychaud), and ½ teaspoon superfine sugar together with ice and strain into a small cocktail glass. Add a twist of lemon peel.

SIDECAR Shake 1½ ounces brandy and ½ ounce Triple Sec or Curacao together with ice in a cocktail shaker and strain into a small cocktail glass.

STINGER Stir 1½ ounces brandy and ½ ounce white crème de menthe together with ice in a cocktail shaker and strain into a small cocktail glass. Variations include vodka stingers and Galliano stingers, in which the named ingredients replace the brandy.

TUXEDO COCKTAIL Combine 1 ounce gin, 1 ounce dry vermouth, 2 dashes Pernod, and a dash bitters in a cocktail shaker with ice. Shake well and strain into a cocktail glass; garnish with a maraschino cherry.

ABOVE: The scene is set for
a black-tie winter cocktail
party in a high-up Manhattan
apartment.

LEFT: On the bar, crystal
decanters and glasses, a
silver cocktail shaker, and
a soda syphon catch the
last glints of daylight.

A Bartender's Cocktail-Making Hints

In the classic *Savoy Cocktail Book*, a compilation of cock-tails served at London's Savoy Hotel published in 1930, the following advice is offered to "the young mixer." Harry Craddock, referred to below, was the legendary bartender at the Savoy during its—and the cocktail's—heydey in the twenties and thirties.

1. Ice is nearly always an absolute essential in any cock-tail.

2. Never use the same ice twice.

3. Remember that the ingredients mix better in a shaker rather larger than is necessary to contain them.

4. Shake the shaker as hard as you can, don't just rock it; you are trying to wake it up, not send it to sleep!

5. Drink your cocktail as soon as possible. Harry Crad-dock was once asked what was the best way to drink a cock-tail. "*Quickly*," replied the great man, "while it's laughing at you."

Mustard-Deviled Pecans

MAKES 4 CUPS

These nuts are great to have on hand to serve with drinks. They'll keep up to a week stored in a tightly covered tin.

⅓ cup Dijon mustard
3 tablespoons honey
¼ cup (½ stick) butter, melted
½ teaspoon hot pepper sauce
¼ teaspoon freshly ground black pepper
1 pound pecan halves

1. Preheat the oven to 275°F. Line a large baking sheet or 2 medium baking sheets with aluminum foil.

2. Combine all ingredients except the pecans in a shallow bowl and blend well. Add the pecans and toss them to coat completely.

3. Spread the pecans in a single even layer on the baking sheet(s). Bake for 10 minutes. Turn the pecans and bake 10 minutes longer. Remove the pans to wire racks and cool completely. Transfer the nuts to tightly covered containers and store in a cool, dry place.

Duck Pâté with Cranberries

MAKES 2 SMALL PÂTÉS, ABOUT 40 HORS D'OEUVRE SERVINGS

This cranberry-studded pâté is baked without the usual pork fat or bacon casing, giving a leaner result. I use two small loaf pans rather than one large one, so the pâté can be cut into hors d'oeuvre-size slices.

4 skinned and boned duck breast halves
⅔ cup cranberries
Grated rind of 1 large orange
2 shallots, finely chopped
¼ cup applejack or Calvados
½ pound chicken livers
2 pounds ground pork
⅔ cup fine dry bread crumbs
1 large egg
½ teaspoon salt
½ teaspoon freshly ground black pepper
1 teaspoon ground allspice

1. Cut the duck breasts into ⅛-inch strips. Place the strips in a large mixing bowl with the cranberries, grated orange rind, and shallots and pour the apple-jack over all. Toss well, cover, place in the refrigera-tor, and marinate for at least 3 hours, or overnight.

2. Place the remaining ingredients in the bowl of a food processor fitted with the steel chopping blade. Process until the mixture is finely chopped and well blended. Add this mixture to the bowl with the duck mixture and blend together. Cover and refrigerate for 1 hour.

3. Preheat the oven to 350°F. Lightly oil two 3-cup loaf pans. Divide the pâté mixture between the 2 pans and smooth out the top.

4. Cover the pans tightly with aluminum foil and place them in a large, shallow baking or roasting pan in the oven. Pour hot water into the large pan halfway up the sides of the loaf pans. Bake for 1½ hours. Re-move the loaf pans from the large pan and pour off and discard any juices. Remove to wire racks to cool, re-cover with aluminum foil, and refrigerate overnight before serving.

BLACK AND RED CAVIAR TORTE

•

MAKES ABOUT 20 HORS D'OEUVRE SERVINGS

This idea's certainly not new, but I think it makes a nice contribution to a fancy party. It disappears quickly, so it's best to splurge and make two.

6 hard-boiled large eggs, peeled and finely
   chopped
1/3 cup (2/3 stick) butter, softened
2 teaspoons chopped dill
1 teaspoon Dijon mustard
1 teaspoon red wine vinegar
1/8 teaspoon salt
6 scallions, white and green parts, finely chopped
1 8-ounce package cream cheese, softened
1/2 cup sour cream
2 tablespoons mayonnaise, approximately
1 3-ounce jar black lumpfish caviar, rinsed and
   drained
1 3-ounce jar red lumpfish caviar, rinsed and
   drained

1. Combine the eggs, butter, dill, mustard, vinegar, and salt and mash with a fork to form a smooth paste. Spread this mixture into the bottom of a 9-inch springform pan. Scatter the scallions evenly over the egg mixture.

2. In a small bowl, blend together the cream cheese and sour cream. Spread this mixture over the scallions. Cover and refrigerate until firm, about 2 hours. *(Can be made up to 24 hours in advance up to this point.)*

3. Just before serving, spread a very thin layer of mayonnaise over the firm cream cheese mixture. Spoon the caviar on top, making alternating stripes of red and black caviar. Garnish with a lemon slice and sprigs of dill. Serve with Black and White Melba Toasts (page 148).

"I always wake up at the crack of ice."
Joe E. Lewis

PROSCIUTTO-STUFFED MUSHROOMS

•

MAKES ABOUT 4 DOZEN

I don't know why, but for some reason stuffed mushrooms, which were once popular finger foods, have fallen into disfavor. Maybe this flavorful version will help bring them back.

1½ pounds small button mushrooms, about 1
   inch in diameter
3 tablespoons butter
1 pound shiitake mushrooms, coarsely chopped
3 tablespoons chopped chives
3 tablespoons chopped flat-leaf parsley
1 teaspoon Hungarian paprika
1/8 teaspoon cayenne pepper
1/2 cup fine, dry bread crumbs
1 ounce prosciutto, finely chopped
1/2 cup sour cream
Parsley leaves, for garnish

1. Using a small paring knife, cut the stems from the button mushrooms and chop them coarsely. Reserve the mushroom caps.

2. Melt the butter in a skillet over medium heat. Add the chopped mushroom stems and the shiitake mushrooms and sauté until the mushrooms have darkened and given up most of their liquid, about 10 minutes. Stir in the chives and the parsley and sauté 1 minute longer. Remove from the heat and stir in the remaining ingredients, except garnish.

3. While the filling mixture is cooking, blanche the mushroom caps in boiling water for 3 minutes. Drain very well.

4. Place the mushroom caps on a baking sheet, cut side up. Using a small spoon, mound some of the filling into each. *(Can be prepared up to this point a few hours in advance, covered, and refrigerated.)*

5. Preheat the oven to 400°F. Bake the mushrooms until the filling is bubbly, about 15 minutes. Serve warm, each mushroom garnished with a parsley leaf.

ABOVE: Hot crab and goat cheese kisses and prosciutto-stuffed mushrooms are passed on a silver platter.

BELOW: A salmon and red pepper mousse is surrounded with cucumber slices and garnished with sprigs of dill.

OPPOSITE: Cavier torte, served with black melba toasts, and jumbo shrimp with three pretty sauces for dipping.

Salmon and Red Pepper Mousse

•

MAKES ONE 4-CUP MOUSSE

A salmon mousse in one form or another is one of the most popular foods I serve at large parties, so hardly a party (or a book) goes by without one. I'm always experimenting, and here's the latest version. Serve this with thin slices of toasted baguette or pumpernickel.

1 tablespoon unflavored gelatin
¼ cup cold water
⅓ cup boiling water
⅓ cup sour cream
⅓ cup Homemade Mayonnaise (page 221)
2 large red peppers, roasted, seeded, and peeled
* (page 64)*
1 tablespoon lemon juice
1 small onion, coarsely chopped
¼ teaspoon salt
⅛ teaspoon cayenne pepper
¼ teaspoon paprika
1 cup heavy cream
1¾ cups flaked poached salmon or 1 15½-ounce
* can red salmon, picked over to remove skin and*
* bones*
1 red pepper, cut into strips, for garnish
Sprigs of dill, for garnish

1. In a large mixing bowl, sprinkle the gelatin over the cold water and let stand for 2 or 3 minutes to soften. Gradually stir in the boiling water and stir until the gelatin is dissolved. Refrigerate for 2 to 3 minutes to cool.

2. Place the remaining ingredients except the cream and salmon in the bowl of a food processor fitted with the steel chopping blade and process until completely blended and smooth. Blend this mixture into the gelatin and chill about 15 minutes, or until slightly thickened.

3. While the mixture is chilling, whip the cream in a separate chilled bowl. Fold the cream and salmon into the chilled mixture.

4. Oil a 4-cup mold and transfer the mousse to it, cover with plastic wrap, and refrigerate until firm, at least 3 hours. To serve, unmold the mousse and garnish with red pepper strips and dill sprigs. Serve with cucumber slices or black and white melba toasts.

Black and White Melba Toasts

•

1. Preheat the oven to 325°F. Cut the crusts from thinly sliced firm white and pumpernickel bread and cut each slice into quarters, making triangles or strips. Or use cookie cutters to make decorative shapes, such as stars or hearts.

2. Spread the bread on a baking sheet in 1 layer and bake for 15 to 20 minutes, or until the bread is dry and just beginning to brown. Cool the toasts on wire racks and store in airtight containers at room temperature for up to 2 weeks.

Jumbo Shrimp with Three Dipping Sauces

•

Since there are only about 10 jumbo shrimp to an expensive pound, I splurge and serve them at a party only once in a blue moon. Don't worry about having enough—there never are; I pass these rather than put them out on the buffet table. They disappear quickly, so by passing them, everyone gets a few. On the tray are small bowls of these three simple sauces.

CUCUMBER – DILL SAUCE Combine 1 large peeled, seeded, and finely chopped cucumber; 2 finely chopped scallions; ¼ cup chopped parsley; 1 tablespoon white wine vinegar; and 1 tablespoon chopped dill with 1 cup sour cream. Mix well and season to taste with salt and white pepper.

RED PEPPER–CAPER MAYONNAISE Combine 2 roasted, peeled, and seeded red peppers (page 64); 1 cup Homemade Mayonnaise (page 221); 1 large garlic clove; and ⅛ teaspoon cayenne pepper in the bowl of a food processor fitted with the steel chopping blade and process until smooth. Stir in 1 teaspoon capers.

TARRAGON MUSTARD SAUCE Combine 3 tablespoons Dijon mustard, 1 teaspoon chopped tarragon, 1 tablespoon red wine vinegar, ½ cup sour cream, and ½ cup Homemade Mayonnaise (page 221). Mix well and season to taste with salt and white pepper.

CRAB AND GOAT CHEESE KISSES

MAKES 40

Here's a nice combination of flavors and textures. Even though these are best when assembled and baked just before serving, it's rather impractical with a crowd of this size. Make them a few hours in advance, underbaking slightly, and reheat them briefly before serving.

½ pound flaked crabmeat
½ pound soft mild goat cheese
1 shallot, very finely chopped
2 tablespoons finely chopped parsley
¼ teaspoon freshly ground black pepper
6 sheets phyllo dough
½ cup (1 stick) butter, melted

1. Blend the crabmeat, goat cheese, shallot, parsley, and pepper in a small mixing bowl. Reserve.

2. Preheat the oven to 350°F. Lightly grease baking sheets. Spread out the layered sheets of phyllo dough and cover with a damp cloth.

3. Quickly and carefully transfer a sheet of dough onto the work surface and brush lightly but completely with melted butter. Spread the second sheet of phyllo smoothly over the first sheet and brush with additional butter; repeat with the third sheet.

4. Cut the layered phyllo into 20 squares and place a teaspoonful of the filling mixture in the center of each square. Gather the corners of the phyllo up over the filling and twist them together, forming a "kiss." Brush the kisses lightly with additional butter and place them on the baking sheets about 1 inch apart.

5. Repeat steps 3 and 4. Place the baking sheets in the oven and bake until the phyllo is nicely browned, about 10 minutes. Transfer the kisses to a platter and serve.

RUM-DOUSED LEMON POPPY-SEED CAKE

MAKES ONE 10-INCH TUBE CAKE

A simple, elegant cake that takes no time to make. I've been known to sneak a slice of this cake with a cup of tea as a late-night snack.

1 cup (2 sticks) butter, softened
4 ounces cream cheese, softened
1¾ cups sugar
3 large eggs
1 tablespoon grated lemon rind
1½ cups all-purpose flour
1 teaspoon baking powder
2 tablespoons poppy seeds
¼ cup light rum

1. Preheat the oven to 375°F. Grease a 10-inch tube or Bundt pan very well.

2. In a large mixing bowl, beat together the butter and cream cheese until well blended, then beat in the sugar, eggs, and lemon rind, beating until the mixture is light and fluffy. In a separate bowl, sift together the flour and baking powder, then beat this into the butter mixture. Stir in the poppy seeds.

3. Spoon the batter into the prepared pan and bake until the cake is a light golden brown and springs back firmly when pressed, 55 to 60 minutes. Cool for 15 minutes in the pan, then invert onto a wire rack to cool. Drizzle the rum over the cake a little at a time, allowing it to be absorbed by the cake before drizzling on more. Transfer to a cake plate or cake stand, cover, and let stand 2 or 3 hours before serving.

"Why don't you slip out of that wet swimsuit and into a dry Martini?"
Robert Benchley

Strawberries with Hazelnut Cream

•

An out-of-season extravagance.

1 cup sour cream
1 cup skim-milk ricotta
½ cup confectioners' sugar
½ cup hazelnuts, toasted and ground
2 tablespoons Frangelico liqueur
½ teaspoon vanilla extract
4 pints strawberries, with stems attached, if possible

In a small bowl, combine all the ingredients except the strawberries and mix until smooth and well blended. Cover and refrigerate until just before serving. Place the bowl on a platter or in a shallow basket and surround with the berries.

Coconut Lace Wafers

•

MAKES ABOUT 5 DOZEN COOKIES

Light and delicate, these cookies are also delicious after dinner for dessert, served with a citrus ice or sherbet.

⅓ cup (⅔ stick) butter, softened
½ cup sugar
¼ cup light corn syrup
½ teaspoon vanilla extract
½ teaspoon lemon juice
½ cup all-purpose flour
1 cup shredded coconut

1. Preheat the oven to 350°F. Lightly grease baking sheets.

2. In a mixing bowl, cream the butter and sugar together until light and fluffy and then beat in the corn syrup, vanilla, and lemon juice. Add the flour and beat until smooth, and then stir in the coconut.

3. Drop the dough by scant teaspoonfuls about 3 inches apart onto the baking sheets. Bake until the edges are lightly browned, about 5 minutes.

4. Remove the baking sheets to wire racks and allow the cookies to cool for about 5 minutes. Transfer the cookies to the racks and cool completely. Store in an airtight container in a cool place.

Mocha Macadamia Truffles

•

MAKES ABOUT 3 DOZEN

6 tablespoons heavy cream
¼ cup (½ stick) butter
2 tablespoons coffee liqueur
2 tablespoons sugar
1 pound semisweet chocolate, chopped
2 teaspoons very finely ground espresso beans
30 macadamia nuts
¼ cup unsweetened cocoa
½ teaspoon ground cinnamon

1. Combine the cream and butter in a small, heavy saucepan over medium heat and bring to a simmer. Turn down the heat, add the liqueur and sugar, and stir until the sugar dissolves. Remove from the heat, add the chocolate and espresso, and stir with a heavy spoon until the chocolate is melted and the mixture is smooth.

2. Transfer the mixture to a small bowl and cool. Cover and refrigerate until the mixture is thick and pliable, about 30 minutes.

3. Line a baking sheet with wax paper (or use a nonstick baking sheet). Using your fingers, mold about 1 tablespoon of the chocolate mixture around each macadamia nut. Place on the baking sheet and refrigerate until firm but still slightly pliable, about 15 minutes.

4. Mix the cocoa and cinnamon together in a small bowl. Dip each truffle in the cocoa mixture to coat lightly. Return to the baking sheet and freeze until firm, about 1 hour.

5. Transfer the truffles to a wax paper–lined airtight container in single layers with wax paper between each layer and store in a cool place (do not refrigerate).

OPPOSITE: **I always include a few sweets and coffee or espresso at cocktail parties. Here, with a crystal vase filled with paper whites, are lacy coconut wafers, extravagant long-stemmed strawberries with hazelnut cream for dipping, cocoa-dusted mocha macadamia truffles, and rum-doused lemon poppy-seed cake.**

A
Fireside
Christmas
Eve Supper

for 6 to 8

•

Menu

RIES'S DUTCH BROWN BEAN SOUP

TRIPLE-GRAIN BROWN BREAD

QUICK CABBAGE SLAW WITH
PINEAPPLE-HORSERADISH DRESSING

• • •

CRANBERRY-ALMOND TART

Christmas Eve may be the most enchanted evening of all. So much legend, myth, and mystery, both religious and secular, are part of the night of December 24. And for those who celebrate Christmas, there are more personal and family traditions attached to this night than to any other night of the year.

In some households, the main holiday celebration is held on Christmas Eve, with a big dinner and the opening of the gifts before or afterward. In other homes decorating the tree and then setting out milk and cookies for Santa is the big event. At our house, there's always a simple supper served hearthside, and then it's off to church for the candlelit reenactment of the Christmas story at midnight and the singing of carols.

A few years ago, when my friend Ries Fess was visiting from Amsterdam, he made this traditional Dutch bean soup for us on Christmas Eve. We served it American style with slaw (which, incidentally, is orig-

inally Dutch) and a hearty bread. The tart adds a note of colorful festivity to this otherwise simple and homey supper.

GETTING READY Both the soup and the bread can be made well in advance and frozen. Or make the soup a day in advance and bake the bread early on the day it is to be served. The slaw can be made a day in advance as well; it only takes a few minutes. The tart can be made anytime up to 24 hours before serving.

BEVERAGES I like beer or cider with the soup and slaw; more cider or coffee with the dessert. If it's a cold night, a hot buttered cider (with or without rum) or hot toddy is perfect at the beginning or end of the evening.

Ries's Dutch Brown Bean Soup

•

SERVES 6 TO 8

A simple soup with a surprisingly rich and complex flavor.

> 1½ pounds dried brown (pinto) beans
> ½ teaspoon salt
> ½ pound bacon, coarsely chopped
> 2 medium onions, chopped
> ½ pound white turnips, peeled and diced
> ½ pound carrots, peeled and diced
> 2 medium leeks, white part only, chopped
> ¾ pound boiling potatoes, peeled and diced
> 5 cups water
> 1 6-ounce can tomato paste
> ½ teaspoon dried savory
> ⅛ teaspoon grated nutmeg
> 1 teaspoon brown sugar
> 1 tablespoon grated fresh gingerroot or
> ½ teaspoon ground ginger
> Salt and freshly ground black pepper
> 1 pound smoked sausage (Dutch rookworst,
> French garlic sausage, or Polish kielbasa)
> ¼ cup chopped parsley

1. Place the beans in a large, heavy soup pot, add water to cover by 2 inches, and place over high heat. Bring to a rolling boil and boil for 2 minutes. Remove from the heat and let stand for 1 hour. Add salt, return to high heat, and bring to a boil. Reduce the heat and simmer the beans until they are just tender, but not mushy, about 1 hour. Drain the beans, rinse well, and reserve.

2. In a large Dutch oven over medium heat, cook the bacon until it begins to render some of its fat. Add the onions, turnips, carrots, and leeks and sauté for 10 minutes. Add the remaining ingredients up to and including the ginger. Bring to a simmer, cover, and cook, barely simmering, for 1½ hours, or until all the vegetables are very soft. Remove from the heat and cool slightly.

3. Puree one-third to one-half of the soup (depending on the desired consistency of the finished soup) in a food processor fitted with the steel chopping blade. Stir the puree back into the soup and season to taste with salt and pepper.

4. Preheat the broiler. Cut the sausage diagonally into ¼-inch-thick slices. Place the slices on a rack in a shallow pan and broil until lightly browned on both sides. Transfer to absorbent paper to drain excess fat and then add the sausage to the soup. (*Can be made up to this point up to 2 days ahead, transferred to tightly covered containers, and refrigerated, or it can be made up to a month in advance and frozen.*)

5. To reheat the soup, first skim off any fat from the surface and then allow the soup to come to room temperature. Transfer the soup to the Dutch oven and place over low heat. Stir in 2 tablespoons of the parsley, bring to a simmer, and cook 5 minutes. Serve in the Dutch oven or transfer to a tureen. Garnish with the remaining parsley.

• •

Winter's Warming Drinks

While the chestnuts are roasting on an open fire, there are all kinds of wonderful drinks (with and without alcohol) that can warm body and soul. Here are a few favorites:

◆ *Hot Citrus Toddy* For 4 drinks, combine 2 cups orange juice, 1½ cups water, 1 tablespoon lemon juice, and 2 tablespoons sugar in a small saucepan and bring to a simmer. Add 2 cinnamon sticks broken in half and 4 lemon or lime slices stuck with cloves. Simmer 2 minutes, stir in ¼ cup Scotch (optional), and pour into mugs.

◆ *Hot Buttered Cider* (non-alcoholic) For 4 drinks, combine 1 quart cider, 1 tablespoon molasses, 1 tablespoon lemon juice, 6 whole cloves, and a cinnamon stick broken in half in a medium saucepan and bring to a boil. Simmer 10 minutes and ladle into mugs. Top each drink with a thin pat of butter and garnish with a cinnamon stick.

◆ *Hot Madras* For 4 drinks, combine 2 cups cranberry juice cocktail, 2 cups orange juice, ¼ cup water, and 6 whole cloves in a medium saucepan and bring to a boil. Simmer 10 minutes and stir in ⅓ cup vodka or rum. Ladle into mugs and garnish each with an orange slice.

• •

*T*RIPLE-GRAIN BROWN BREAD

•

MAKES 1 ROUND LOAF, ABOUT
9 INCHES IN DIAMETER

The oatmeal and cornmeal give this bread a grainy texture, which compliments the smooth soup quite nicely.

1½ cups rolled oats
1 cup stone-ground yellow cornmeal
1½ cups boiling water
½ cup cold milk, plus extra for top
3 tablespoons molasses
2 envelopes active dry yeast
¼ cup (½ stick) corn oil margarine, melted and cooled
1 teaspoon salt
1 cup whole wheat flour
2½ to 3 cups all-purpose flour

1. In a large mixing bowl, stir the oats (reserving 1 tablespoon) and cornmeal together. Pour the boiling water over the mixture and let it stand until just warm, about 15 minutes. Stir in the milk and molasses, then sprinkle the yeast over the mixture. Stir in the margarine, salt, and whole wheat flour. Gradually stir in all-purpose flour, about ½ cup at a time, until the mixture is difficult to stir.

2. Turn the mixture out onto a lightly floured board and, using floured hands, knead the dough, adding more all-purpose flour, about ¼ cup at a time, until the dough is no longer sticky and becomes smooth and satiny. Continue kneading 2 minutes more.

3. Roll the dough into a ball and place in a lightly oiled bowl. Cover with a clean cloth, place in a draft-free place, and let rise until doubled in bulk, 50 to 60 minutes.

4. Punch down the dough and knead it in the bowl for a minute. Form it into a ball again and place it on a lightly greased baking sheet. Brush the surface with milk and sprinkle the reserved oats over the top. Cover again with the cloth and allow the dough to double again, 40 to 50 minutes.

5. Preheat the oven to 375°F. Bake for about 45 minutes, or until the bread is well browned and sounds hollow when tapped. Transfer to a wire rack and serve warm or at room temperature.

ABOVE: On Christmas Eve, I like serving a simple supper in front of the tree and a roaring fire. RIGHT: Dutch bean soup with sausage is served from a Victorian china tureen, and oatmeal-topped triple-grain brown bread on an old English bread board.

OPPOSITE: A vibrant cranberry-almond tart with a crunchy almond shortbread crust is served on a favorite Victorian pressed glass cakestand.

Quick Cabbage Slaw with Pineapple-Horseradish dressing

•

SERVES 8

1 small head red or green cabbage, shredded
1 small red or green pepper, coarsely grated
⅔ cup Homemade Mayonnaise (page 221)
⅓ cup Jezebel Sauce (recipe follows)

Place the cabbage and pepper in a medium bowl. In a separate small bowl, combine the mayonnaise and Jezebel Sauce and blend well. Pour the dressing over the cabbage and toss to coat. Cover and refrigerate for a few hours, or overnight, before serving.

Jezebel Sauce

•

MAKES ABOUT 3 CUPS

In addition to being a primary ingredient in the preceding slaw dressing, this easy sauce is delicious with simple roasted or grilled ham, pork, and duck or grilled sausages. It's great on a ham sandwich, too.

1 12-ounce jar pineapple preserves
1 12-ounce jar apple jelly
1 5-ounce jar prepared horseradish, drained
1 1½-ounce can dry mustard
½ teaspoon hot red pepper flakes

Combine all the ingredients in a small bowl and mix well. Transfer to a jar (or jars) and refrigerate at least 48 hours before using.

Cranberry-Almond Tart

•

MAKES ONE 10-INCH TART

I like a surprise ending to a homey meal, and this elegant-looking tart, with its wonderful combination of textures and flavors, finishes this supper off with a bang.

ALMOND SHORTBREAD CRUST
1 cup all-purpose flour
¼ teaspoon salt
¼ cup confectioners' sugar
⅓ cup ground almonds
½ cup (1 stick) butter, melted and cooled
½ teaspoon almond extract

CRANBERRY FILLING
¾ cup red currant jelly
¼ cup cranberry juice cocktail or orange juice
¼ cup sugar
⅛ teaspoon ground cloves
3 cups (1 12-ounce bag) cranberries
1 tablespoon unflavored gelatin
¼ cup water
2 tablespoons lightly toasted slivered almonds

1. Preheat the oven to 350°F. Lightly butter a 10-inch tart pan with a removable bottom.

2. To make the crust, sift together the flour, salt, and confectioners' sugar in a small mixing bowl. Blend in the almonds and then beat in the cooled melted butter and almond extract until thoroughly combined, forming a thick dough.

3. Using your fingers, press the dough into the tart pan, evenly lining the bottom and sides. Place the pan in the oven and bake for 30 to 35 minutes, or until golden brown, and then transfer the tart pan to a wire rack to cool.

4. To make the filling, place the jelly, juice, and sugar in a small saucepan over medium heat and bring to a simmer, stirring until the jelly and sugar are dissolved. Stir in the ground cloves. Reduce the heat and simmer about 10 minutes, stirring occasionally. Add the cranberries and simmer, stirring occasionally, until the berries begin to pop, about 5 minutes. Remove from the heat.

5. Sprinkle the gelatin over the water and let stand 5 minutes to soften. Stir the gelatin into the cranberry mixture until it is dissolved and blended in. Allow the mixture to cool thoroughly.

6. Spoon the cooled cranberry mixture into the cooled crust. Cover loosely with aluminum foil and chill at least 2 hours before serving. Garnish by scattering the toasted almonds around the edges of the tart. Remove the sides of the pan and serve the tart cut into thin wedges, with dollops of unsweetened whipped cream.

A
HOLIDAY
DESSERT
PARTY
for 30

◆

Years ago, it was common practice to invite a few friends over for coffee and cake. The evening may have also included a card game or board game, or it may not have had any planned agenda at all—just a simple excuse to get together (and you can be assured there was plenty of tongue-wagging). Somehow, that practice waned over the years. I don't know whether it's because we've cut back on everyday dessert eating, or just that we've become too "sophisticated" for such simple pleasures, but I can't think of a better reason than dessert for having a party.

I throw a big dessert party every year during the holidays, which seems like the best time for such extravagance. Everyone forgets waistline watching and our health-conscious reasons for skipping desserts during the rest of the year. My party is held late on a Friday evening or early on a Sunday evening, and when I invite everyone, I give them fair warning there'll be plenty to eat so they can have a light meal (or none at all) beforehand. One of the advantages of this party for the host is that all the cooking (and there's a good bit of it, here) is done ahead of time. Once the party begins, all I have to worry about is keeping the punchbowl filled and replenishing the buffet when it needs it.

The menu offers all the traditional tastes and colors of the holiday season, from cranberries and mincemeat to chocolate and rum; there's something to satisfy everyone. To me, the holidays wouldn't be the holidays without an assortment of homemade cookies. (There are more cookies here than needed for this party; choose three or four varieties or make them all to carry you through the season.) Rather than eggnog,

Menu

WINTER WHITE PUNCH   CHAMPAGNE

COFFEE AND LIQUEURS (PAGES 212 TO 214)

· · ·

CHOCOLATE CHOCOLATE CHOCOLATE CAKE

BAKED RUMMY PINEAPPLE

PEAR-PECAN TART

MAIDS OF HONOUR

CHOCOLATE HOLIDAY STOLLEN

BAVARIAN CHRISTMAS PUDDING

CRANBERRY WINTER PUDDING

APPLE-MINCEMEAT CAKE

WINTER FRUITS

· · ·

CHRISTMAS COOKIES:

POPPY-SEED PINWHEELS

AL'S CHOCOLATE WHISKEY BALLS

MARBLE TILES

CREAM CHEESE CHRISTMAS COOKIES

JAM THUMBPRINTS

ORANGE GINGER SNAPS

PECAN CHESS BARS

CHOCOLATE CHIP SHORTBREAD

BROWN SUGAR–WALNUT SHORTBREAD

which would be too sweet and rich, I've included a light, refreshing punch along with an urn of coffee.

GETTING READY There's a good bit of preparation here, but the work can be stretched over a period of days or even weeks.

The stollen and the layers for the chocolate cake can be baked far in advance and frozen. The cookies can all be made well ahead; check the individual recipes for advance timing.

Up to two days in advance, make the apple-mince-meat cake and the Bavarian pudding.

The day before the party, make the cranberry pudding, the filling for the chocolate cake, the pear tart, and the maids of honour.

On the day of the party, assemble and frost the chocolate cake. An hour or two in advance, prepare the pineapple; it can be baked just before serving.

WINTER WHITE PUNCH
·
MAKES ABOUT SIXTY 6-OUNCE SERVINGS

When making punch it's always a good idea to chill all the liquid ingredients if you have room in the refrigerator (or stash everything on the porch for an hour or two) to keep the punch as cold as possible. I usually make two batches of this punch, one with the rum and one without.

1 cup lemon juice
½ cup sugar
6 star anise
½ teaspoon almond extract
2 liters chilled light rum (optional)
2 liters chilled dry white wine
2½ quarts chilled grapefruit juice
2 quarts chilled white grape juice
3 liters chilled seltzer or club soda

Mint sprigs, for garnish
Lime slices, for garnish

1. Combine the lemon juice, sugar, and star anise in a small saucepan, place over medium heat, and stir until sugar is dissolved, forming a thin syrup. Remove from the heat, stir in the almond extract, and cool.

2. Just before serving, place a molded block of ice in a large punch bowl. Pour the syrup into the bowl and stir in the remaining ingredients. Garnish with the mint and lime slices.

BELOW: Winter white punch is served before the tree. The punch bowl set is one of my best tag sale finds.

OPPOSITE: Served on old silver platters and trays and glass cake stands, an opulent array of festive desserts is laid out on the candle-bedecked dining table.

CHOCOLATE CHOCOLATE CHOCOLATE CAKE

•

MAKES ONE 3-LAYER CAKE

I know some think I'm crazy, but, to my mind, some chocolate cakes can be *too* chocolatey—too "Johnny One-Note" in flavor. There's plenty of chocolate here (half a pound!) to satisfy even the most maniacal choc-oholic, but a hint of orange and cinnamon in the lay-ers and rum in the filling add a bit of zing to this cake.

LAYERS
3 ounces unsweetened chocolate, melted
3 ounces semisweet chocolate, melted
⅓ cup hot strong-brewed coffee
1 cup (2 sticks) butter, at room temperature
1½ cups sugar
4 large eggs, separated and at room temperature
2⅔ cups sifted cake flour
1½ teaspoons baking powder
¼ teaspoon salt
½ teaspoon ground cinnamon
1 cup milk
1 teaspoon vanilla extract
Grated rind of 1 orange

1. Preheat the oven to 350°F. Grease three 9-inch round cake pans, line them with wax paper, and grease the wax paper.

2. Melt the chocolate in the top of a double boiler over simmering water and stir in the hot coffee. Re-move from the heat and set aside to cool.

3. In a large mixing bowl, cream the butter and sugar together until light and fluffy. One at a time, beat in the egg yolks until well blended. Beat in the cooled chocolate mixture.

4. In a separate bowl, sift together the flour, baking powder, salt, and cinnamon. In three batches, beat this into the wet mixture, alternating with the milk. Beat in the vanilla and orange rind.

5. In a separate bowl, beat the egg whites until stiff but not dry. Fold the egg whites into the batter and then divide the batter among the 3 pans.

6. Bake the cake until the edges of the cake come away from the pan and a toothpick or cake tester in-serted in the center comes out clean, 25 to 30 minutes. Cool in the pan 5 minutes and then turn out onto wire racks to cool. *(The layers can be baked well in advance and frozen, tightly wrapped.)*

FILLING
2 ounces unsweetened chocolate
¾ cup heavy cream
¼ cup dark rum
⅔ cup sugar
⅓ cup all-purpose flour
¼ teaspoon salt
3 large egg yolks
2 tablespoons (¼ stick) butter, softened
1 teaspoon vanilla extract

1. Melt the chocolate in the top of a double boiler and stir in the cream and rum. Combine the sugar, flour, and salt in a mixing bowl and then beat in the egg yolks. Gradually beat the chocolate mixture into the egg yolk mixture.

2. Pour the mixture back into the top of the double boiler and cook, stirring continuously, until the filling has thickened and thickly coats the spoon. *Do not allow the custard to simmer at any point.*

3. Remove the top of the double boiler from the heat and dip it into a large bowl of cold water to stop the filling from cooking any further. Beat briskly for 5 minutes to help it cool off rapidly, then beat in the butter and the vanilla. Allow the filling to cool and then cover tightly and chill. *(Can be made up to a day ahead and stored in the refrigerator.)*

4. Place one cooled cake layer on a cake plate or cake stand and spread half the filling evenly on top. Place the second layer on the filling and top the layer with the remaining filling. Top with the third cake layer.

FROSTING
⅓ cup (⅔ stick) butter
2 ounces semisweet chocolate
1 teaspoon all-purpose flour
¾ cup milk
¼ cup strong brewed coffee
2 cups sugar
1 teaspoon vanilla extract
Strips of candied orange peel, for garnish

1. Melt the butter and chocolate in the top of a double boiler over simmering water and then stir in the flour. Gradually stir in the milk and coffee and then stir in the sugar.

2. Place the pan directly over medium-low heat and bring to a boil, stirring constantly. Continue cooking until the mixture reaches the soft ball stage (234°F.) on a candy thermometer. Remove the pan from the heat and stir in the vanilla.

3. Beat the frosting until it cools slightly and becomes spreadable. Working quickly, frost the top and sides of the cake, dipping the knife into hot water to make the surface of the frosting smooth. If the frosting gets too thick and hard while spreading it onto the cake, place the pan over simmering water for a few moments until it softens again.

4. To garnish, arrange strips of candied orange peel in a flower pattern on top of the cake. Cover the cake and store it in the refrigerator until serving time.

*B*AKED RUMMY PINEAPPLE

•

SERVES 16

2 ripe medium pineapples
½ cup firmly packed dark brown sugar
½ cup molasses
2 teaspoons ground cinnamon
2 tablespoons butter, softened
⅓ cup dark rum

1. Preheat the oven to 350°F. Line a large baking sheet with aluminum foil.

2. Cut the pineapples, including the leafy tops, in half lengthwise and then into quarters. Cut the core from each quarter and then neatly cut the pineapple away from the skin. Cut the pineapple into ½-inch-thick slices and then push the slices back into their original positions in the shells.

3. In a small bowl, combine the brown sugar, molasses, cinnamon, butter, and rum to form a paste. Spread this paste over the pineapple. Arrange the pineapple on the baking sheet and cover the leafy tops with aluminum foil.

4. Bake the pineapple until it's glazed and browned, 12 to 15 minutes. Arrange the pineapple quarters on a round platter with the tops pointing out. Serve warm or at room temperature with bamboo skewers or toothpicks.

*P*EAR-PECAN TART

•

MAKES ONE 10-INCH TART

CRUST
2 cups all-purpose flour
¾ cup firmly packed dark brown sugar
1 teaspoon baking soda
½ teaspoon ground allspice
½ teaspoon ground ginger
½ cup quick-cooking oats
½ cup finely chopped pecans
½ cup (1 stick) butter
4 tablespoons ice water, approximately

FILLING
5 large ripe pears cored, peeled, and sliced
½ cup coarsely chopped pecans
2 tablespoons butter
¼ cup firmly packed dark brown sugar
¼ cup granulated sugar

1 cup heavy cream, whipped

1. To make the crust, combine the flour, brown sugar, baking soda, and spices in a mixing bowl and blend well. Blend in the oats and pecans. Using a pastry blender or your fingers, cut in the butter until the mixture is uniformly crumbly. Mix in the water and work the mixture with your fingers just until it forms a dough that holds together—add a bit more water if necessary.

2. Preheat the oven to 375°F. Press the dough into a 10-inch tart pan with a removable bottom, lining the bottom and sides. Fill the tart shell with the pears and scatter the pecans over the pears.

3. In a small saucepan over medium heat, melt the butter and the brown and white sugars together, stirring constantly. Drizzle the mixture over the tart with a spoon, covering the pears and nuts.

4. Bake until the pears are tender and the crust is well browned. Remove to a wire rack to cool. Cut the tart into thin wedges and serve with a dollop of unsweetened whipped cream.

"Dessert has always been my favorite vegetable. To me, having just fruit for dessert reminds me of being a little kid and getting clothes for Christmas: what kind of treat is that?"
Malcolm Forbes

Sugar-dusted apple mincemeat cake, pear pecan tart, and fruit-studded chocolate holiday stollen. OPPOSITE: Maids of Honour (rich little tarts filled with jam and nuts and other good things) and a triple chocolate cake, served on old glass cake stands.

Maids of Honour

According to legend, Anne Boleyn was the creator of these little almond tarts when she was a lady-in-waiting to the Queen, Catherine of Aragon. Catherine's husband, Henry VIII, a gourmand if there ever was one, tasted one of Anne's tarts and—well, you know the rest of the story.

CRUST
1½ cups (3 sticks) butter, softened
1 cup sugar
3 large egg yolks
3½ cups all-purpose flour
¼ teaspoon salt
1½ teaspoons vanilla extract

FILLING
1 cup strawberry or raspberry jam, approximately
2 large eggs
¾ cup sugar
½ teaspoon almond extract
Grated rind of 1 lemon
2 tablespoons dry sherry
1 tablespoon all-purpose flour
¾ cup ground almonds
¼ teaspoon salt
½ teaspoon ground cinnamon
¼ teaspoon grated nutmeg
Confectioners' sugar, for dusting

1. To make the crust, cream the butter and sugar together in the bowl of an electric mixer and continue beating until light and fluffy. Beat in the egg yolks, one at a time, and then beat in the flour, salt, and vanilla to form a stiff dough.

2. Preheat the oven to 350°F. Grease miniature muffin pans.

3. Pull off pieces of dough about the size of a small walnut and shape into balls. Press the dough balls into the pan to line each muffin cup. Spread each dough piece with about ½ teaspoon jam. Set pans aside.

4. To make the filling, beat the eggs until light and lemon colored and then beat in the sugar. Stir in the almond extract, lemon rind, and sherry. In a separate bowl, stir together the flour, almonds, salt, and spices. Gradually beat this into the egg mixture and continue beating until smooth.

5. Fill each lined muffin cup with filling mixture. Place the pans in the oven and bake until the filling is set and the crust is nicely browned, 20 to 25 minutes. Carefully remove the pastries from the pans and transfer to a wire rack to cool. *(Can be made a day in advance, covered, and stored in a cool place; do not refrigerate.)*

6. Decorate the pastries no more than an hour or two before serving: Closely cover half of each pastry with a small square of wax paper. Dust the other half lightly with confectioners' sugar and carefully remove the paper.

Chocolate Holiday Stollen

Traditionally, fruit stollen is a breakfast or tea bread especially popular during the holiday season, but this chocolate version can make an appearance any time of day. Last year I bought an extra-long baking sheet and, rather than making the two shorter loaves, I made one very long loaf, which looked spectacular on the dessert table. The stollen is best made a day in advance to allow the texture and flavors to mellow.

¾ cup milk
2 teaspoons instant coffee granules
¾ cup sugar
½ teaspoon salt
2 packages active dry yeast
⅔ cup lukewarm water
5 to 6 cups all-purpose flour
2 large eggs, lightly beaten
1 teaspoon vanilla extract
⅔ cup (1⅓ sticks) butter, softened
8 ounces semisweet chocolate, melted and cooled
½ teaspoon ground cinnamon
¼ teaspoon grated nutmeg
1½ cups golden raisins
½ cup chopped candied citron
½ cup chopped candied orange peel
½ cup chopped candied red cherries
Grated rind of 1 small lemon
½ cup coarsely chopped almonds
½ cup (1 stick) butter, melted
Confectioners' sugar, for dusting

1. In a small saucepan over medium heat, scald the milk; add the coffee granules, sugar, and salt and stir until dissolved and blended. Remove from the heat and allow to cool to room temperature.

2. In a large mixing bowl, dissolve the yeast in the lukewarm water, then stir in 1 cup of the flour. Gradually pour in the cooled milk mixture, then mix until blended. Cover the bowl with a clean dish towel and let the mixture, called a sponge, rise in a warm place until doubled in bulk, about 1 hour.

3. When sponge has risen, add the eggs, vanilla, softened butter, chocolate, 4 cups flour, and the cinnamon and nutmeg; mix well. Fold in the raisins, candied fruits, grated lemon rind, and the nuts.

4. Remove the dough to a floured board and knead until the dough is very elastic. Add a bit of flour, if necessary, to keep the dough from sticking.

5. Transfer the dough to a buttered mixing bowl and brush the surface with some of the melted butter. Cover the bowl with the towel and let the dough rise again until doubled in bulk, 30 to 40 minutes.

6. Punch down the dough and divide it into 2 equal portions. Roll each half into a long oval about ½ inch thick and brush the surface with the remaining melted butter. Fold the dough over lengthwise, not quite in half, and place on a lightly greased baking sheet. Cover the loaves with the towel and let rise again until doubled in bulk.

7. Preheat the oven to 350°F. Bake the loaves about 50 minutes, or until they are nicely browned and sound hollow when tapped. Remove the loaves to wire racks and allow to cool. *(The stollen freezes extremely well and can be made up to 6 months in advance.)* Just before serving, dust the loaves lightly with confectioners' sugar.

*B*AVARIAN CHRISTMAS PUDDING

•

SERVES 12 TO 14

Here I've adapted a very old recipe from my great-grandmother to serve as an alternative to the more usual plum pudding.

½ cup dried currants
⅔ cup brandy
2 tablespoons unflavored gelatin
1 cup sugar
½ teaspoon salt
2 cups milk
4 large eggs, separated

1 teaspoon ground cinnamon
½ teaspoon grated nutmeg
½ teaspoon ground ginger
1 teaspoon vanilla extract
½ cup finely chopped candied cherries
½ cup finely chopped candied orange rind
½ cup finely chopped candied ginger
1 pint heavy cream

1. In a small bowl, soak the currants in ⅓ cup of the brandy to soften them. In a separate small bowl, dissolve the gelatin in the remaining ⅓ cup brandy.

2. Combine the sugars and salt in the top of a double boiler. Stir in the milk, place the mixture over simmering water, and heat to just below the simmering point.

3. While the milk mixture is heating, beat the egg yolks in a mixing bowl until they are thick and pale in color. Gradually pour the hot milk mixture into the egg yolks, beating continuously.

4. Pour the yolk mixture back into the top of the double boiler and cook, stirring continuously, until the custard has thickened and thickly coats the spoon. *Do not allow the custard to simmer at any point.* Remove from the heat and set aside.

5. Whisk the gelatin mixture into the custard. Stir in the spices, the vanilla, and the currants and brandy. Dip the pan into a large bowl of cold water to stop the custard from cooking any further and stir for a few minutes until it cools slightly. Stir in the candied cherries, orange rind, and ginger.

6. Transfer the custard to a large mixing bowl, place a piece of plastic wrap directly on the surface of the custard to prevent a skin from forming, and place in the refrigerator for about 10 minutes to thicken and chill slightly.

7. In a clean bowl, beat the egg whites until stiff but not dry. Remove the custard from the refrigerator and gently fold the egg whites into the custard. In a separate bowl, whip the cream until soft peaks form, and then fold the cream into the custard mixture.

8. Oil a 2-quart round mold very well. Transfer the mixture to the mold and cover tightly with plastic wrap. Chill for at least 8 hours before serving. *(The pudding can be completely prepared up to 2 days in advance.)*

9. Just before serving, dip the mold into warm water and then invert onto a serving platter. To serve, cut the pudding into thin slices.

CRANBERRY WINTER PUDDING

MAKES 8 TO 10 SERVINGS

Summer pudding, a traditional English dessert made with fresh summer berries, is one of the prettiest and most luscious desserts there is. This winter version, made with cranberries and a touch of apple and orange, and served with a dab of whipped cream, can make anyone forget balmy July evenings and glorious summer puddings—at least for a few minutes.

Use a firm, dense, good-quality white bread for this pudding or the end result will be mush.

1 12-ounce bag cranberries
2 large tart apples, peeled, cored, and diced
1½ cups sugar
Juice and grated rind of 1 orange
¼ teaspoon ground cloves
12 slices, approximately, of day-old firm white
  bread

½ pint heavy cream, whipped

1. Combine the cranberries, apples, and sugar in a heavy saucepan. Pour the orange juice into a measuring cup and add enough water to make 2 cups; pour this mixture into the pan and add the orange rind and cloves.

2. Place the saucepan over medium-high heat and bring the contents to a boil. Reduce the heat and cook until all the berries pop and the liquid is syrupy, 12 to 15 minutes. Drain the fruit, reserving the syrup, and set aside.

3. Trim the crusts from the bread and cut each slice into rectangular halves. Completely line the bottom and sides of an 8-inch round casserole or shallow 2-quart mold with bread, cutting bread to fit where necessary. Reserve the remaining bread.

4. Moisten the bread by spooning some of the reserved syrup over it. Using about one-fourth of the berry mixture, spread a thin layer of fruit over the bread; cover with a single layer of bread and again

OPPOSITE TOP: **A dome-shaped cranberry winter pudding with a tray of cookies (decorated cream cheese Christmas cookies, poppy seed pinwheels, brown sugar-walnut shortbread, and cheesecake-like marble tiles) and in the background, baked rummy pineapple.**
OPPOSITE BOTTOM: **A fruit-studded Bavarian Christmas pudding, chocolate whiskey balls, and more cookies.**

moisten the bread with some of the syrup. Repeat until all the fruit is used up and top with a final layer of bread. Spoon the remaining syrup over the bread, saturating it completely. Let stand for 30 minutes.

5. Place a small plate on top of the pudding and cover the mold with plastic wrap. Top with a weight (canned goods are useful here) and chill overnight.

6. Just before serving, carefully invert the pudding onto a serving plate with a lip to catch any juices. Serve with whipped cream.

APPLE-MINCEMEAT CAKE

MAKES ONE 10-INCH TUBE CAKE

3 cups all-purpose flour
4 teaspoons baking powder
1 teaspoon ground cinnamon
½ teaspoon ground ginger
½ teaspoon ground allspice
½ teaspoon salt
1 cup vegetable oil
½ cup (1 stick) butter, melted and cooled
1½ cups firmly packed dark brown sugar
3 large eggs, lightly beaten
1½ cups grated tart baking apples
1½ cups mincemeat, preferably homemade
½ cup chopped walnuts or pecans
1 teaspoon vanilla extract
Whipped cream or confectioners' sugar

1. Preheat the oven to 350°F. Grease a 10-inch Bundt or other tube pan very well.

2. In a medium mixing bowl, sift together the flour, baking powder, spices, and salt. In a separate large mixing bowl, combine the oil, butter, and brown sugar and beat until smooth.

3. Beat the flour mixture into the sugar mixture, adding a third of the flour mixture at a time, and beating until smooth after each addition. Beat in the eggs, one a time. Stir in the grated apple, the mincemeat, pecans, and vanilla.

4. Pour the batter into the prepared pan and bake for about 1 hour, or until a cake tester inserted in the thickest part of the cake comes out clean.

5. Turn the cake out onto a serving platter and serve warm with unsweetened whipped cream. Or turn the cake out onto a wire rack and allow it to cool completely and then dust the cake lightly with confectioners' sugar.

Poppy-Seed Pinwheels

•

MAKES ABOUT 4 DOZEN COOKIES

Here's an old Czech recipe from my father's side of the family. My grandmother used to grind the poppy seeds with a mortar and pestle, but I do it in the food processor.

DOUGH
1 cup (2 sticks) butter
⅔ cup sugar
2 large eggs
¼ cup milk
4 cups all-purpose flour
½ teaspoon salt
Grated rind of 1 lemon

FILLING
2 cups poppy seeds
¼ cup sugar
1 teaspoon ground allspice
½ teaspoon grated nutmeg
½ teaspoon ground cloves
¾ cup milk
¼ cup honey

1. In a medium bowl, cream the butter and sugar together until light and fluffy and then beat in the eggs and milk. Combine the flour, salt, and lemon rind in a separate bowl and then beat this mixture into the butter mixture, a third at a time, to form a stiff dough. Divide the dough into 2 parts, cover, and set aside.

2. To make the filling, combine the poppy seeds, sugar, and spices in the bowl of a food processor fitted with the steel chopping blade and process until the seeds are ground.

3. Add the milk and honey and pulse to blend. Transfer the mixture to a saucepan and place over medium heat. Bring to a boil, reduce heat, and simmer 5 minutes, stirring frequently. Remove from the heat and cool.

4. Roll out each dough ball into a rectangle about ¼ inch thick. Divide the filling between the 2 rectangles and spread it in an even layer onto the dough. Roll up the dough, jelly-roll fashion. Wrap each dough roll in wax paper or plastic wrap and chill for at least 1 hour. (*Can be made ahead up to this point, wrapped tightly, and frozen; thaw in the refrigerator before proceeding.*)

5. Preheat the oven to 350°F. Lightly grease baking sheets.

6. Cut the dough into ¼-inch slices, place them about 1½ inches apart on the baking sheets, and bake until golden brown, about 30 to 35 minutes. Remove the cookies to wire racks to cool and store in tightly covered containers in a cool place.

VARIATIONS Use any of the following for the filling: grated semisweet chocolate and chopped walnuts; a thin layer of fruit preserves with or without a sprinkling of finely chopped nuts; a thin layer of honey and a sprinkling of chopped dried apricots; a sprinkling of brown sugar, chopped nuts, and cinnamon.

Al's Chocolate Whiskey Balls

•

MAKES ABOUT 6 DOZEN

In *The Holidays*, I rhapsodized about my friend Lindsay Miller's bourbon balls. Last Christmas I discovered this even more sinful chocolate version, a holiday specialty of my friend Al Stefanic, whose wife, Lorraine, packages them for gift giving. Make these a month or so in advance, since, as Al says, these just get better and better with age.

6 ounces semisweet chocolate
3 tablespoons dark corn syrup
½ cup whiskey (Scotch, Bourbon, or Irish)
2½ cups crushed store-bought chocolate wafers
1 cup finely chopped pecans or *walnuts*
¼ cup finely chopped candied cherries
½ cup confectioners' sugar
Granulated sugar, for rolling

1. In the top of a double boiler over simmering water, melt the chocolate. Remove from the heat and stir in the corn syrup and whiskey.

2. In a mixing bowl, mix the cookie crumbs, nuts, cherries, and confectioners' sugar. Add the melted chocolate mixture and mix well. Let stand 30 minutes.

3. Form the mixture into ¾-inch balls and roll them in granulated sugar. Pack the balls into wax paper–lined tins and store in a cool place. To keep the balls from drying out, add a few sugar cubes soaked in whiskey to each tin.

Marble Tiles

CRUST
1 cup (2 sticks) butter, softened
1 cup firmly packed light brown sugar
3 cups all-purpose flour
1½ cups ground walnuts

TOPPING
3 8-ounce packages cream cheese, softened
¾ cup granulated sugar
3 large eggs
⅓ cup milk
Grated rind of 1 small lemon
1 teaspoon vanilla extract
1 ounce semisweet chocolate, coarsely grated

1. Preheat the oven to 350°F. Lightly grease a 9 x 13-inch baking pan.

2. To make the crust, cream the butter and brown sugar together in the bowl of an electric mixer until light and fluffy. Add the flour and walnuts and beat until smooth.

3. Press this mixture evenly into the prepared pan and bake until the edges just begin to turn golden brown, about 12 minutes. Remove to a wire rack to cool slightly while making the topping.

4. To make the topping, mix the cream cheese and granulated sugar together until light and fluffy and then beat in the eggs. Add the milk, lemon rind, and vanilla. Spread this mixture over the crust and bake until the edges are very lightly browned, about 25 minutes.

5. Remove from the oven to the wire rack. Immediately scatter the grated chocolate evenly over the top. Allow to cool completely and cut into 1½-inch squares. Refrigerate until serving.

· · · · · · · · · · · · · ·

Quicker Cookie Dough

Most butter-and-sugar–based cookie doughs can be mixed together in a flash in a food processor. First cream the butter and sugar together in the bowl of a food processor fitted with the steel chopping blade. Add the other ingredients as the recipe indicates, processing until smooth after each addition. Ingredients such as chopped nuts or chocolate chips should be stirred in at the end with a wooden spoon, or they will become too finely chopped in the processor.

· · · · · · · · · · · · · ·

Cream Cheese Christmas Cookies

I think it's just about a necessity to have cut-out decorated cookies at Christmastime and during the year I'm always on the lookout for unusual cutters.

¾ cups (1½ sticks) butter, softened
1 3-ounce package cream cheese, softened
¾ cup sugar
2 cups all-purpose flour
¼ teaspoon baking soda
¼ teaspoon baking powder
¼ teaspoon salt
2 teaspoons lemon juice
1 teaspoon vanilla extract

FOR DECORATING
Colored sugars
Chocolate jimmies
Multicolored hundreds and thousands

1. In the bowl of an electric mixer, cream the butter, cream cheese, and sugar together until light and fluffy. Add the flour, baking soda, baking powder, and salt all at once, and beat on low speed until the mixture is smooth. Add the lemon juice and vanilla and beat until blended.

2. Roll the dough into a ball, wrap in wax paper or plastic wrap, and refrigerate until firm, about 1 hour. (*The dough can be made up to 2 days in advance and stored in the refrigerator or made well in advance and frozen.*)

3. Roll out the dough to a thickness of slightly more than ⅛ inch. Using Christmas-shape cookie cutters, cut out the dough and place the cookies about 1 inch apart on ungreased baking sheets.

4. Preheat the oven to 350°F. Decorate the cookies using colored sugars, etc. Bake for 10 to 12 minutes, or until lightly browned. Remove to wire racks to cool and store in tightly covered tins in a cool place.

VARIATIONS Two-thirds cup finely chopped nuts can be added to the dough. The soft cookie dough can also be rolled into two 2-inch-diameter rolls, wrapped, and chilled. Roll the dough rolls in colored sugar or finely chopped nuts, then slice into ¼-inch-thick disks. Bake until lightly browned, 12 to 15 minutes.

JAM THUMBPRINTS
·
MAKES ABOUT 4 DOZEN

1 recipe dough for Cream Cheese Christmas
    Cookies (preceding recipe)
Seedless raspberry jam
Confectioners' sugar, for dusting

1. Preheat the oven to 350°F.

2. Place the soft cookie dough in a pastry tube fitted with a large star tip and pipe 1½-inch rosettes about 2 inches apart onto ungreased baking sheets. Using a floured fingertip, make a depression in the center of each rosette and spoon ¼ teaspoonful of jam into each.

3. Bake until lightly browned, 8 to 10 minutes. Transfer the cookies to wire racks to cool. Lightly dust the cookies with confectioners' sugar, taking care not to cover the jam. Transfer the cookies to airtight containers and store in a cool, dry place.

ORANGE GINGER SNAPS
·
MAKES ABOUT 4 DOZEN COOKIES

2½ cups sifted all-purpose flour
2 teaspoons baking soda
½ teaspoon salt
1 tablespoon ground ginger
½ teaspoon ground cinnamon
½ teaspoon ground allspice
¾ cup (1½ sticks) butter, softened
1 cup firmly packed dark brown sugar
¼ cup dark molasses
1 large egg
Grated rind of 2 oranges
Coarse sugar, for rolling

1. Preheat the oven to 350°F.

2. Combine the flour, baking soda, salt, and spices in a mixing bowl and stir well with a fork to blend. In a separate bowl, cream the butter and brown sugar together until light and fluffy and then beat in the molasses, egg, and orange rind. Beat in the dry ingredients in 3 parts, beating well after each addition, forming a stiff dough.

3. Pull off pieces of dough the size of small walnuts and shape into balls. Roll each dough ball in the coarse sugar to coat generously and place the balls on ungreased baking sheets about 2 inches apart. (The cookies will flatten as they bake.)

4. Bake until the edges of the cookies are flattened and nicely browned, about 10 minutes. Transfer to wire racks to cool. Store the cookies in tightly covered tins in a cool place.

PECAN CHESS BARS
·
MAKES ABOUT 4 DOZEN COOKIES

This Southern-style cookie tastes almost like pecan pie, and what could be better than that?

CRUST
½ cup (1 stick) butter, softened
½ cup vegetable shortening
½ cup confectioners' sugar
2 cups all-purpose flour

TOPPING
¼ cup (½ stick) butter, melted
1 cup dark corn syrup
1½ cups firmly packed light brown sugar
¼ teaspoon salt
6 large eggs, lightly beaten
1½ teaspoons vanilla extract
3 cups coarsely chopped pecans

1. Preheat the oven to 350°F.

2. In the bowl of an electric mixer, cream the butter, shortening, and confectioners' sugar together until light and fluffy. Add the flour and beat until smooth.

3. Evenly press the mixture into the bottom of a 9 x 13-inch baking pan. Bake until the edges are lightly browned, about 15 minutes. Remove the pan to a wire rack to cool slightly while you make the topping.

4. In the mixer bowl, combine the melted butter, dark corn syrup, brown sugar, and salt and beat until smooth. Beat in the eggs and vanilla. Stir in the pecans. Spread this mixture over the crust.

5. Bake until the topping is set and lightly crusted, 30 to 40 minutes. Remove to a wire rack to cool completely and then cut into 1 x 2½-inch bars.

CHOCOLATE CHIP SHORTBREAD

•

MAKES 32

Here's a classic shortbread—butter, sugar, and flour—with little chocolate chips added. It's easy to double the dough mixture for this shortbread and then bake it in two batches.

1 cup (2 sticks) butter, softened
½ cup confectioners' sugar
⅛ teaspoon salt
1 teaspoon vanilla extract
2 cups all-purpose flour
⅔ cup miniature semisweet chocolate chips

1. Preheat the oven to 300°F. Generously butter two 8-inch round cake pans.

2. In a mixing bowl, cream the butter, confectioners' sugar, and salt together until light and fluffy, and then beat in vanilla. Add the flour and knead to form a stiff dough. Add the chocolate chips and knead them into the dough.

3. Divide the dough into 2 equal parts and press each part into a cake pan. Prick the dough all over with a fork and then score each circle into 16 wedges.

4. Bake the shortbread until firm and evenly golden but not brown, 30 to 35 minutes (if the shortbread begins to brown too quickly, cover it loosely with aluminum foil).

5. Remove from the oven and cut the shortbread along the scored lines. Place the pans on wire racks and allow the shortbread to cool. Transfer to a tin, cover tightly, and store in a cool place.

BROWN SUGAR–WALNUT SHORTBREAD Substitute ⅔ cup firmly packed dark brown sugar for the confectioners' sugar and omit the vanilla. Substitute ⅔ cup finely chopped walnuts for the chocolate chips.

On the sideboard, some of my favorite electrified Santas are all aglow from watching over the proceedings.

Winter Vacation Barbecue

for 10 to 12

•

Menu

PIMM'S PUNCH

POLENTA-FETA SQUARES

· · ·

MIXED GRILL:

GRILLED LAMB MARINATED IN
MERLOT AND SPICES

GRILLED ASSORTED SAUSAGES

BEER MUSTARD
FLAVORED MUSTARDS
JEZEBEL SAUCE (PAGE 156)

GRANDMA STAPLETON'S FRIED PEPPERS

MOM'S WINTER TOMATO PUDDING

WHITE BEAN AND CAULIFLOWER SALAD

· · ·

GRILLED ORANGE-PECAN BREAD

TROPICAL FRUIT

By the time the dead of winter settles in, I'm ready again for summer, so I always try to sneak off for a week or ten days to someplace warm. This barbecue took place under the stars on a perfect warm evening in Palm Beach, but there's no reason why a summer-style bar-

becue with the same lazy mood couldn't take place indoors in Alaska. In fact, in New York I've been known to grill on a small hibachi set in the fireplace. And I have some friends who keep their outdoor grills at the ready throughout the year, using them on cold, even snowy, days. Even at home, this event can be a good time to relax and start making those big plans for next summer.

GETTING READY The beer mustard, flavored mustards, and Jezebel Sauce should be prepared at least two days in advance, and stored in the refrigerator so they have a little time to mellow.

A day in advance, prepare the polenta-feta squares up to the end of step 3. Also bake the orange-pecan bread so it has a chance to mellow and firm up.

Early in the day of the dinner, marinate the lamb and pare the peppers. Make the bean and cauliflower salad.

An hour and a half before you plan to serve dinner, light the fire in the grill. (If you're broiling the lamb, the broiler needs only to be preheated a few minutes.) An hour or so before dinner, start the tomato pudding, and once it's in the oven, start the peppers. Put the lamb on the grill about fifteen or twenty minutes before it's to be served.

Toast the bread for dessert just before serving.

BEVERAGES The obvious wine choice would be Merlot; if another wine is used for the marinade, use the same one for drinking. With the warm dessert, I like iced coffee or espresso.

Pimm's Punch

•

MAKES TWENTY 6-OUNCE DRINKS

3 cups Pimm's No.1 Cup
1 liter ginger ale, chilled
1 liter bitter lemon mixer, chilled
1 liter seltzer or club soda, chilled
1 small orange, sliced
1 lemon, sliced
1 small cucumber, thinly sliced
Mint sprigs, for garnish

In a large pitcher or punch bowl, combine all the ingredients except mint sprigs and mix well. Serve in ice-filled tall glasses and garnish each serving with a mint sprig.

POLENTA-FETA SQUARES

•

MAKES 3 DOZEN

The flavor and texture combination here is pretty powerful—it really wakes up the palate without over-powering the rest of dinner.

1½ cups milk
¼ cup (½ stick) butter
3 tablespoons finely chopped sun-dried tomatoes
⅛ teaspoon cayenne pepper
1½ cups stone-ground yellow cornmeal
1½ cups water
1 large egg, lightly beaten
1 cup feta cheese, finely crumbled
1 cup grated Swiss cheese
1 scallion, white and green parts, finely chopped
1 teaspoon fresh thyme leaves or ½ teaspoon dried thyme

1. In a large, heavy saucepan, combine the milk, butter, sun-dried tomatoes, and cayenne. Place over low heat and bring to just below the simmering point.

2. In a mixing bowl, combine the cornmeal and water and stir until smooth. Gradually add this mixture to the pan, stirring until smooth. Bring the mixture to a simmer, stirring constantly, and cook until thickened, 5 to 7 minutes. Remove from the heat and stir in the egg, ½ cup of each cheese, the scallions, and thyme.

3. Lightly grease a 9-inch baking pan, line the bottom with waxed paper, and lightly grease the waxed paper. Pour the polenta mixture into the pan and allow to cool. *(Can be made a day in advance, covered tightly with plastic wrap, and refrigerated; return to room temperature before proceeding.)*

4. Preheat the oven to 400°F. Scatter the remaining cheese over the polenta. Bake until the cheese is melted and lightly browned, 20 to 25 minutes. Cut the polenta into 1½ -inch squares and serve warm or at room temperature.

VARIATIONS Substitute crumbled Gorgonzola for the feta. For Southwestern polenta squares, add ¼ teaspoon ground cumin in step 1, add 1 tablespoon finely chopped jalapeño in step 2, and substitute grated Monterey Jack for the feta and Swiss cheeses; omit the thyme. For Southern-style polenta squares, add ¼ cup finely chopped country ham or crisp bacon in step 1, add 2 tablespoons chopped pimiento in step 2, and substitute sharp Cheddar for the feta and Swiss cheeses; omit the thyme.

GRILLED LAMB MARINATED IN MERLOT AND SPICES

•

SERVES 10 TO 12

MARINADE
⅓ cup olive oil
⅓ cup Merlot or other dry, medium-bodied red wine
Juice of 1 lemon
1 large garlic clove, chopped
1 small onion, coarsely chopped
1 tablespoon finely chopped gingerroot
1 teaspoon ground cumin
½ teaspoon grated nutmeg
½ teaspoon ground cardamom
1 teaspoon ground cloves
½ teaspoon freshly ground black pepper
2 tablespoons paprika

4 medium onions
4 pounds boneless lamb shoulder or leg, cut into 1½-inch cubes

1. Combine the marinade ingredients in a blender or bowl of a food processor fitted with the steel chopping blade and blend or process until smooth.

2. Peel the onions and parboil them 5 minutes. Cut into wedges. Place the onions and lamb in a plastic bag, add the marinade, and seal the bag. (The lamb can also be marinated in a shallow nonmetallic bowl, covered.) Squeeze the bag to cover all sides of the meat with the marinade. Refrigerate 2 to 4 hours—longer than 4 hours will overseason the lamb.

3. Preheat the broiler (or prepare a charcoal fire). Skewer the lamb and onion wedges and place the skewers on a broiling pan or grill about 4 inches from the heat. Broil or grill the lamb about 7 minutes per side for rare, longer for more well done.

Above: A kitschy old souvenir plate and a tropical "bouquet" with visiting flamingos help set the mood.
Below: A platter of polenta-feta squares and Pimm's punch, garnished with mint, citrus slices, and cucumbers.

ABOVE AND BELOW: The main course is served on Russell Wright dishes: sautéed peppers, winter tomato pudding, white bean and cauliflower salad, and grilled skewered lamb and sausages with mustards and Jezebel sauce.

GRILLED ASSORTED SAUSAGES

•

There are many varieties of sausages that are delicious when grilled or broiled, from Italian sweet or hot sausages to French garlic sausages and Polish kielbasa. If you have a specialty butcher in your area, ask there for particular recommendations. When sausages are being served as part of a mixed grill, allow about ⅓ pound per person.

Before grilling sausages, prick them all over with a fork so they release some of the fat during cooking. Very fatty sausages should be parboiled before grilling. Have a spray bottle of water ready to squelch any flareups that may occur when fat drips onto the coals. Serve with Beer Mustard (recipe follows). Jezebel Sauce (page 156), or flavored mustards (recipes follow).

BEER MUSTARD

•

MAKES ABOUT 2 HALF-PINTS

Make this mustard at least a day or so in advance to allow the flavors to blend and mellow. Serve the mustard with all kinds of grilled sausages, ham steaks, and simple grilled chicken.

1 12-ounce can dark beer
2 cups dry mustard
1 cup firmly packed dark brown sugar
2 teaspoons salt
½ teaspoon turmeric
2 tablespoons malt vinegar or cider vinegar
1 tablespoon mustard seeds, cracked

1. Pour the beer into a shallow bowl and let stand for 1 hour.

2. Combine the beer and remaining ingredients in a saucepan over medium heat and whisk to blend. Bring to a simmer, whisking constantly. Remove from the heat and allow to cool. Transfer to 2 half-pint jars, cover, and store in the refrigerator.

"Mustard's no good without roast beef."
Chico Marx

Flavored Mustards

I like mixing flavored mustards myself rather than splurging on buying pricy store-bought ones; it takes no time at all, and homemade always has a fresher flavor. Blend any of the following combinations into 1 cup of Dijon mustard:

1 tablespoon each chopped parsley, tarragon, and dill
2 finely chopped shallots and 2 tablespoons chopped chervil
   or parsley
Juice of ½ lime and 2 teaspoons dark brown sugar or honey
1 tablespoon mixed *fines herbes*
1 finely chopped garlic clove and ¼ cup chopped basil
½ teaspoon ground cumin and ⅛ teaspoon cayenne pepper
2 tablespoons prepared horseradish and 2 finely chopped
   scallions

GRANDMA STAPLETON'S FRIED PEPPERS

•

SERVES 10

This was always a summer treat when I was growing up, but nowadays peppers are "all season" vegetables. These simply prepared peppers aren't really fried at all, but that's what we always used to call them. Grandma used to "fry" her peppers in lard, but I now use olive oil.

2 tablespoons olive oil
3 medium onions, sliced
3 pounds green and/or red peppers, cut into
   ½-inch strips
1 teaspoon cider vinegar
Pinch of sugar
Salt and freshly ground black pepper

Coat the bottom of a skillet with the oil and place over high heat. When the oil begins to sizzle, add the onions and peppers. Stir-fry until the vegetables begin to wilt, 5 to 7 minutes, then turn down the heat and sauté until tender, an additional 5 minutes or so. Add the vinegar and sugar and toss; season to taste with salt and pepper. Serve warm or at room temperature.

Mom's Winter Tomato Pudding

•

SERVES 10 TO 12

At the end of every summer, Mom would can bushels and bushels of tomatoes, ending up with several hundred jars. The worst part of the process was parboiling and peeling the tomatoes, a task always assigned to us kids. During the course of the winter those tomatoes would appear in many guises; this tomato pudding was one of my favorites. If you have home-canned tomatoes, by all means use them; the best store-bought substitute is imported Italian plum tomatoes, as listed here.

¼ cup (½ stick) butter, plus 2 tablespoons for top
1 medium onion, finely chopped
2 tablespoons firmly packed dark brown sugar
1 teaspoon salt
½ teaspoon freshly ground black pepper
1 teaspoon dried marjoram
3 cups white or whole wheat bread cubes, toasted
2 28-ounce cans imported plum tomatoes
1 6-ounce can tomato paste
1 small onion, thinly sliced

1. Melt the butter in a skillet over medium-low heat and add the chopped onion. Sauté until the onion is transparent, about 10 minutes. Add the brown sugar, salt, pepper, and marjoram and stir well to combine. Add the bread cubes and toss to coat with the seasoned butter. Remove from the heat and reserve.

2. Place the tomatoes in a mixing bowl and break them up into chunks by crushing against the side of the bowl with the back of a heavy spoon. Add the tomato paste and blend until smooth. Reserve.

3. Preheat the oven to 350°F. Generously butter a shallow 2½-quart baking dish. Spoon about half of the tomato mixture into the baking dish and top with half of the bread mixture. Repeat. Scatter the sliced onion over the bread cubes and dot with additional butter.

4. Bake for 35 to 40 minutes, or until tomatoes are thick and bubbling and onion is nicely browned. Serve warm.

White Bean and Cauliflower Salad

•

SERVES 12

A complimentary combination, this is a crossbreed salad, based on the white bean salads of Tuscany and the cauliflower salads of Sicily.

1 cup dried great northern or white kidney beans
  (cannellini)
1 teaspoon salt
1 medium head cauliflower, broken into flowerets
1 small red pepper, chopped
10 black ripe olives, pitted and quartered
2 tablespoons capers
2 tablespoons chopped parsley
4 scallions, white and green parts, thinly sliced
¾ cup White Wine Vinaigrette (page 220)
Chicory leaves
Rings of red onion, for garnish
Freshly ground black pepper

1. Place the beans in a large saucepan, add water to cover by 2 inches, and place over high heat. Bring to a rolling boil and boil for 2 minutes. Remove from the heat and let stand 1 hour. Add ½ teaspoon salt, return to high heat, and bring to a boil. Reduce the heat and simmer the beans until they are just tender, but not mushy, about 1 hour. Drain the beans, rinse well, and reserve.

2. Place the cauliflower in a saucepan with water to cover and ½ teaspoon salt. Place over high heat and bring to a boil. Reduce the heat and simmer until crisp-tender, 3 to 5 minutes. Drain the cauliflower, rinse with cold water to stop the cooking, and drain again.

3. In a large mixing bowl, combine the beans and cauliflower with the remaining ingredients. Add the dressing and toss. Serve warm or at room temperature. *(The salad can be prepared a day in advance and refrigerated; return to room temperature before serving.)*

4. To serve, mound the salad in a bowl lined with chicory and garnish with the red onion rings and a generous grinding of black pepper.

GRILLED ORANGE-PECAN BREAD

•

MAKES TWO 8½" X 4½" X 3" LOAVES

Serve warm toasted slices of this fragrant bread as a hand-held accompaniment to coffee; or, if you're feeling decadent, serve the bread on plates topped with whipped cream or Vanilla Bean Ice Cream.

3 cups all-purpose flour
1 tablespoon baking powder
½ teaspoon baking soda
¼ teaspoon salt
¾ cup sugar
Grated rind of 2 large oranges
1 cup lightly toasted chopped pecans
1 large egg
½ cup orange juice
¼ cup (½ stick) butter, melted
¾ cup milk

1. Preheat the oven to 350°F. Lightly grease two 8½ x 4½ x 3-inch loaf pans.

2. Combine the flour, baking powder, baking soda, salt, and sugar in a medium mixing bowl and mix well. Add the orange rind and blend well. Add the nuts to the bowl but do not blend in.

3. In a separate bowl, combine the egg, orange juice, and butter, and beat with a fork to blend well. Beat in the milk. Pour the liquid mixture over the dry mixture and beat with the fork until the dry ingredients are just moistened—it's okay if the batter is a little lumpy.

4. Divide the batter between the prepared pans and bake until the loaves are lightly browned and a cake tester or toothpick inserted in the center comes out clean, 50 to 60 minutes.

5. Remove the pan to a wire rack and cool for 30 minutes. Remove the loaves from the pan, place them on their sides, and allow to cool completely. Wrap the loaves tightly with plastic wrap and store in the refrigerator for 1 to 2 days.

6. To grill the bread, cut it into ⅜-inch-thick slices. Place on a grill over glowing ash-covered coals or under a preheated broiler, 3 inches from the heat, and toast on both sides.

ABOVE: An assortment of colorful tropical fruits and grilled slices of orange pecan bread.

A HEARTY SKI LODGE DINNER

for 8

·

Menu

HOT BULLSHOTS

ONION AND PEPPER PUFF-PASTRY STRAWS
(PAGE 45)

· · ·

ROLLED LASAGNE WITH SPINACH, WILD
MUSHROOMS, AND THREE CHEESES

CHICORY SALAD WITH HOT GARLIC DRESSING

· · ·

ICED TANGERINES IN SAMBUCA AND RUM

ANISE-SEED SHORTBREAD

On a frosty winter weekend I'm always ready to head for the hills and a little lodge near the slopes. In fact, I like everything about ski weekends except the skiing itself. Where I come from, it's flat as a pancake, and ice skating was our favorite winter pastime; by the time I came to New York, I was no longer quite as brave as I once had been, so I never did learn to downhill ski. Cross-country is one thing, but don't ask me to go up or down those hills!

But I do love the rustic comforts of a ski lodge: gas lanterns, a blazing fire, and sleeping in a chilly room under piles of blankets. While everyone else is off all day zigging and zagging through the snow, I'm usually back inside after a few hours, curled up by the fire with a book or puttering around in the kitchen. After a day of exhilarating exercise in the icy air, everyone finds a warming drink and a hearty dinner really welcoming.

The lasagne here is meatless, but it's outrageously rich and intensely flavored, so the rest of the meal is kept simple and uncomplicated. Hot drinks and peppery puff-pastry straws welcome everyone in from the cold and tide them over until dinner's ready. After the hearty lasagne and salad, icy cold tangerines, served with an unusual shortbread, are a light and refreshing finish.

GETTING READY The only dish that requires much work here is the lasagne, but it can be accomplished in stages. Preparing the rest of the menu is a breeze, and even some of that work can be done ahead.

The shortbread can be baked anytime during the week and packed into tins (if it's traveling, line the tin with a thick layer of crumpled paper towels to prevent the cookies from breaking). The tangerines can be prepared a day or two in advance; in any case they should be made a few hours before serving.

The sauce and filling for the lasagne can be made a day ahead; boil the lasagne itself and assemble the dish just before baking.

The puff-pastry straws, bullshots, and salad each take only a few minutes and should be prepared just before serving. (The salad greens can be washed, torn, and refrigerated anytime during the day.)

BEVERAGES With the lasagne, a medium-dry California Zinfandel or an Italian Chianti. With this dessert, I like strongly brewed aromatic Earl Grey tea.

*H*OT BULLSHOT
·
MAKES 1 DRINK

A bullshot is usually served on the rocks, but I serve this hot version as a winter warmer-upper.

1½ ounces (1 jigger) vodka
¾ cup hot beef boullion
Dash of Worcestershire sauce
Dash of hot pepper sauce
Twist of lemon

Pour the vodka into individual mugs or sturdy wine glasses and add the boullion and Worcestershire and hot pepper sauces to taste. Stir to blend, add a twist of lemon, and serve.

*R*OLLED LASAGNE WITH SPINACH, WILD MUSHROOMS, AND THREE CHEESES
·
SERVES 6 TO 8

Flavor abounds in this hearty vegetarian lasagne. Rolling the pasta rather than layering it helps make the lasagne much easier to serve. Lasagne that's been assembled too far in advance tends to become mushy. It's worth taking the time to assemble this lasagne just before baking.

SAUCE AND FILLING
3 tablespoons olive oil
2 garlic cloves, finely chopped
3 shallots, finely chopped
¾ pound button mushrooms, chopped
½ pound shiitake mushrooms, chopped

SAUCE
¼ cup (½ stick) butter
¼ cup all-purpose flour
3 cups milk
½ cup crumbled Gorgonzola
¾ cup freshly grated Parmesan
2 tablespoons tomato paste
Salt and freshly ground black pepper

FILLING
3 10-ounce packages frozen chopped spinach,
*   thawed and squeezed dry*
1½ cups ricotta
¾ cup freshly grated Parmesan
3 large eggs, lightly beaten
1½ teaspoons dried basil
⅛ teaspoon grated nutmeg
Salt and freshly ground black pepper

1 pound curly lasagne, cooked until al dente

1. Place the olive oil in a large, heavy skillet over medium heat. Add the garlic and shallots and sauté until they're translucent, about 5 minutes. Add the mushrooms and sauté until they turn brown and most of the liquid is evaporated, about 10 minutes. With a slotted spoon transfer to a large bowl and reserve.

2. Melt the butter in the skillet, blend in the flour, and cook for 2 minutes, stirring constantly. Gradually whisk in the milk and bring to a simmer. Cook, stirring constantly, until the sauce thickens, about 5 minutes.

Stir in the Gorgonzola, ½ cup of the Parmesan, and the tomato paste and continue cooking and stirring until the cheese is melted and blended in.

3. Stir half the mushroom mixture into the sauce. Season the sauce with salt and fresh pepper to taste. Remove from the heat and reserve.

4. In a large mixing bowl, combine the filling ingredients with the remaining mushroom mixture and stir just until the mixture is evenly blended. (*Both the sauce and the filling can be made a day in advance, covered tightly, and refrigerated; reheat before assembling the lasagne.*)

5. Preheat the oven to 375°F. To assemble, lay one lasagne noodle at a time on a clean work surface. Spread a thin layer of filling (about ¼ cup) onto the lasagne. Carefully roll up the lasagne, making the roll as tight as possible without squeezing out the filling. Place the roll, standing on its end, in a greased shallow baking dish large enough to hold the rolls compactly. Repeat with the remaining lasagne and filling.

6. Spoon the sauce evenly over the lasagne rolls to cover them completely. Sprinkle the remaining ¼ cup Parmesan over the sauce. Place the pan in the oven and bake until browned and bubbly, about 25 to 30 minutes. (If the top browns before the sauce is bubbly, cover loosely with aluminum foil.) Serve hot.

Chicory Salad with Hot Garlic Dressing

•

SERVES 6

This garlicky adaptation of a Midwestern favorite, hot sweet-and-sour dressing, is especially good tossed with pungent chicory. The dressing can be made in advance and quickly reheated just before serving.

4 slices bacon, coarsely chopped
½ cup olive oil
3 large garlic cloves, very thinly sliced crosswise
2 thick slices firm white bread, diced
¼ cup red wine vinegar
1 tablespoon sugar
½ teaspoon dried oregano
Salt and freshly ground black pepper

1 large head chicory (curly endive), about 1 pound, washed well and torn into bite-size pieces

1. In a small skillet over medium heat, sauté the bacon in 2 tablespoons of the oil over low heat until crisp. Remove with a slotted spoon and reserve. Add the remaining oil, the garlic, and the bread cubes to the pan and sauté until the garlic is tender and the bread is lightly browned, about 10 minutes. Remove the bread cubes and reserve.

2. Gradually whisk in the vinegar. Add the sugar and cook another minute or so, until it is dissolved and blended in. Stir in the oregano and season the dressing to taste with salt and plenty of pepper.

3. Place the chicory in a serving bowl, add the reserved bacon and bread cubes, and pour the hot dressing over all. Toss the salad and serve immediately.

VARIATIONS To make this a completely meatless menu, eliminate the bacon and substitute balsamic vinegar for the wine vinegar. For a more subtly flavored dressing, crush the garlic clove rather than slicing it and remove it from the pan after sautéeing 3 or 4 minutes.

Iced Tangerines in Sambuca and Rum

•

SERVES 6 TO 8

A refreshing dessert after a rich dinner.

1 cup light rum
½ cup sugar
6 whole cloves
6 star anise
2 tablespoons Sambuca liqueur
10 tangerines, peeled, cut crosswise into thin slices, and seeded

1. Combine the rum, sugar, cloves, and star anise in a small, heavy saucepan over medium heat. Bring to a simmer and cook until syrupy, about 10 minutes. Remove from the heat and allow to cool, then stir in the Sambuca.

2. Place the orange slices in a shallow bowl and pour the syrup over them. Cover and refrigerate for at least 2 or 3 hours. (*Can be made up to a day before serving.*) Place the oranges in the freezer for 30 minutes before serving, so they're icy cold.

ANISE-SEED SHORTBREAD
•
MAKES ABOUT 2 DOZEN COOKIES

Whether it's plain and simple or fancified, I love short-bread just about any way. This "fancy" version is especially good with the tangerines.

1 cup (2 sticks) butter, softened
½ cup sifted confectioners' sugar
⅛ teaspoon salt
1 teaspoon vanilla extract
2 cups sifted all-purpose flour
¼ teaspoon baking powder
¼ teaspoon ground cinnamon
1½ tablespoons crushed anise seeds

1. Preheat the oven to 300°F. Generously butter a 9-inch square cake pan.

2. In a mixing bowl, cream the butter, confectioners' sugar, and salt together until light and fluffy and then beat in the vanilla. Add the flour, baking powder, and cinnamon and knead to form a stiff dough. Add the anise seeds and knead them into the dough. Wrap the dough in plastic wrap and chill for 30 minutes.

3. Divide the dough into 2 equal parts and press into the prepared pan. Prick the dough all over with a fork and then score it into 3 x 1-inch bars.

4. Bake the shortbread until firm and evenly golden but not brown, 30 to 35 minutes. (If the shortbread begins to brown too quickly, cover it loosely with aluminum foil.)

5. Remove from the oven and cut the shortbread along the scored lines. Place the pan on a wire rack and allow the shortbread to cool. Transfer to a tin, cover tightly, and store in a cool place.

ABOVE LEFT: A hearty rolled lasagne, stuffed with spinach, wild mushrooms, and three cheeses, is served with a simple chicory salad with hot garlic dressing.

LEFT: A simple and refreshing dessert of icy marinated tangerines with fingers of anise-seed shortbread.

OPPOSITE: It's "nothing fancy" when dinner is served in the lodge's main room, unmatched plates and all.

A WEEKNIGHT KITCHEN SUPPER

for 6

•

Menu

HURON COUNTY PORK STEW

CARAWAY CORN BREAD

STEPHANIE'S CAJUN COLESLAW

• • •

STEAMED BUTTERSCOTCH PUDDING WITH
MAPLE-BUTTERSCOTCH SAUCE

Most of us tend to confine our entertaining to weekends and holidays, but occasionally I like to break up the week by inviting a few friends in for a very casual supper. I plan a make-ahead menu and tell everyone to come straight from work.

When my guests arrive, I bring them right into the kitchen; there's no pretense of formality here. While they sip a cocktail and maybe nibble on a few spiced nuts, I take care of the few last-minute tasks at the stove, without missing a beat of the conversation. After dinner we move to the living room and gather around the fireplace for coffee.

The menu centers on a real stick-to-the-ribs main course: a hearty pork stew flavored with onion and apples, based on a recipe that's been in my family for years. And supper ends with a warm, comforting dessert.

GETTING READY The stew, coleslaw, pudding, and sauce can all be fully prepared a day in advance.

The corn bread is best baked just before serving, but if the dry ingredients are measured and mixed in advance, it can be ready to go into the oven in just a few minutes. While the corn bread is baking, reheat the stew and rewarm the pudding.

BEVERAGES Try a dry Johannisberg Riesling or Gewürztraminer from California. A good nonalcoholic choice would be a not-too-sweet apple cider.

*H*URON COUNTY PORK STEW

•

SERVES 6

Huron County, Ohio, that is.

> 2 pounds boneless pork butt or shoulder
> All-purpose flour, for dredging
> 4 slices bacon, coarsely chopped
> 12 small white onions, peeled
> 1 garlic clove, finely chopped
> 2 carrots, peeled and cut into ½-inch slices
> ½ cup diced celery
> 4 Granny Smith apples, peeled, cored, and diced
> 1½ pounds russet potatoes, scrubbed and
>   quartered
> 1 tablespoon chopped fresh sage leaves or
>   1 teaspoon dried rubbed sage
> 1 teaspoon fresh thyme leaves or ¼ teaspoon dried
>   thyme
> 1 cup apple cider
> 1 cup chicken stock
> Salt and freshly ground black pepper

1. Trim the pork of excess fat and cut it into ¾-inch cubes. Place the flour in a shallow bowl and dredge the pork cubes in the flour. Spread the pork cubes out on a board to allow the flour to dry while you render the bacon.

2. Place the bacon in a Dutch oven or large, heavy saucepan over medium heat and sauté until it begins to render its fat. Brown all the pork cubes on all sides, a few at a time. Remove the pork from the pan and reserve. Remove all but 2 tablespoons bacon fat.

3. Place the onions, garlic, carrots, and celery in the pan and sauté until the onions are golden brown, about 15 minutes. Return the pork to the pan and add the remaining ingredients. Bring the mixture to a simmer and simmer, loosely covered, for 1 hour or until the pork is tender. Season to taste with salt and pepper and serve.

NOTE If you prefer a thicker sauce, whisk ½ cup of the sauce together with 1 or 2 tablespoons flour. Stir this mixture back into the Dutch oven and cook for an additional 7 to 10 minutes, or until the sauce is thickened and the flour is cooked.

CARAWAY CORN BREAD

SERVES 6 TO 8

I like corn bread in any shape or form and vary it in many ways. This is a traditional buttermilk corn bread, but the flavor of caraway seeds makes it a great partner for the pork stew.

1¾ cups stone-ground yellow cornmeal
1¼ cups all-purpose flour
4 teaspoons baking powder
1 teaspoon baking soda
2 teaspoons sugar
1 teaspoon salt
¼ teaspoon grated nutmeg
1 tablespoon caraway seeds
3 large eggs
1½ cups buttermilk
⅓ cup (⅔ stick) butter or vegetable shortening, melted

1. Preheat the oven to 425°F. Grease a 9-inch square baking pan.

2. Combine the cornmeal, flour, baking powder, baking soda, sugar, salt, and nutmeg in a mixing bowl and stir well with a fork to blend thoroughly. Stir in the caraway seeds.

3. Combine the eggs, buttermilk, and melted butter or shortening in a separate bowl and beat with the fork to blend. Pour the wet mixture over the dry mixture and mix with a fork until the dry ingredients are just moistened. *Do not overmix.*

4. Transfer the batter to the prepared pan and bake until a toothpick or cake tester inserted in the center comes out clean and the top is golden brown, 25 to 30 minutes. Cut into squares and serve hot with butter.

STEPHANIE'S CAJUN COLESLAW

SERVES 6 TO 8

Stephanie Chalmers O'Rourke hails from down N'Orleans way, and this is how her family makes slaw.

DRESSING
¾ cup Homemade Mayonnaise (page 221)
¼ cup red wine vinegar
3 tablespoons grainy mustard
2 large garlic cloves, very finely chopped
⅛ teaspoon cayenne pepper

1 medium head green cabbage, coarsely shredded
½ cup coarsely chopped pecans

1. Combine the mayonnaise, vinegar, mustard, garlic, and cayenne in a small bowl and whisk to blend. Set aside.

2. Place the cabbage and pecans in a large bowl, add the dressing, and toss well. Cover and let stand in the refrigerator for at least 3 hours before serving. *(Can be made a day or two in advance.)*

. . . .

"It'll Stick to Your Ribs"

When you were young, did you ever wonder about that expression? On cold winter days, before we kids were allowed to go outside, Grandma Wynn would prepare a hearty meal and make sure we cleaned our plates, telling us that, yes, it would stick to our ribs. I used to wonder how my arms and legs would ever grow if all that food was going straight to my rib cage. But then again, I also wondered how eating burnt toast would give me rosy cheeks or how eating carrots would make my hair curl, neither of which ever happened!

. . . .

Huron County pork stew and caraway corn bread.

Slices of the steamed pudding with the warm sauce.

STEAMED BUTTERSCOTCH PUDDING WITH MAPLE-BUTTERSCOTCH SAUCE

•

SERVES 6 TO 8

1 teaspoon instant coffee granules
3 tablespoons brandy
1 cup golden raisins
¼ cup (½ stick) butter, softened
⅔ cup firmly packed light brown sugar
4 large eggs, lightly beaten
1¼ cups all-purpose flour, sifted
1 teaspoon baking powder
¼ teaspoon salt

1. In a small bowl, combine the instant coffee granules and brandy and stir to dissolve the coffee. Add the raisins, toss well, and let stand for an hour or so to plump the raisins.

2. In a medium bowl, cream the butter and brown sugar together until light and fluffy. Gradually beat in the eggs. Slowly stir in the flour, baking powder, and salt. Fold the raisins into the batter.

3. Preheat the oven to 350°F. Butter a 6-cup pudding mold or other heatproof mold very well. Have ready a kettle of boiling water.

4. Pour the batter into the mold and cover tightly with its lid or aluminum foil. Place the mold into a Dutch oven or round casserole and pour hot water into the pan to come two-thirds up the side of the mold. Cover tightly with lid or aluminum foil.

5. Place the pudding in the oven and steam it until a toothpick or cake tester inserted in the center comes out clean, 50 to 60 minutes. *(The pudding can be prepared a day in advance, stored in the covered mold in a cool place; to reheat, steam the pudding 15 to 20 minutes in a pan of hot water on top of the stove.)* Serve the pudding warm, cut into thick slices and topped with maple-butterscotch sauce.

MAPLE-BUTTERSCOTCH SAUCE

¼ cup (½ stick) butter
⅓ cup firmly packed light brown sugar
½ cup maple syrup
½ cup light corn syrup
½ cup light cream or half-and-half

1. In a small, heavy saucepan, combine the butter, brown sugar, and syrup. Over medium heat stir until the sugar is dissolved and the mixture is smooth. Bring the mixture to a simmer and cook gently for 10 minutes, stirring frequently.

2. Gradually stir in the cream. Return the mixture to a simmer, stirring constantly, and remove from the heat. *(The sauce can be made a few days in advance, stored in a covered jar, and refrigerated. To rewarm, bring the jar to room temperature, place it in a small pan of water, and place over low heat.)*

Supper is served from the countertop
of an old Hoosier cabinet: squares of caraway
corn bread, a pot of pork stew flavored with
apples and herbs, and a big bowl of garlicky,
pecan-studded Cajun cole slaw.

DINNER FOR AN ICY EVENING

for 2

•

Menu

HOT LEMONADE

BRIE EN CROUTE STUFFED WITH OLIVES
AND PEPPERS

•   •   •

OSSO BUCO WITH GREMOLATA

ORZO MILANESE

•   •   •

SPINACH SALAD WITH PEARS AND PIGNOLI

•   •   •

BAKED FROZEN TORTONIS

Ice skating followed by a carriage ride, bundled under thick wooly blankets—that's my idea of a romantic winter evening in the country. When I was young, I'd go skating on the frozen pond nestled between two low rises in the back pasture. Now I transfer that simple pleasure to the city: skating on the rink in Central Park between the high rises of Manhattan, followed perhaps by a ride through the park in a horse-drawn hansom cab.

After being out for a while in the icy air, I find a hearty hearthside dinner is especially satisfying. Spiked hot lemonade served with a warm, runny stuffed brie should help take the chill off. The richly flavored osso buco that follows helps warm both body and soul. The surprise here is the hot-and-cold dessert, a baked frozen tortoni based on that mid-century favorite, baked Alaska.

GETTING READY The osso buco can be made a day in advance; the brie can be assembled and wrapped a day ahead and stored in the refrigerator until a half-hour or so before baking.

A few hours before dinner, get the spinach and dressing ready; cut up the pear and toss the salad just before serving.

About 45 minutes ahead, put the cheese in the oven. Begin rewarming the osso buco. Start the orzo about 30 minutes before serving.

The dessert needs to be assembled before baking, and it does take a few minutes; having all the ingredients ready ahead of time can help speed things up.

BEVERAGES As an alternative to the hot lemonade, try a full-bodied Zinfandel or a Petite Sirah with the cheese. These wines are good ones to serve with the main course as well. An interesting twist might be to switch to Champagne with dessert, followed by espresso with a twist of orange peel.

BRIE EN CROUTE STUFFED WITH OLIVES AND PEPPERS

•

SERVES 2

Warm and runny is the way I like Brie best. Here it's stuffed with roasted peppers and olives and then baked in a golden puff-pastry crust to serve as a hot antipasto.

1 4-ounce wheel of Brie, chilled
½ small red or green pepper, roasted, peeled,
*   seeded, and coarsely chopped (page 64)*
2 tablespoons coarsely chopped ripe black olives
½ sheet (about ¼ pound) frozen puff pastry,
*   thawed*
1 large egg yolk, beaten with 1 tablespoon water

1. Place the Brie on a cutting board and, using a serrated knife, carefully slice it in half horizontally. Scatter the chopped pepper and olives over the bottom half and replace the top half. Reserve.

2. Fold the corners of the puff pastry over itself to form a rough circle. Roll the pastry out to a circle approximately 12 inches in diameter. Trim the edges of the pastry with a pastry wheel.

3. Carefully place the Brie on the center of the pastry and lift the edges of the pastry up over the cheese to enclose it. Gather the pastry in the center and tie it together with kitchen string. Let the pastry edges fall back over the package and arrange them attractively.

Wrap the package well in plastic wrap and refrigerate until needed. *(Can be made up to a day in advance.)*

4. About 45 minutes before serving, preheat the oven to 400°F. Remove the plastic wrap from the Brie package and place it on a lightly greased baking sheet. Brush the surface of the pastry lightly with the beaten egg-yolk mixture. Bake until a rich golden brown, about 30 to 35 minutes. Remove to a wire rack to cool about 10 minutes before serving.

5. To serve, place the warm cheese package on a small cutting board and slice into small wedges.

NOTE To serve a crowd, use a large wheel of Brie, about 3 pounds, and 2 sheets of frozen puff pastry, about 1 pound. Use 2 large peppers and ⅓ cup chopped olives.

VARIATIONS Try any of the following as stuffing ingredients: sun-dried tomatoes in oil, well drained and chopped; grated hard sharp cheese, such as Asiago or Pecorino Romano; coarsely chopped prosciutto; mushrooms sautéed in olive oil with garlic; toasted chopped almonds, pecans, or walnuts; chopped apples or pears tossed with a little sugar and cinnamon.

Osso Buco with Gremolata

•

SERVES 2 GENEROUSLY

I haven't fiddled much with the traditional way of making osso buco (which means "hollow bones"), a Milanese dish of braised veal shanks. It's here because this is one of my favorite standbys.

Osso buco is usually served with a risotto Milanese; here I prefer the texture of orzo, the tiny rice-shaped pasta, which also happens to be easier to prepare than a laborious risotto.

4 3-inch pieces veal shank
All-purpose flour, for dredging
3 tablespoons olive oil
1 small garlic clove, finely chopped
1 small onion, chopped
¼ cup finely diced carrot
¼ cup finely diced celery
¼ cup dry white wine
2 plum tomatoes, seeded and chopped
1 tablespoon tomato paste
½ cup veal or chicken stock

1 teaspoon chopped fresh sage leaves or
  ¼ teaspoon dried sage
1 tablespoon chopped flat-leaf parsley
Salt and freshly ground black pepper

GREMOLATA
1 small garlic clove, finely chopped
Grated rind of 1 lemon
2 tablespoons chopped flat-leaf parsley
1 tablespoon toasted pignoli, for garnish

1. Dredge the veal shanks lightly with flour and let stand for 10 minutes. In a small Dutch oven or flameproof casserole over medium-high heat, heat the oil to sizzling. Brown the veal on all sides; with a slotted spoon, remove pieces to a plate and reserve.

2. Reduce the heat to medium-low. Add the garlic, onion, carrot, and celery to the Dutch oven and sauté until the onion is softened and transparent, 7 to 10 minutes. Add the remaining ingredients and stir to mix well. Raise the heat to medium-high and bring to a simmer. Season the sauce lightly with salt and generously with pepper.

3. Preheat the oven to 350°F. Arrange the veal in a single layer in the Dutch oven. Cover the Dutch oven and bake until the veal is very tender, about 1½ hours. *(The osso buco can be prepared a day in advance and stored in the refrigerator or a few weeks in advance and frozen in an airtight container.)*

4. Just before serving, make the gremolata by combining the ingredients in a small bowl and mixing well. Serve the osso buco on a bed of Orzo Milanese (page 192) and garnish each serving with a spoonful of gremolata.

· ·

Hot Lemonade

Most hot alcoholic drinks served in the wintertime not only warm you up but can knock you out as well. Here's a light warmer-upper:

Make a not-too-sweet lemonade using boiling water. (If using frozen lemonade, use one more canful of water than the instructions call for and add a generous squeeze of fresh lemon juice.) Pour an ounce of vodka into a heavy glass mug, add hot lemonade, and garnish with a slice of lemon studded with cloves.

· ·

"Colors seen by candlelight
Will not look the same by day."
Elizabeth Barrett Browning

OPPOSITE TOP: On an icy night, dinner is served before a blazing fire. Unmatched pink and green depression glass catch the glimmering flames.

OPPOSITE BOTTOM: For starters, a small wheel of warm and runny brie, stuffed with olives and roasted peppers and wrapped in puff pastry.

ABOVE: Comforting osso buco is served with orzo and a salad of spinach with slivers of pear and toasted pignoli.

LEFT: A baked frozen tortoni, with its macaroon-like cloak, is a descendant of the sixties classic dessert, baked Alaska.

ORZO MILANESE

•

SERVES 2

1 cup orzo, cooked al dente according to package
*   directions and drained*
1 tablespoon olive oil
2 tablespoons grated Parmesan
1 tablespoon chopped flat-leaf parsley
Generous pinch of saffron, crumbled
Salt and freshly ground black pepper to taste

Immediately after draining the orzo, combine all ingredients in a bowl and toss well to combine.

SPINACH SALAD WITH
PEARS AND PIGNOLI

•

SERVES 2

1 small ripe pear or apple, peeled and diced
1 teaspoon lemon juice
1½ cups spinach leaves, washed and torn into
*   bite-size pieces*
1 tablespoon toasted pignoli
1 tablespoon coarsely grated Asiago or Pecorino
*   Romano cheese*
Balsamic Vinaigrette (page 226)
Cracked black pepper

Toss the pear with the lemon juice. Arrange the spinach on 2 salad plates and distribute the pear, pignoli, and cheese over the spinach. Drizzle with vinaigrette and season generously with the black pepper.

WARM SPINACH SALAD Place the washed spinach in a small saucepan with just the water that clings to the leaves. Place over medium heat and allow the spinach to steam until it just begins to wilt, about 7 minutes. Remove the pan from the heat, add the remaining ingredients, and toss well. Serve immediately.

BAKED FROZEN TORTONIS

•

SERVES 2

A generation ago, baked Alaska became "the" dessert on the dinner party circuit, the spectacular finale to a dinner meant to impress—one that perhaps consisted of such foreign and exotic dishes as onion soup gratinée and coq au vin or beef Wellington accompanied by green beans amondine and duchess potatoes. Well, even though we've come a long way in the kitchen since then, the very idea of baked Alaska continues to intrigue me: a dessert that remains frozen on the inside while the meringue coating is baked at a high temperature.

Since I'm not much of a fan of plain meringue, I came up with a macaroonlike topping, with little pockets of hazelnut liqueur in the frozen interior. Here's the "new and improved" result of my experimentation.

If all the ingredients are prepared in advance, this only takes a few minutes to make: just whip the egg whites, assemble, and bake. This recipe is an easy one to multiply for a larger number of guests.

2 large egg whites
¼ cup sugar
¼ cup lightly toasted chopped hazelnuts
½ cup shredded coconut

2 3-inch cubes rock-hard vanilla, chocolate fudge,
*   or toasted almond ice cream (or make rounds of*
*   ice cream by molding in 2 half-cup measuring*
*   cups and freezing until hard)*
2 tablespoons Frangelico liqueur or sherry
2 ¾-inch-thick slices of day-old pound cake,
*   about 3 inches square (or cut out circles using a*
*   half-cup measuring cup as a template)*

1. In a spotlessly clean, small mixing bowl, beat the egg whites until foamy. Beat in the sugar a tablespoon at a time and continue beating until stiff peaks form. Fold in the hazelnuts and the coconut. Reserve.

2. Preheat the oven to 450°F. Line a small baking sheet with a double layer of parchment paper.

3. Work very quickly: using an ice pick, poke holes in the ice cream and then drizzle the liqueur into the holes. Place the pieces of cake on the baking sheet, spaced well apart and carefully put a piece of ice cream on each piece of cake.

4. Continuing to work quickly, frost the ice cream and cake with the meringue, making sure that they are completely covered and sealed, leaving no holes for hot air to seep in and melt the ice cream.

5. Immediately place the pan in the oven and bake until the meringue is lightly browned, 5 or 6 minutes. Using a spatula, transfer the baked tortonis to individual serving plates and serve immediately.

A POTLUCK SUPPER

for a crowd

•

In the summer there are family reunions, and in the fall and winter there are potluck suppers (although there's no law saying you can't have one in the summer). In fact, potlucks were originally held in the summer, when farmers would help each other out making hay, raising barns, and getting in the harvest. The farmers would work outside all day while the farm women worked inside, preparing their favorite "covered dishes." This ritual evolved into a cool-weather tradition, with friends and families getting together for a big feast. Now potlucks are held by church and community groups, after meetings, ball games, and other events. And the potluck is still used as a means of enjoying good food and fellowship.

Quite a few times in New York, I've gotten together with a big group of friends and planned potlucks. A few years ago we had a Southern barbecue dinner with all the fixin's, and most recently we threw a barn-raising potluck (no, we didn't raise a barn in Manhattan, but the food was all classic Midwestern dishes). Everyone always has a terrific time. And no wonder. Since everyone contributes, potluck suppers give each person a feeling of really being an essential part of the party.

Here are some of my favorite tried-and-true potluck dishes: dishes that are easy to make and that travel well, from old family recipes to new ones from friends. I'm certainly not suggesting anyone make this as a whole menu, but there's plenty to choose from when next time you're invited for potluck or when you organize one of your own.

Menu

MOM'S SIMPLE SIMON CHICKEN

JOE'S BAKED EGGPLANT ROLLATINI

PAULA'S OVEN-BRAISED SWISS STEAK

CHILI COBBLER

NOLAN'S WALNUT-AND-MUSHROOM–STUFFED PEPPERS WITH RED PEPPER SAUCE

CARROT PUDDING   OHIO CORN PUDDING

DAD'S FAVORITE CABBAGE AND POTATO CASSEROLE

ROSE'S SPAGHETTI PIE

JANET'S APPLE-GLAZED HAM AND PORK LOAF

BAKED LIMAS AND HOMINY (PAGE 113)

•   •   •

JAN'S BEET PERFECTION SALAD

LILLIAN'S LENTIL SALAD

IDAHO POTATO SALAD WITH BOILED DRESSING

TOM'S CHEESE AND PEAS SALAD

CORINNE'S "GUESS AGAIN" SALAD (PAGE 116)

STEPHANIE'S CAJUN COLESLAW (PAGE 185)

•   •   •

PINEAPPLE CHOCOLATE SQUARES

SUGAR-CREAM PIE

APPLE-GINGERBREAD UPSIDE-DOWN CAKE

FRAN'S ORANGE COFFEE CAKE

MARY ANN'S SPICY PEAR BREAD PUDDING

LINDA'S MOM'S NOODLE PUDDING

JEAN'S MOLDED RICE PUDDING

JOE'S "GERMAN" BANANA CAKE (PAGE 109)

APPLE-STRAWBERRY COBBLER (PAGE 67)

RIGHT: A pot luck assortment of hearty dishes is spread out buffet-style on the chintz-covered dining table.

"I never see any home cooking.
All I get is fancy stuff."
HRH Prince Phillip, Duke of Edinburgh

Mom's Simple Simon Chicken

•

MAKES 16 PIECES

COATING
1½ cups cracker meal or fine cracker crumbs
⅓ cup grated Parmesan
1 teaspoon dry mustard
2 garlic cloves, very finely chopped
¼ teaspoon salt
⅛ teaspoon paprika
⅛ teaspoon cayenne pepper

2 broiler-fryer chickens cut into eighths
½ cup corn oil, approximately

Preheat the oven to 375°F. Combine the coating ingredients in a shallow bowl. Brush the chicken pieces lightly with oil and then roll them in the coating mixture. Arrange the chicken in a single layer on a foil-lined baking sheet. Bake for 1 hour, or until tender and well browned.

Joe's Baked Eggplant Rollatini

•

SERVES 8

Joe Brescia's mother always made this for big family gatherings. It's a great dish to have stashed away in the freezer. When I have it for supper, I like to serve it with steamed spinach drizzled with a few drops of extra-virgin olive oil.

FILLING
½ pound sweet Italian sausage
½ cup shredded mozzarella
¼ cup grated Parmesan
½ cup ricotta
1 large egg, lightly beaten
½ teaspoon salt
¼ teaspoon freshly ground black pepper
1 large garlic clove, finely chopped
¼ cup chopped parsley
1 tablespoon chopped basil

1 1¼-pound eggplant
2 large eggs, lightly beaten
½ cup all-purpose flour, approximately
3 tablespoons olive oil

1½ cups tomato sauce
½ cup shredded mozzarella
¼ cup grated Parmesan

1. Make the filling. Remove the casings from the sausage and place the sausage meat in a skillet over low heat. Sauté, chopping up the meat, until nicely browned, about 10 minutes. Remove with a slotted spoon to a plate lined with absorbent paper.

2. In a mixing bowl, combine the 3 cheeses, egg, salt, pepper, garlic, parsley, and basil and stir until smoothly blended. Stir in the sausage. Place in the refrigerator to chill.

3. Cut the eggplant (do not peel) into slices slightly less than ¼ inch thick. Dip the slices into the beaten eggs and then dip into flour to coat lightly. Heat the oil to sizzling in a skillet over medium heat and, a few at a time, sauté the eggplant slices on both sides until nicely browned. Remove to absorbent paper to drain excess oil.

4. Preheat the oven to 375°F. Spoon about half the tomato sauce evenly across the bottom of a shallow 2-quart baking pan.

5. One slice at a time, spread a thin layer of filling onto each eggplant slice. Roll up the eggplant and place seam side down into the prepared dish. Spoon the remaining sauce over the eggplant. Sprinkle the mozzarella and then the Parmesan over the sauce. (Can be prepared up to this point, tightly wrapped, and frozen; thaw before proceeding.)

6. Cover the pan with aluminum foil and place in the oven. Bake until the sauce is bubbling, 20 to 30 minutes. Remove the foil and continue baking until the cheese is nicely browned, about 15 minutes longer. Serve hot.

"Some people's food always tastes better than others, even if they are cooking the same dish at the same dinner. Now I will tell you why—because one person has much more life in them—more fire, more vitality, more guts—than others."
Rosa Lewis, London hotelier

Paula's Oven-Braised Swiss Steak

SERVES 10

3 pounds boneless beef round, ½ inch thick
1 cup dry red wine
6 tablespoons olive oil
½ teaspoon salt
½ teaspoon freshly ground black pepper
1 teaspoon dried rosemary, crumbled
2 garlic cloves, finely chopped
3 tablespoons all-purpose flour
3 cups thinly sliced onions
1 cup well-seasoned beef broth
2 cups peeled and coarsely chopped tomatoes
¼ cup chopped parsley

1. Cut the meat into small serving-size pieces. Place in a shallow bowl and add the wine, 2 tablespoons olive oil, salt, pepper, rosemary, and garlic. Toss to coat the meat with the marinade, cover, and refrigerate for 2 hours.

2. Drain the marinade from the meat, reserving the marinade, and wipe meat dry. Place the flour in a shallow bowl and lightly dredge the meat.

3. In a skillet over medium-high heat, heat the remaining olive oil to sizzling. Quickly brown the meat pieces on both sides. Remove the meat to a shallow 3-quart baking dish. Scatter the sliced onions over the meat.

4. Preheat the oven to 325°F.

5. Stir any remaining flour into the skillet and brown. Slowly stir reserved marinade and the beef stock into the skillet. Bring to a simmer, stir in the tomatoes, and simmer 5 minutes. Pour the sauce over the meat and onions and cover the baking dish with its lid or aluminum foil.

6. Place the dish in the oven and bake for 2 hours. (*Can be made in advance up to this point, cooled, tightly wrapped, and refrigerated or frozen.*) Uncover the casserole and bake 1 hour longer. Let stand 10 minutes and skim off any excess fat. Sprinkle the parsley over the meat and serve.

Chili Cobbler

SERVES 6 TO 8

CHILI
2 tablespoons olive oil
1½ pounds lean ground beef
1 large garlic clove, finely chopped
4 scallions, white and green parts, chopped
1 15½-ounce can black beans, drained and rinsed
½ teaspoon dried oregano
¼ teaspoon salt
1 teaspoon ground mild chili (not prepared chili powder)
1 teaspoon ground cumin
Pinch of cayenne pepper, or to taste
4 cups thick tomato sauce

CORN BREAD TOPPING
¾ cup sifted all-purpose flour
3 teaspoons baking powder
½ teaspoon salt
1 teaspoon sugar
1 cup stone-ground yellow cornmeal
¾ cup milk
1 large egg
3 tablespoons vegetable shortening, melted and cooled
2 scallions, white and green parts, chopped
½ cup grated sharp Cheddar

1. To make the chili, heat the oil in a skillet over medium-high heat. Add the beef, garlic, and scallions and sauté until the meat is browned, about 7 minutes. Stir in the remaining chili ingredients, bring to a simmer, and cook uncovered for 45 minutes, stirring occasionally to prevent sticking.

2. Preheat the oven to 425°F. Pour the chili into a 9½-inch deep-dish pie pan or a shallow 2-quart casserole.

3. To make the topping, stir the flour, baking powder, salt, and sugar together with a fork in a medium mixing bowl. Add the cornmeal and stir to blend well. In a separate bowl, mix the milk, egg, and shortening. Pour the wet mixture over the dry mixture and stir until all the dry ingredients are just moistened. Stir in the scallions and cheese.

4. Drop the topping mixture by large tablespoonfuls onto the chili, leaving a bit of space between the mounds of batter to allow the chili to bubble up. Place the pan in the oven and bake until the topping is nicely browned, about 20 to 25 minutes. Serve hot.

Lentil salad, eggplant rollatini, and
chili cobbler. OPPOSITE: Cajun cole
slaw, beet perfection salad, and
apple-glazed ham and pork loaf.

NOLAN'S WALNUT-AND-MUSHROOM–STUFFED PEPPERS WITH RED PEPPER SAUCE

·

SERVES 8 AS A SIDE DISH,
4 AS A MAIN COURSE

My friend Nolan Drummond created this hearty main dish when he was a vegetarian. He's a carnivore again, but he still makes these often.

1 medium green pepper, seeded and chopped
1 medium onion, chopped
3 tablespoons olive oil
12 ounces button mushrooms, coarsely chopped
1 large egg, lightly beaten
½ cup milk
2½ cups coarse soft whole wheat bread crumbs
1 cup chopped walnuts
2 teaspoons crumbled fresh thyme leaves or ¾
   teaspoon dried thyme
¼ cup chopped parsley
¼ teaspoon salt
¼ teaspoon freshly ground black pepper
4 medium green peppers, cut in half lengthwise
   and cored

1. In a skillet over medium heat, sauté the chopped pepper and onion in the oil until transparent, about 10 minutes. Add the mushrooms and sauté until brown, about 10 minutes. Transfer the mixture, including its liquid, to a large mixing bowl.

2. In a separate bowl, beat the egg and milk together to blend. Add the bread crumbs and toss; let stand 5 minutes. Add the bread mixture to the mushroom mixture and add the walnuts, thyme, parsley, salt, and pepper. Toss well to combine all ingredients.

3. Preheat the oven to 400°F. Lightly oil a shallow baking pan just large enough to fit all the pepper halves in a single layer.

4. Spoon the stuffing compactly into the pepper halves and arrange them in the baking pan. Cover the pan tightly with its lid or with aluminum foil. Bake for 1 hour, or until the peppers are tender. Serve with Red Pepper Sauce (recipe follows).

RED PEPPER SAUCE

1 small garlic clove
6 large red peppers, roasted, peeled, and seeded
   (page 64)
2 tablespoons olive oil
1 teaspoon crumbled fresh thyme leaves or ½
   teaspoon dried thyme
1 large sprig parsley
¼ teaspoon salt
⅛ teaspoon cayenne pepper

With the motor running, drop the garlic through the tube of a food processor, and process until finely chopped. Add the remaining ingredients and process to a coarse puree. (*Can be made a day or two in advance.*) Warm the sauce in a small heavy saucepan over low heat.

CARROT PUDDING

·

SERVES 8 TO 10

⅓ cup (⅔ stick) butter, melted
1 small onion, finely chopped
3 cups cooked carrots, mashed
1½ cups milk
3 large eggs, lightly beaten
1 cup fine dry bread crumbs
½ teaspoon salt
⅛ teaspoon grated nutmeg
⅛ teaspoon freshly ground black pepper

1. In a small skillet over medium heat, melt the butter. Add the onion and sauté until transparent, about 7 minutes.

2. Preheat the oven to 350°F. Grease a 2-quart baking dish.

3. Transfer the sautéed onion and butter to a mixing bowl. Add the remaining ingredients, mix well, and transfer the mixture to the prepared baking dish. Smooth the surface with a knife, then create a crisscross pattern on the surface with a fork. Bake until the surface is lightly browned, about 1 hour.

Ohio Corn Pudding

•

SERVES 8

Back home, one or two corn puddings invariably appeared at every potluck. Over the years I've tried a lot of different recipes, and this is the one I like best. A few variations are listed at the end of the recipe.

3 large eggs, lightly beaten
2 cups milk
1 teaspoon salt
½ teaspoon freshly ground black pepper
2 tablespoons butter
4 scallions, white and green parts, finely chopped
1 tablespoon all-purpose flour
3 cups fresh corn kernels or 2 10-ounce packages frozen corn, thawed

1. Preheat the oven to 325°F. Generously butter a shallow 2-quart baking dish and place the baking dish in a slightly larger baking dish or pan.

2. In a mixing bowl, beat the eggs, milk, salt, and pepper together until well blended. Reserve.

3. In a small skillet over low heat, melt the butter and add the scallions. Sauté until wilted, 7 to 10 minutes. Stir in the flour and blend well. Transfer the contents of the skillet to the mixing bowl, add the corn, and mix well.

4. Pour the mixture into the buttered baking dish. Pour hot water into the large pan to come halfway up the sides of the baking dish. Bake for 1 hour, or until the custard is set and the edges of the pudding are lightly browned. Serve warm.

EXTRA-RICH CORN PUDDING Substitute sour cream for the milk and add 1 teaspoon sugar in step 2.

OTHER VARIATIONS Substitute 1 cup cooked lima beans for 1 cup of the corn. Or add any of the following: ¼ cup crumbled crisp bacon, ½ cup finely chopped ham, or ½ cup chopped green or red pepper sautéed with the scallions.

Dad's Favorite Cabbage and Potato Casserole

•

SERVES 8

One of my father's favorite dishes and a many-generations-old Hadamuscin recipe.

6 slices thick bacon, coarsely chopped
2 medium onions, coarsely chopped
1 garlic clove, finely chopped
1 medium head green cabbage, coarsely shredded
1 cup chicken stock
1 tablespoon cider vinegar
3 pounds boiling potatoes, unpeeled and quartered
Salt
3 tablespoons butter, cut into small pieces
¼ cup milk
2 large eggs, lightly beaten
¼ cup chopped parsley
Freshly ground black pepper

1. In a skillet over medium heat, sauté the bacon until crisp. Remove the bacon with a slotted spoon and drain on absorbent paper. Reserve. Remove all but 3 tablespoons of the fat from the skillet.

2. Add the onions, garlic, and cabbage to the pan and sauté until well browned, about 20 minutes. Turn the heat up to high and add the stock and vinegar. Cook, stirring frequently, until most of the liquid has evaporated, about 10 minutes.

3. Place the potatoes in a large saucepan with salted water to cover. Place over high heat and bring to a boil. Reduce the heat to medium and cook until tender, about 20 minutes. Drain potatoes and place in a large mixing bowl. Mash the potatoes and beat in the butter, milk, and eggs.

4. Preheat the oven to 400°F. Grease a shallow 3-quart baking dish. Add the cabbage mixture, the reserved bacon, parsley, and pepper to the potatoes and mix well. Mound the mixture into the baking dish, leaving the surface "hilly."

5. Bake until nicely browned, about 20 minutes. *(The casserole can be prepared a day in advance, covered with plastic wrap, and refrigerated. Bring to room temperature and reheat in a 350°F. oven for about 30 minutes.)*

Rose's Spaghetti Pie

•

SERVES 8 TO 10

This is one of those dishes that seemed exotic and "foreign" a generation or two ago; it's one of those Italian dishes that I'm sure no one in Italy would recognize. There are a zillion versions of this, but Rose Meola's is the best I've ever tasted.

1 pound spaghetti
Salt
4 tablespoons olive oil
2 medium onions, coarsely chopped
1 green pepper, coarsely chopped
3 garlic cloves, finely chopped
3 large eggs, lightly beaten
2 cups ricotta
¾ cup grated Parmesan
1 tablespoon chopped fresh oregano leaves or 1
    teaspoon dried oregano
½ cup chopped fresh basil or 1 teaspoon dried
    basil and ½ cup chopped parsley
¼ teaspoon salt
½ teaspoon hot red pepper flakes
¼ pound Swiss cheese, coarsely grated

1. Cook the spaghetti in salted boiling water until *al dente.* Drain, transfer to a large mixing bowl, and toss with 2 tablespoons of the oil. Reserve.

2. Heat the remaining oil in a skillet over medium heat to sizzling. Add the onion, green pepper, and garlic, and sauté until the vegetables are soft and golden, 12 to 15 minutes.

3. While the onion mixture is cooking, preheat the oven to 350°F. Lightly oil a 9½-inch deep-dish pie pan or a 10-inch springform pan.

4. With a slotted spoon, transfer the contents of the skillet to the mixing bowl (reserve the oil in the skillet). In a separate bowl, combine the eggs, cheeses, oregano, basil, salt, and hot pepper flakes. Beat with a spoon to blend well, then add this mixture to the spaghetti and toss until evenly combined.

5. Transfer half the spaghetti mixture to the prepared pan. Scatter half the Swiss cheese over the spaghetti. Repeat, and drizzle the reserved oil from the skillet over the top layer of cheese.

6. Bake for 1 hour, or until the pie is set and the top is well browned. Remove from the oven and let stand 20 minutes before serving (or let cool to room temperature). Cut into thin wedges to serve.

Janet's Apple-Glazed Ham and Pork Loaf

•

SERVES 10 TO 12

A cross between a French pâté and an American meatloaf from my friend Janet Sutherland.

1 pound cooked ham, coarsely ground
1 pound ground pork or mild pork bulk sausage
½ cup unsweetened applesauce
2 tablespoons orange juice
1 small onion, chopped
1 small green pepper, chopped
2 cups soft coarse bread crumbs
2 large eggs, lightly beaten
1 teaspoon curry powder
1 teaspoon dry mustard
⅛ teaspoon cayenne pepper
⅛ teaspoon paprika

GLAZE
1 cup apple jelly
¼ cup cider vinegar
1 teaspoon prepared yellow mustard
⅛ teaspoon cayenne pepper

1. Preheat the oven to 325°F. Lightly oil a medium rectangular baking dish or shallow roasting pan.

2. In a large mixing bowl, combine all ingredients (except the glaze) and mix well with your hands. Shape the mixture into a loaf. (*Can be made in advance, wrapped tightly, and refrigerated overnight; or make well in advance and freeze.*) Place in the pan and bake for 1 hour.

3. While the loaf is baking, combine the glaze ingredients in a small saucepan over medium heat. Stir until the jelly is melted and the mixture is smoothly blended. Remove from the heat.

4. Remove the loaf from the oven and carefully pour off the fatty pan juices. Spoon glaze over the loaf and bake an additional 30 minutes, basting frequently with the pan juices. Let stand at least 15 minutes before slicing. Serve hot, warm, or at room temperature with Beer Mustard (page 176).

OPPOSITE: A confetti-like cheese and peas salad, golden cheese-topped spaghetti pie, and walnut- and mushroom-stuffed pepper halves with red pepper sauce.

JAN'S BEET PERFECTION SALAD

SERVES 10

A recipe from Mom's pal Jan Robinson, this is a molded gelatin salad that's really good, as opposed to some of those overly sweet and silly concoctions that give these salads a bad name.

2 envelopes unflavored gelatin
½ cup cold water
2 cups boiling water (see note)
⅓ cup sugar
½ teaspoon salt
½ cup cider vinegar
Juice of 1 lemon
1 tablespoon prepared horseradish
2 cups grated red cabbage
2 cups julienned cooked beets

1. Soften the gelatin in the cold water; gradually add the boiling water, stirring until the gelatin is dissolved. Add the sugar and salt and stir until dissolved. Stir in the vinegar, lemon juice, and horseradish. Add the cabbage and beets and mix well.

2. Pour the mixture into a lightly oiled 6-cup mold and chill until firm, about 4 hours. Once firm, cover the mold with plastic wrap until serving. To serve, dip the mold in a pan of warm water and invert onto a serving plate. Serve with mayonnaise.

NOTE If you boil the beets, the cooking water from the beets can be used instead of water.

LILLIAN'S LENTIL SALAD

SERVES 10 TO 12

2½ cups (1 pound) dried lentils
8 cups water
1 medium onion, quartered
2 large carrots, trimmed and peeled
2 large garlic cloves, slightly crushed
1 bay leaf
1 teaspoon salt
1 small onion, chopped
½ cup chopped parsley
10 cherry tomatoes, seeded and chopped
1½ teaspoons chopped fresh marjoram leaves or ½
    teaspoon dried marjoram
1 small garlic clove, finely chopped
1 cup Red Wine Vinaigrette (page 220)
1 tablespoon lemon juice

1. Rinse the lentils well. Place in a large saucepan with the water, quartered onion, carrot, garlic, bay leaf, and salt. Place over high heat and bring to a boil. Reduce the heat and simmer until just tender, 15 to 20 minutes. Drain and transfer to a mixing bowl.

2. Discard the onion and garlic. Remove the carrot, dice it fine, and add it to the mixing bowl. Add all the remaining ingredients and mix well. Cover and let marinate in the refrigerator for a few hours before serving.

3. Remove the salad from the refrigerator about an hour before serving.

Idaho Potato Salad with Boiled Dressing

This potato salad with an old-fashioned boiled dressing was a standard years ago, before Mr. Hellman and Mr. Kraft put jars of mayonnaise on grocery shelves. The dressing is absorbed by floury Idaho baking potatoes more readily than by waxy boiling potatoes.

8 large Idaho potatoes, peeled, boiled, and cut into ½-inch dice
1 medium red onion, chopped
1 small green pepper, seeded and diced
¼ cup chopped parsley

6 slices bacon, chopped
2 tablespoons all-purpose flour
½ teaspoon celery seeds
1 tablespoon sugar
¼ teaspoon salt
¼ teaspoon freshly ground black pepper
⅓ cup milk
⅓ cup cider vinegar

1. Place the potatoes, red onion, green pepper, and parsley in a large bowl and reserve.

2. In a medium skillet, sauté the bacon over medium heat until crisp. With a slotted spoon, remove the bacon to absorbent paper to drain. Sprinkle the flour over the bacon fat in the pan and stir until smooth. Stir in the celery seeds, sugar, salt, and pepper. Stir in milk and cook 5 minutes, stirring constantly. Stir in the vinegar.

3. Pour the skillet mixture over the vegetables in the bowl and toss well to coat the vegetables. Sprinkle the bacon over the salad. Serve warm or at room temperature.

Tom's Cheese and Peas Salad

Strange as it seems, I never heard of this salad before I came to New York, but Tom Barnes says this is a Midwestern classic. Tom's paternal grandmother's family, the Schleys, were Iowa cheesemakers for several generations, and this is their recipe. It may sound like an odd combination to the uninitiated, but it's delicious.

3 cups shelled peas, cooked, or 2 10-ounce packages frozen peas, thawed
¼ pound Colby cheese or mild Cheddar, diced
1 cup finely diced celery
1 small onion, finely chopped
¼ cup chopped pimiento
2 hard-boiled eggs, coarsely chopped

DRESSING
1 cup Homemade Mayonnaise (page 221)
¼ cup cider vinegar
2 tablespoons sugar
1 teaspoon prepared yellow mustard
Salt and cayenne pepper to taste

In a large bowl, combine the salad ingredients. Combine the dressing ingredients in a small bowl and blend well. Pour the dressing over the salad and toss well to blend. Cover and refrigerate until serving.

VARIATIONS Substitute grated Swiss or crumbled blue cheese for the Colby cheese. Or add ¼ cup chopped pimiento and/or 2 tablespoons drained sweet pickle relish.

Pineapple Chocolate Squares

MAKES 25

Pineapple and chocolate? Sounds strange, but it's scrumptious, I assure you. The recipe came from a little square mimeographed and stapled booklet of cookie square recipes I bought at a flea market some years ago, and I've been making them ever since. The booklet is called (what else?) "The Square Cookbook" and was put together by the Grafton Baptist Women, but there's no mention of which state Grafton is in. Anyway, Grafton Baptist Women—wherever you are —thanks.

¾ cup vegetable shortening
1½ cups sugar
1 teaspoon vanilla extract
3 large eggs
1 cup all-purpose flour
1 teaspoon baking powder
½ teaspoon salt
1 teaspoon ground cinnamon
¼ cup chopped walnuts or pecans
2 1-ounce squares unsweetened chocolate, melted and cooled
1 8¾-ounce can crushed pineapple, well drained
½ cup miniature semisweet chocolate chips

1. Preheat the oven to 350°F. Grease a 9-inch square baking pan.

2. In a mixing bowl, cream the shortening, sugar, and vanilla together. Beat in the eggs. In a separate bowl, stir the flour, baking powder, salt, and cinnamon together with a fork until well blended. Add the dry mixture to the wet mixture and beat with a fork until well blended.

3. Transfer half the batter into the other bowl. Add the chocolate and nuts to one portion of batter and blend well. Spread this mixture into the prepared pan. Add the pineapple to the remaining batter and blend well. Carefully spread the pineapple batter over the chocolate batter. Sprinkle the chocolate chips over the top.

4. Bake for 35 minutes, or until lightly browned and a toothpick or cake tester inserted in the center comes out clean. Let cool in the pan and cut into 1¾-inch squares. Store in an airtight container in a cool place up to 1 week.

Sugar-Cream Pie

MAKES ONE 9-INCH PIE

Here's a simple, old-fashioned pie that used to be a favorite back home when fruit was scarce; in the summer, the pie is good topped with slightly crushed and lightly sweetened berries or sliced peaches. Some cooks like to use half brown sugar and half white, or they may add a little cinnamon to the filling or dust it with nutmeg after it's baked, but I like it just the way it is.

1 cup sugar
¼ cup all-purpose flour
⅛ teaspoon salt
1 cup heavy cream
½ cup light cream (see note)
¾ teaspoon vanilla extract
1 recipe Basic Pastry for a 9-inch pie (page 226)

1. In a mixing bowl, stir the sugar, flour, and salt together with a fork until well blended. Add the 2 creams and the vanilla and beat with an electric mixer at high speed until the mixture is smooth, fluffy, and thickened, 5 or 6 minutes. Cover and refrigerate for 1 hour.

2. Preheat the oven to 425°F. Line a 9-inch pie pan with the pastry. Cut the pastry scraps into decorative shapes and place on a small baking sheet. Pour the filling into the pie shell and bake 10 minutes. Reduce the heat to 375°F. and put the decorative pastry into the oven. Bake for 20 minutes longer, or until the pastry is golden brown and a knife inserted in the center of the pie comes out clean.

3. Remove the pie and decorative pastry to a wire rack to cool. Arrange the decorative pastry on the pie, cover the pie with aluminum foil or plastic wrap, and refrigerate until serving.

NOTE In many areas, it's not as easy as it used to be to find light cream at the market. If necessary, substitute half-and-half.

"All people are made alike. They are made of bones, flesh and dinners. Only the dinners are different."
Gertrude Louise Cheyney

APPLE-GINGERBREAD UPSIDE-DOWN CAKE

•

MAKES ONE 9-INCH SQUARE CAKE

Winter pot luck desserts are decorated with forced early spring blossoms (left to right): upside-down apple gingerbread, spicy pear bread pudding, pineapple-chocolate squares, and a pecan-coated orange coffee cake.

How could this be anything but one of the most comforting desserts in the world? To be totally decadent, serve it topped with a scoop of Vanilla Bean Ice Cream (page 221).

½ cup vegetable shortening
½ cup boiling water
1 cup dark molasses
2½ cups all-purpose flour
1 teaspoon baking soda
¼ teaspoon salt
2 teaspoons ground ginger
2 teaspoons ground cinnamon
⅓ cup firmly packed light brown sugar
2 baking apples, peeled, cored, and sliced

1. Preheat the oven to 350°F. Grease a 9-inch square cake pan.

2. In a mixing bowl, combine the shortening with the boiling water and stir until the shortening is melted. Stir in the molasses.

3. In a separate bowl, sift the flour, baking soda, salt, ginger, and 1 teaspoon cinnamon together. Gradually beat this mixture into the wet mixture until well blended.

4. Combine the brown sugar with the remaining 1 teaspoon cinnamon and sprinkle over the bottom of the pan. Arrange the apples in a single layer over the brown sugar. Spoon the batter over the apples. Bake for 45 minutes, or until a cake tester or toothpick inserted in the center comes out clean.

5. Invert the cake onto a wire rack to cool. Carefully slide the cake onto a cake plate and cover until serving. To serve, cut into squares.

Fran's Orange Coffee Cake

•

MAKES ONE 10-INCH TUBE CAKE

From my friend Fran Barnes, a fragrant cake with a crunchy pecan topping that is good any time of day.

TOPPING
1½ cups finely chopped pecans
¾ cup fine, dry bread crumbs
⅓ cup (⅔ stick) butter, melted
¾ cup fine dry bread crumbs
½ cup firmly packed dark brown sugar
¼ teaspoon salt
½ teaspoon ground cinnamon

CAKE BATTER
½ cup (1 stick) butter, softened
½ cup vegetable shortening
1½ cups granulated sugar
Grated rind of 2 large oranges
1 teaspoon vanilla extract
4 large eggs
¼ cup orange juice
½ cup milk
2½ cups sifted all-purpose flour
2 teaspoons baking powder
½ teaspoon salt
¼ teaspoon ground cloves
½ teaspoon ground cinnamon

1. In a mixing bowl, combine the topping ingredients and blend well. Press the topping into the bottom and up the sides of an ungreased 10-inch tube or Bundt pan. Set aside.

2. Preheat the oven to 375°F.

3. In a large mixing bowl, cream the butter, shortening, and sugar until light and fluffy. Beat in the orange rind and the vanilla. Beat in the eggs, one at a time, beating until smooth after adding each one. Beat in the orange juice and then the milk.

4. In a separate bowl, combine the flour, baking powder, salt, cloves, and cinnamon and mix well. A third at a time, beat the dry ingredients into the butter-egg mixture, beating until smooth after adding each third. Carefully spoon the batter into the cake pan.

5. Bake until the cake is nicely browned and a toothpick or cake tester comes out clean, 60 to 65 minutes. Transfer the pan to a wire rack to cool for 30 minutes. Invert the cake onto a cake plate or cake stand and cool completely.

Mary Ann's Spicy Pear Bread Pudding

•

SERVES 8 TO 10

The whole wheat bread gives this old-fashioned bread pudding extra flavor. Mary Ann says the pudding is good when made with apples, too.

6 cups cubed day-old firm whole wheat bread
   (¼-inch cubes)
3 cups milk, scalded
⅓ cup (⅔ stick) butter, melted and cooled
¾ cup firmly packed light brown sugar
3 large eggs, lightly beaten
1 teaspoon ground cinnamon
¼ teaspoon ground ginger
¼ teaspoon ground cloves
¼ teaspoon grated nutmeg
2 cups sliced firm ripe pears

1. Preheat the oven to 350°F. Butter a shallow 3-quart baking dish. Place the bread cubes in a large mixing bowl and pour the milk over them. Let stand 5 minutes.

2. In a separate bowl, beat the remaining ingredients except the pears together until smoothly blended. Add this mixture and the pears to the bread and milk and mix well.

3. Transfer the mixture to the buttered baking dish and bake until the custard is set and the pudding is nicely browned, 40 to 45 minutes. Serve warm, at room temperature, or cold.

Linda's Mom's Noodle Pudding

•

My friend Linda Sunshine writes funny books, among them *Plain Jane's Thrill of Very Fattening Foods Cookbook*. This very fattening, but irresistible, recipe from Linda's mom, Norma, is no joke. A note about the ingredients: Linda says not to panic when you come to the "non-fattening" cottage cheese—you'll never taste it.

1 pound medium egg noodles
Salt
¼ cup (½ stick) butter
1 cup sugar
4 large eggs, lightly beaten
½ pound pot-style cottage cheese
1 pint sour cream
2 cups milk
2 tart apples, peeled, cored, and diced
2 medium ripe peaches, peeled, pitted, and diced
½ cup orange marmalade
½ cup raisins
1 teaspoon vanilla extract
½ cup fine dry bread crumbs
2 tablespoons butter
2 tablespoons sugar combined with ½ teaspoon
    ground cinnamon

1. Preheat the oven to 350°F.

2. Parboil the noodles for 5 minutes in 4 quarts of salted water. Drain the noodles and transfer to a large mixing bowl. Add the butter and toss well to coat all the noodles.

3. In a separate bowl, beat the sugar and eggs together and then beat in the cottage cheese, sour cream, and milk. Fold in the apples, peaches, marmalade, raisins, and vanilla.

4. Add the wet mixture to the noodles and toss well to combine. Transfer to a greased 9 x 13-inch baking dish (the dish should be only about three-fourths full,

since the pudding will rise when baking). Dot with butter and sprinkle with the bread crumbs and the cinnamon sugar.

5. Bake until the top is crusty and browned, about 1 hour. Serve warm, at room temperature, or chilled.

Jean's Molded Rice Pudding

•

SERVES 8

1½ cups long-grain white rice
3¾ cups milk
½ teaspoon salt
⅔ cup golden raisins
⅓ cup sugar
¼ teaspoon ground cinnamon
⅛ teaspoon grated nutmeg
Grated rind of 1 orange
1 8-ounce can crushed pineapple in juice, drained
⅔ cup heavy cream, whipped

1. Place the rice in a shallow bowl with water to cover and soak for 30 minutes. Drain the rice, rinse, and drain again. Transfer the rice to a heavy medium saucepan. Add the milk, salt, and raisins, then place over medium heat and bring to a boil. Turn down the heat, cover the pan loosely, and simmer until the rice is very soft and creamy, about 30 minutes.

2. Remove the pan from the heat, cover it tightly, and allow to cool 10 minutes. Add the sugar, spices, orange rind, and pineapple, and mix well. Cool the mixture 10 minutes longer and fold in the whipped cream.

3. Transfer the mixture to a lightly oiled 6-cup mold and refrigerate 6 hours, or until firm. Unmold just before serving.

AFTER-DINNER TREATS

◆

GINGER-CURRANT WINE

RASPBERRY LIQUEUR   BLUEBERRY LIQUEUR

TANGERINE BRANDY   SPICED PLUM BRANDY

SOUR CHERRY BOURBON CORDIAL

RAY'S ROCK AND RYE

•   •   •

STILTON-WALNUT TORTE

APRICOT-CHUTNEY CHEESE

RASPBERRY CAMEMBERT CHEESE

•   •   •

BUTTERMINTS

ORANGE BITTERSWEET BITES

CHOCOLATE-PRALINE TRUFFLES

SPICED BERRY JELLIES

GOLDEN-GLAZED GRAPES

BROWN SUGAR–BLACK WALNUT FUDGE

ESPRESSO-ALMOND FUDGE

EVERGLAZED PECANS

SESAME CRUNCH

CHOCOLATE-DIPPED CHIPS

RIGHT: Homemade after-dinner drinks "under development." Sour cherry bourbon cordial, rock and rye, blueberry liqueur, and spiced plum brandy.

After dinner is often my favorite part of the evening. The meal has been served and savored, the table is cleared, and I'm officially off duty. Now I can sit back and enjoy the pleasure of my guests' company without interruption. But, as the old saying goes, "it ain't over till it's over!" So I always like to have a few treats—after-dinner drinks, savories, and sweets—to enjoy as we sit back and chat or perhaps play a game. (Having a few of these treats stashed away in the pantry also makes it easy to invite a few people in on the spur of the moment for a nightcap after a movie, concert, or restaurant dinner.) These little extras always make my guests feel special and pampered—and I don't mind pampering myself now and then, either.

Ginger-Currant Wine

•

MAKES APPROXIMATELY 3 QUARTS

This is my version of an old English favorite. I can't think of a better way to while away the end of a cold country evening than sipping a glass of this wine while I'm nestled in a well-cushioned chair in front of a cracking fire.

2 cups water
½ cup sugar
½ cup finely chopped gingerroot
1 cup dried currants
3 liters dry white wine

1. Combine the water, sugar, and ginger in a small saucepan over medium-high heat and bring to a boil. Reduce the heat and stir in the currants. Cover the pan and simmer for 20 minutes, or until the currants are very soft. Remove the cover, raise the heat, and boil until the liquid is reduced by half.

2. Transfer the mixture to a large jar or jug and pour in the wine. Cover tightly and let stand in a cool, dark place for 24 hours. Strain the mixture through a double layer of cheesecloth and transfer to three 1-quart bottles. Cover tightly and store in a very cool place or the refrigerator.

"After the coffee, things ain't so bad."
Henry Herbert Knibbs

Tangerine Brandy

•

MAKES 1 QUART

Juice and grated rind of 10 tangerines
2 cups sugar
¼ teaspoon ground coriander
¼ teaspoon ground cloves
¼ teaspoon ground cinnamon
3 cups brandy
1 cup vodka

1. Combine the tangerine juice, grated rind, and the sugar in a small saucepan over low heat and stir until sugar is dissolved. Stir in the coriander, cloves, and cinnamon and remove from the heat. Transfer the mixture to a jar, add the brandy and vodka, and mix well.

2. Let stand at room temperature for 1 month. Strain through a double thickness of cheesecloth and repeat until the liquid is clear. Pour the liqueur into one 1-quart or two 1-pint decanters or bottles, cover tightly, and store in a cool, dark place for a week before using.

Raspberry Liqueur

•

MAKES 2 QUARTS

Here's one of the prettiest liqueurs there is, with an intense magenta color. This is a light after-dinner drink, especially welcome on a cool summer evening. It's also a refreshing cocktail when served on the rocks with soda and a sprig of mint.

1 cup sugar
1 cup water
2 quarts vodka
2 pints raspberries
1 1-inch wide strip orange peel

1. In a medium saucepan over low heat, combine the sugar and water and stir until the sugar is dissolved. Increase the heat to medium-high, bring the mixture to a boil, and set aside to cool. When cool, stir in the vodka.

2. Place the berries and orange peel in a 3- to 4-quart glass jar. Pour the vodka mixture over the berries and cover the jar tightly. Set in a cool, dark place and let stand for 4 weeks, inverting the jar once or twice a week.

3. Strain the liquid through a double thickness of cheesecloth, crushing the berries to exude their juices; discard the crushed berry pulp and seeds. Strain the liquid again through a clean double thickness of cheesecloth. Pour the liqueur into two 1-quart or four 1-pint decanters or bottles, cover tightly, and store in a cool, dark place for 1 week before using.

BLUEBERRY LIQUEUR Substitute 2 pints blueberries for the raspberries. Add the blueberries to the saucepan once the sugar dissolves in step 1.

. . . .

Dessert Wines — the Final Flourish

Most of us seldom think much about wine after the main course. While I'm not always partial to wine with dessert, I often end a dinner with a dessert wine. We Americans are just beginning to explore dessert wines in a big way, and nowadays there is a wider selection available than ever before. Visit a wine shop with a good selection and ask a knowledgable merchant for some recommendations. Here are a few of my suggestions:
- ◆ *Port* The English have long considered this heady fortified Spanish wine to be king when it comes to after-dinner sipping, but for some reason Port has never gained widespread popularity in America. I love a Tawny Port to finish off a meal, perhaps with a hunk of good Stilton and plain crackers. Or, on very special occasions, a few sips of an old (and very expensive!) vintage port.
- ◆ *Madeira* was popular throughout the eighteenth and nineteenth centuries. In fact, America's first "gourmet," Thomas Jefferson, declared it to be "as soft as rainwater." Nowadays we tend to think of Madeira only as a cooking wine, but it's well worth a try *after* dinner rather than *in* it. I like it especially as a companion to fresh plums or peaches. The same goes for Madeira's Sicilian cousin, Marsala.
- ◆ *Sherry* We tend to associate Spain's Sherry with sweet little old ladies who keep it stashed in the refrigerator "for cooking" and then sneak sips to "calm the nerves." Forget the old ladies and end a special dinner on a high note by offering small glasses of cream Sherry.
- ◆ A few other European dessert wines to consider are sweet French *Sauternes* and Hungarian *Tokay*.
- ◆ As far as American entries go, I like some of the late-harvest varietals from California, sweetened by the sugary grapes from the end of the harvest, such as *Late Harvest Rieslings* and *Late Harvest Zinfandels*, or one I recently discovered, Essence of Petite Sirah.

. . . .

*R*AY'S ROCK AND RYE
•
MAKES 1 QUART

Aside from being a warming after-dinner drink on a cold evening, this is, as my grandfather used to say, "good for what ails you." I stir a few tablespoons of rock and rye into a hot cup of tea to help soothe the aches and pains that come along with a cold.

1 12-inch string rock candy (about ⅔ cup)
1 lemon, cut into wedges
1 orange, cut into wedges
1 quart Canadian whiskey

Drop the rock candy into a 1½-quart jar or wide-mouthed bottle. Gently squeeze the lemon and orange wedges into the jar and then drop them into the jar. Pour the whiskey into the jar, seal tightly, and store in a cool, dark place. Gently shake the bottle every day or so. The mixture is ready to drink after 3 weeks.

*S*OUR CHERRY BOURBON CORDIAL
•
MAKES 1 QUART

3 pounds very ripe sour cherries
1 cup sugar
1 teaspoon grated lemon rind
2 cups vodka
2 cups bourbon

1. Place the cherries in a large jar, sprinkle the sugar and lemon rind over them, and pour the vodka and bourbon over them. Stir the mixture with a wooden spoon, crushing the cherries slightly. Even out the cherries so they are completely covered with the liquors.

2. Cover the jar tightly and let stand in a cool, dark place for 1 month.

3. Strain the liquid through a double thickness of cheesecloth and repeat until the liquid is clear. Crush the cherries to exude all their juices and discard the pulp and pits. Pour the liqueur into a 1-quart decanter or bottle, cover tightly, and store in a cool, dark place for 2 weeks before using.

Spiced Plum Brandy

·

MAKES 2 QUARTS

2 *pounds firm, ripe prune plums, pitted and*
   quartered
4 *cinnamon sticks*
2 *teaspoons whole cloves*
5 *star anise*
4 *cups dry white wine*
4 *cups sugar*
4 *cups brandy*

1. In a medium saucepan over medium heat, combine the plums, spices, and ½ cup of the wine. Bring to a simmer and cook, loosely covered, until the plums begin to soften, 8 to 10 minutes. Stir in the sugar and continue cooking until the sugar is dissolved.

2. Combine the plum mixture, the remaining wine, and the brandy in a large glass container. Cover tightly and store in a cool, dark place, shaking the container every 2 or 3 days, for 3 weeks.

3. Strain the liquid through a double thickness of cheesecloth and repeat until the liquid is clear. Reserve the "drunken" plums for another use (they're excellent over ice cream). Pour the liqueur into two 1-quart or four 1-pint decanters or bottles, cover tightly, and store in a cool, dark place for 1 or 2 weeks before using.

Stilton-Walnut Torte

·

SERVES 8 TO 10

The perfect finish to an elegant fall or winter dinner. I like serving this with a glass of Port in the living room after a light dessert, or even in place of dessert with plums or tart apples.

2 *8-ounce packages of cream cheese, softened*
1 *cup (2 sticks) butter, softened*
¼ *cup Port*
¼ *pound Stilton, crumbled*
¾ *cup coarsely chopped toasted walnuts*

1. Lightly oil a 9-inch springform pan.

2. In a large mixing bowl, beat the cream cheese and butter together until completely blended and light and fluffy. Beat in the Port.

3. Spread about one-third of the cheese-butter mixture in an even layer in the bottom of the prepared pan. Scatter half the Stilton over the cheese-butter mixture and scatter one-third of the walnuts over the Stilton. Press down lightly with your fingers and repeat. Top with the last third of the cheese-butter mixture and scatter the remaining walnuts over the top.

4. Cover the pan with plastic wrap and refrigerate until firm, at least 3 hours. (*Can be made up to 3 days in advance.*)

5. To serve, press a warm, wet towel around the sides of the pan and remove the sides. Serve the torte with stoned wheat, whole wheat, or rye crackers.

Apricot-Chutney Cheese

·

SERVES 8

Serve this with fruit and plain crackers after a highly seasoned dinner. Who needs dessert?

⅓ *cup finely chopped Major Grey's chutney*
⅔ *cup finely chopped dried apricots*
1 *cup applejack or Calvados*
¼ *pound sharp white Cheddar, finely grated*
3 *4-ounce packages cream cheese, softened*

1. Combine the chutney, apricots, and applejack in a small, heavy saucepan and place over medium heat. Bring the mixture to a boil, reduce the heat to low, and cook until most of the liquid has been absorbed and evaporated and the mixture is thick, 7 to 10 minutes. Remove from the heat and cool.

2. Meanwhile, in a large mixing bowl, beat the cheeses until completely blended and smooth. Add the apricot mixture and beat until well blended.

3. Transfer the mixture to a crock (or crocks), cover tightly, and store in the refrigerator. (*Can be made up to a week in advance.*) Remove from the refrigerator about 45 minutes before serving and serve with plain crackers.

OPPOSITE: **Special treats enjoyed before the fire.** TOP: **Ginger-currant wine, raspberry Camembert with crackers, and on the saucers, praline truffles.** BOTTOM: **Stilton-walnut torte with water biscuits, and brown sugar-black walnut fudge.**

Raspberry Camembert Cheese

•

MAKES ABOUT 2½ CUPS

This spread is perfect with coffee for those times when you don't want to fuss with a real dessert. Serve with plain water biscuits.

8 ounces Camembert, rind removed
1 8-ounce package cream cheese, softened
1½ cups raspberries, crushed and tossed with
    ¼ cup sugar, or 1 10-ounce package frozen
    raspberries, thawed and drained
¾ cup toasted walnut or pecan halves

1. Place the Camembert, cream cheese, and raspberries (reserving a few for garnish) in a food processor fitted with the steel chopping blade. Process until smooth. Add the nuts, and pulse until the nuts are chopped and blended in.

2. Transfer the mixture to a crock (or crocks) and smooth the top. Garnish with the reserved raspberries, cover with plastic wrap, and refrigerate at least 3 hours, or overnight. Remove from the refrigerator about 30 minutes before serving.

Golden-Glazed Grapes

•

MAKES APPROXIMATELY 1½ POUNDS

A tasty bit of edible decoration on a coffee or tea saucer, these also make a beautiful dessert garnish. Try glazing strawberries, too.

1 cup sugar
¼ cup water
Approximately 1½ pounds red and green seedless
    grapes

1. Combine the sugar and water in a small, heavy saucepan over medium heat and stir until sugar is dissolved. Bring the mixture to a boil. Boil without stirring until the mixture turns a light golden color, 5 to 7 minutes, and remove the pan from the heat.

2. Place a wire rack over a large sheet of wax paper. Working quickly, use small tongs or tweezers to dip the grapes, one at a time or small springs at a time, into the syrup, coating them completely. Place the fruit on the wire rack to drain, cool, and harden.

Transfer to a wax paper–lined container and store in a cool place (do not refrigerate). The fruit should be eaten within 36 hours.

Chocolate-Praline Truffles

•

MAKES ABOUT 3 DOZEN

¼ cup sugar
1 teaspoon water
¼ cup coarsely chopped pecans
12 squares semisweet chocolate
¼ cup strong black coffee
2 tablespoons Frangelico liqueur or brandy
½ cup (1 stick) butter, softened
2 tablespoons heavy cream
¼ cup unsweetened cocoa
¼ teaspoon ground cinnamon

1. Combine the sugar and water in a small, heavy saucepan and stir over low heat until the sugar has dissolved. Raise the heat and boil rapidly without stirring until the syrup turns light golden brown, 5 to 7 minutes.

2. Stir in the pecans, pour the mixture out onto a lightly greased baking sheet, and cool thoroughly. Finely chop the cooled praline in a food processor fitted with the steel chopping blade. *(Can be made any time in advance and stored in a covered jar at room temperature.)*

3. In the top of a double boiler over simmering water, combine the chocolate, coffee, and liqueur. Stir until chocolate is just melted, then remove from the heat. Add the butter and stir until smooth. Transfer to a bowl and allow to cool to lukewarm.

4. Stir in the chopped praline and the cream. Cover the bowl with plastic wrap and refrigerate until firm but still pliable, 3 or 4 hours.

5. Line a baking sheet with wax paper (or use a nonstick baking sheet). Using your fingers, mold the truffle mixture into ½-inch balls.

6. Mix the cocoa and cinnamon in a shallow bowl. Roll each truffle in the cocoa mixture to coat lightly. Set onto the baking sheet again and freeze until firm, about 1 hour. Pack the truffles in wax paper–lined tins with wax paper between the layers. Store in a cool place up to 2 weeks.

CHOCOLATE-DIPPED CHIPS

•

MAKES ABOUT ½ POUND

Chocolate-dipped strawberries, step aside! If you've never had chocolate-coated potato chips, you're missing something. They're not as crazy as they sound.

10 ounces semisweet chocolate, coarsely chopped
2 tablespoons vegetable shortening
4 ounces extra-crispy unsalted potato chips

1. In the top of a double boiler over simmering water, combine the chocolate and shortening and stir until melted and smooth. Keep warm.

2. Using wooden tongs or long tweezers, carefully dip the potato chips, one at a time, into the chocolate. Allow excess chocolate to drip from the chips and place chips on nonstick baking sheets (or regular baking sheets lined with wax paper). Allow the chocolate to cool and then place the baking sheets in the refrigerator until the chocolate hardens, about 30 minutes.

3. Line the bottom of an airtight container with a thin layer of crumpled wax paper for cushioning. Carefully pack the potato chips into the container, cover, and store in a cool place up to 1 week.

BUTTERMINTS

•

MAKES ABOUT 4 DOZEN

Once you taste these old-fashioned, homey candies, you'll remember them. If you want to make them like they were made in grandmother's day, divide the candy mixture into three batches in step 2 and tint the batches pale pink, pale green, and pale yellow with a drop or two of food coloring.

¼ cup (½ stick) butter
⅓ cup light corn syrup
4 cups confectioners' sugar, sifted
½ teaspoon peppermint extract
½ teaspoon vanilla extract

1. In a medium, heavy saucepan, combine the butter, corn syrup, and 2 cups of the confectioners' sugar and stir until smooth. Place over low heat and cook, stirring constantly with a wooden spoon, until the mixture comes to a boil, about 7 minutes. Stir in the remaining sugar about ½ cup at a time, stirring until smooth after each addition.

2. Remove the pan from the heat and stir until the mixture is thick and soft peaks form. Stir in the peppermint and vanilla extracts. Turn the mixture out onto a marble pastry slab or a clean smooth countertop and knead it until very smooth and creamy.

3. Using lightly oiled hands, shape the mixture into ½-inch ovals between the palms. Place on wax paper. Allow the candies to cool completely. Pack in a wax paper–lined airtight container. Store up to 3 weeks in a cool place.

SPICED BERRY JELLIES

•

MAKES ABOUT 2 TO 3 DOZEN,
DEPENDING ON SIZE

Because these are made with pureed fresh fruit, these little candies have an intense burst of flavor no gumdrop ever had.

3 envelopes unflavored gelatin
½ cup cold water
2 pints raspberries, blackberries, or blueberries
2 cups granulated sugar
¼ teaspoon ground cinnamon
¼ teaspoon ground cloves
2 tablespoons butter, softened
½ cup superfine sugar

1. Line a 9 x 12-inch baking pan with wax paper (or use a nonstick pan). Dissolve the gelatin in the water.

2. In the bowl of a food processor fitted with the steel chopping blade, process the berries to form a thick puree.

3. Transfer the puree to a medium, heavy saucepan and stir in the granulated sugar and spices. Place over medium-high heat, bring to a boil, and boil 3 minutes. Stir in the butter, return to a boil, and cook 2 minutes more.

4. Strain the mixture through a fine sieve into a bowl to eliminate the seeds. While the mixture is still hot, stir in the dissolved gelatin. Allow the mixture to cool for 20 minutes or so. Pour the mixture into the baking pan, cover the pan with plastic wrap or aluminum foil, and refrigerate until firmly jelled, 3 or 4 hours.

5. Pour superfine sugar into a shallow bowl. Using small cookie cutters, cut the firm candy into pieces and roll in the sugar. Pack the candies in airtight containers and store in the refrigerator.

Orange Bittersweet Bites

•

MAKES 3 DOZEN

These intensely flavored candies pack a chocolate whollop, so I cut them into small squares, about two bites' worth apiece. The orange adds a surprising extra flavor note.

1 large orange
⅓ cup sugar
⅓ cup raisins
¾ cup chopped brazil nuts or pecans
6 ounces bittersweet chocolate, coarsely chopped
6 ounces semisweet chocolate, coarsely chopped
⅓ cup heavy cream

1. Grate the zest from the orange and reserve. Peel the orange, cutting away all white pith, and chop the flesh into small pieces, discarding the seeds.

2. In a medium, heavy saucepan, combine the orange zest, chopped orange, and sugar. Place over medium-high heat and cook, stirring constantly, until the sugar is dissolved. Continue cooking until the mixture is thick and syrupy, about 5 minutes. Remove the pan from the heat and stir in the raisins and nuts.

3. In the top of a double boiler over simmering heat, combine the chocolate and cream. Cook, stirring constantly, until the chocolate is melted and the mixture is smooth. Immediately remove from the heat and stir into the syrup mixture.

4. Coat a 9-inch square baking pan with vegetable oil spray (or use a nonstick 9-inch square pan). Pour the mixture into the pan and allow to cool to room temperature. Refrigerate until firm, about 30 minutes. Cut the candy in ¾-inch squares. Pack into a wax paper–lined airtight container and store in a cool place.

Sesame Crunch

•

MAKES ABOUT 2 DOZEN CANDIES

These simple sweets are an old favorite of mine, made by one of our neighbors from the South when I was a kid. I remember the store-bought ones, too—they used to be penny candies!

2 cups sesame seeds
½ cup honey
½ cup firmly packed light brown sugar
¼ teaspoon salt

1. Place the sesame seeds in a large, heavy non-reactive (preferably stainless steel or porcelain-coated) skillet over low heat. Stirring or shaking constantly, toast the seeds to a golden brown. Remove the seeds from the skillet and reserve.

2. Combine the honey, brown sugar, and salt in the pan over medium-high heat and bring to a boil, stirring constantly. Boil, continuing to stir, for 2 minutes. Add the seeds to the pan and stir to blend with the syrup.

3. Pour the mixture into a nonstick 9-inch square baking pan and spread in an even layer. Place the pan on a wire rack and cool for 15 minutes.

4. Invert the pan onto a cutting board and tap to release the candy. Cut the candy into ½ x 3-inch sticks. Allow the candy to cool completely and pack into an airtight container with wax paper between layers. Store in a cool place.

Everglazed Pecans

•

MAKES 3 CUPS

1 cup sugar
½ cup water
½ teaspoon ground cinnamon
¼ teaspoon ground ginger
¼ teaspoon ground cloves
Grated rind of 1 tangerine or 1 small orange
3 cups pecan halves

1. Line a large baking sheet with wax paper.

2. In a medium, heavy saucepan, combine all ingredients except the pecans. Place over medium heat and stir until sugar has dissolved. Add the nuts and bring the mixture to a rolling boil. Continue cooking, stirring constantly, until the liquid has evaporated and the nuts are sugar-coated, 5 to 7 minutes.

3. Spread the nuts in a single layer on the baking sheet. When cool enough to handle but still warm, break apart any nuts that may have stuck together. Cool completely and store in an airtight container for up to 2 weeks.

Brown Sugar–Black Walnut Fudge

•

MAKES ABOUT 1 POUND

Place a few small squares of this creamy, caramel-ly fudge on the edge of a saucer of espresso.

2 tablespoons butter
2 cups firmly packed light brown sugar
¼ teaspoon salt
¾ cup half-and-half
½ teaspoon vanilla extract
¾ cup coarsely chopped black walnuts

1. In a medium, heavy saucepan, melt the butter over low heat. Add the brown sugar, salt, and half-and-half, and stir until the sugar dissolves. Raise heat to medium and bring to a boil. Boil until the mixture reaches the soft ball stage, 234°F. on a candy thermometer.

2. Remove the pan from the heat and allow to cool to lukewarm. Stir in the vanilla and beat with a heavy spoon until thick and creamy. Stir in the nuts.

3. Pour the mixture into a lightly oiled or nonstick 8-inch square baking pan. When firm but not hard, cut the fudge into 1-inch squares. Pack into a wax paper–lined airtight container with wax paper between layers and store in a cool place.

Espresso-Almond Fudge

•

MAKES ABOUT 1 POUND

2 cups sugar
1 cup freshly brewed espresso
1 tablespoon heavy cream
1 tablespoon butter
¼ teaspoon salt
¼ teaspoon cream of tartar
½ teaspoon almond extract
1 cup lightly toasted chopped almonds

1. In a heavy saucepan over low heat, combine the sugar, espresso, cream, butter, salt, and cream of tartar and stir until the sugar is dissolved. Raise the heat to medium-high and bring to a boil. Cook, stirring constantly, until the mixture reaches the soft ball stage, 234°F. on a candy thermometer.

2. Remove the pan from the heat and allow to cool to lukewarm. Stir in the almond extract and the chopped almonds. Beat the mixture with a heavy spoon until thick and creamy.

3. Pour the mixture into a lightly oiled or nonstick 8-inch square baking pan. When firm but not hard, cut the fudge into 1-inch squares. Pack into a wax paper–lined airtight container with wax paper between layers and store in a cool place.

BASIC RECIPES

◆

Basic Pastry

◆

MAKES 1 CRUST FOR A 9- OR
10-INCH PIE OR TART

Use this basic crust recipe as is for desserts; for a savory crust omit the sugar. I like using a combination of two shortenings: vegetable shortening for flakiness and butter for flavor. I use my fingers or a pastry blender for pastry making; the texture of the finished product is never quite as good when it's made in the food processor.

FOR A 9-INCH PIE
1½ cups all-purpose flour
Scant ½ teaspoon salt
1½ teaspoons sugar
¼ cup vegetable shortening, chilled
¼ cup (½ stick) butter, chilled
3 to 4 tablespoons very cold water

FOR A 10-INCH PIE
2 cups all-purpose flour
½ teaspoon salt
2 teaspoons sugar
⅓ cup vegetable shortening, chilled
⅓ cup (⅔ stick) butter, chilled
4 to 6 tablespoons very cold water

1. Sift together the flour, salt, and sugar into a large mixing bowl, then add the shortening and butter. Using your fingertips, rub the dry ingredients and fats together until mixture is coarse and crumbly in texture. Do this quickly to keep the fats cold and solid, and do not overwork the dough. Or use a pastry blender to combine the dry ingredients and shortenings.

2. Starting with 3 tablespoonfuls (4 for a 10-inch crust), add the water and work it into the flour-shortening mixture to form a ball of dough. Add 1 or 2 additional tablespoons of water if necessary to hold the dough together. Wrap the dough ball in plastic wrap and chill for 1 hour before using.

3. Roll out the chilled dough ball on a floured pastry board or marble pastry slab into a circle about ⅛ inch thick. For small pies or tartlets, divide the dough and roll out each piece separately.

4. To line the pan, fold the dough into quarters and center the point in the bottom of the pan. Gently unfold the circle and press the dough into the pan without stretching. For pies, trim off the edges and crimp with your fingers. For tarts, simply trim off the excess dough. For further directions, follow the individual recipes.

SCALLION PASTRY Omit the sugar and add 3 tablespoons finely chopped scallions at the end of step 1.

ORANGE PASTRY Double the sugar, substitute very cold orange juice for the water, and add the grated rind of a small orange.

WALNUT PASTRY For a 9-inch pie: reduce the flour to 1⅓ cups and add ⅓ cup finely chopped walnuts. For a 10-inch pie: reduce the flour to 1⅔ cups and add ½ cup finely chopped walnuts.

Red or White Wine Vinaigrette

◆

MAKES 1½ CUPS

½ cup red or white wine vinegar
1 teaspoon Dijon mustard
⅛ teaspoon salt
½ teaspoon freshly ground black pepper
1 cup extra-virgin olive oil

Whisk together the vinegar, mustard, salt, and pepper in a small mixing bowl, then gradually whisk in the oil. *Or* combine all the ingredients in a jar, cover tightly, and shake well. Refrigerate the vinaigrette for up to 1 week tightly covered.

BALSAMIC VINAIGRETTE Substitute balsamic vinegar for the wine vinegar.

HOMEMADE MAYONNAISE

•

MAKES ABOUT 2½ CUPS

2 large egg yolks, at room temperature
1 large whole egg, at room temperature
1 teaspoon Dijon mustard
¼ cup red wine vinegar or lemon juice
1 cup olive oil
1 cup vegetable oil
Pinch of salt
Ground black or red pepper

1. Combine the yolks, whole egg, mustard, and vinegar or lemon juice in a food processor fitted with the steel blade. Process for 1 minute.

2. With the machine running, slowly add the oils through the tube in a thin, steady, stream.

3. After the oil is completely incorporated and the mayonnaise is thick and fluffy, season it with salt and pepper to taste. Add more lemon juice or blend in more oil, depending on the consistency desired. Transfer the mayonnaise to a jar, cover, and refrigerate for up to 1 week.

VANILLA BEAN ICE CREAM

•

MAKES ABOUT 2 QUARTS

This is the ideal topper for baked fruit desserts, cobblers, crisps, pies, and the like. When I was a kid I always thought the dark flecks of vanilla bean in ice cream were black pepper, so I always asked for the ice cream with the pepper in it.

1 cup sugar
1 1-inch piece vanilla bean
½ cup water
7 large egg yolks
Pinch of salt
2 pints heavy cream

1. Combine the sugar and vanilla bean in a small bowl, cover, and let stand overnight. Pick the bean out of the sugar, split it open, and scrape the seeds into the sugar. Discard the pod.

2. Combine the sugar and water in a small, heavy saucepan and place over medium heat. Cook, stirring until the sugar is dissolved, then continue cooking until the syrup forms a thin thread.

3. In a large mixing bowl, beat the egg yolks until light and frothy. Very gradually pour in the syrup, beating constantly, until all the syrup is incorporated and the mixture is cool. Beat in the salt and then beat in the cream until smooth.

4. Pour the mixture into an ice cream maker and freeze according to the manufacturer's directions.

ORANGE ZEST ICE CREAM Skip step 1, omitting the vanilla bean, and beat in ½ teaspoon vanilla extract and the grated zest of 1 large orange at the end of step 3.

INDEX

◆

Page references in italics refer to captions.

After-Dinner Treats, 210–219, *215*
Almond
  Bars, Chocolate-Glazed, 30, 33
  -Espresso Fudge, 219
  Tarts, Maids of Honour, *163*, 164
"Amediteroccan" Chicken, John's, *19*, 20
Angel Food Cake, Chocolate, with
    Raspberries, 79, *81*
Anise-Seed Shortbread, 182, *182*
Apple(s)
  and Beet Slaw, 78, 80
  Cabbage and Fennel Salad, 17
  Cider Pie, *135*, 137
  and Currants in Cinnamon Sauce, Waffle
    Topping, 128
  -Gingerbread Upside-Down Cake, 207, *207*
  -Mincemeat Cake, *162*, 167
  and pears, fall, *115*, 117
  -Strawberry Cobbler, 67, *67*
  -Sweet Potato Pancakes, *106*, 109
  Tartlets with Orange Custard, 94, 96
Apricot-Chutney Cheese, 214
Arugula and Vidalia Onion Salad, 21
Asparagus and Sugar Snap Peas, Steamed with
    Lemon Butter, 35, *37*
Asparagus Tip and Prosciutto Puffs, 27, *29*
Avocado and Hearts of Palm with Lime
    Vinaigrette, 121, *123*
Avocado, Simple Guacamole, 41, *42*

Bacon, Chutney and Cheese Canapes, 102, *102*
Bacon-Horseradish Dip, 100
Banana(s)
  Cake, Joe's "German," *107*, 109
  Chip Ice Cream, 41, *43*
  Frozen Chocolate-Coated, *103*, 104
  in Orange-Rum Sauce, Waffle Topping,
    126, 128
Bavarian Christmas Pudding, 165, *166*
Bean(s)
  Brown, Soup, Ries's Dutch, 152, *154*
  Black, Dip, 100
  Green, in Tomato Vinaigrette, 47, *49*
  Green and Yellow, in Brown Butter, 65, 66
  White, and Cauliflower Salad, *175*, 177
Beef
  Chili Cobbler, 197, *198*
  Garlicky Oven-Braised, with Pan-Roasted
    Vegetables, *15*, 16
  Sweet 'n' Sour Porcupine Meatballs, 101, *102*
  Swiss Steak, Paula's Oven-Braised, 197
Beer Mustard, *175*, 176
Beet(s)
  and Apple Slaw, 78, 80
  and Carrot Salad, Julienned, *47*, 48
  Greens with Bacon and Red Onion, 82, *85*
  Greens with Balsamic Vinaigrette, 85
  Orange-Roasted, 82, 84
  Perfection Salad, Jan's, *199*, 204
Berry Jellies, Spiced, 217
Beverages
  After-Dinner (Brandy, etc.), 210, *212*–214
  bar, the well-equipped, 141
  Cape Code Sunsets, 40
  Cherry Cuba Libres, 99
  cocktail-making hints, bartender's, 144
  Cocktails, Classic, 141–142
  dessert wines (Madeira, Port, etc.), 213
  Frozen Daiquiris, 99
  Harvest Moon Brew, 112
  Mai Tais, 99
  Martini, the perfect, 142
  Punch, Pimm's, *172*, *174*

  Punch, Tropical Tea, 69
  Punch, White Winter, 158, *158*
  Sangria, Golden, 118, *119*
  Whiskey Sours, Blender, 99, *99*
  Wine Spritzers, Red and White, 28
Beverages, hot
  Bullshot, 180
  Buttered Cider, 153
  Citrus Toddy, 153
  Lemonade, 189
  Madras, 153
Blackberry Dumplings, Grandma Wynn's, 54,
  54
Blueberry Crisp, 87, 89
Blueberry, Wild, Cookies, Jennifer's, 58, *61*
Bread
  Batter, Herb and Garlic, 53
  Chocolate Holiday Stollen, *162*, 164
  Corn, Caraway, 185, *186*
  Focaccia with Two Toppings, 70, *73*
  Grilled Orange-Pecan, *178*, *178*
  Popovers, Hot, *135*, 136
  Pudding, Pear, Mary Ann's Spicy, 207, 208
  Puddings, Warm Pineapple, 38, *38*
  Triple-Grain Brown, 153, *154*
  Zucchini-Basil Muffins, 80
Brie en Croute Stuffed with Olives and
    Peppers, 188, *190*
Brussels Sprouts and Root Vegetables, with
    Wild Mushroom Butter, 134, *135*
Bulgur Wheat Salad, 58, 60
Buttermints, 217, *219*
Butternut Squash. *See* Squash
Butterscotch Pudding, Steamed, with Maple-
    Butterscotch Sauce, 186, *186*

Cabbage
  Cajun Coleslaw, Stephanie's, 185, *187*
  Fennel and Apple Salad with Walnut
    Vinaigrette, 17
  and Potato Casserole, Dad's Favorite, 201
  Slaw with Pineapple Horseradish Dressing,
    Quick, 156
Cake
  Apple-Gingerbread Upside-Down, 207, *207*
  Apple-Mincemeat, *162*, 167
  Banana, Joe's "German," *107*, 109
  Chocolate Angel Food, 79, *81*
  Chocolate Chocolate Chocolate, 160, *163*
  Chocolate Holiday Stollen, *162*, 164
  Coffee, Fran's Orange, 207, *208*
  Cupcakes, Coca-Cola, with Tutti-Frutti
    Coconut Frosting, *103*, 104
  Cupcakes, Miniature, Orange-Coconut
    Upside-Down, 31, *32*
  Lemon Poppy-Seed, Rum-Doused, 149, *151*
  Lemon Pudding, Grandma Wynn's, *15*, 17
  Peach Upside-Down, Grandma Stapleton's,
    82, *85*
Camembert Raspberry Cheese, *215*, 216
Canapes, 102, *102*. *See also* Hors d'Oeuvres
Candies, 216–219
  Brown Sugar–Black Walnut Fudge, *215*, 219
  Buttermints, 217, *219*
  Chocolate-Dipped Chips, 217
  Chocolate-Praline Truffles, *215*, 216
  Chow Mein Noodle Candy Clusters, 103,
    103
  Espresso-Almond Fudge, 219
  Everglazed Pecans, 218
  Mocha Macadamia Truffles, 150, *151*
  Orange Bittersweet Bites, 218, *219*
  Sesame Crunch, 218, *219*

  Spiced Berry Jellies, 217
Caraway Corn Bread, 185, *186*
Carrot(s)
  and Beet Salad, Julienned, *47*, 48
  with Herbs, Oven-Braised, *106*, 108
  Pudding, 200
Cauliflower, "Guess Again" Salad, *115*, 116
Cauliflower and White Bean Salad, *175*, 177
Caviar and Pink Radish Dipping Sauce, 25
Caviar Torte, Black and Red, 145, *147*
Cheddar and Linguiça Corn Sticks, 40
Cheese. *See also name of cheese*
  Apricot-Chutney, 214
  Dessert, 214–216, *215*
  and Peas Salad, Tom's, *203*, 205
  Roulades, Herbed, 30, 32
  -Stuffed Pita Wedges, Grilled, 86, 88
Cherry Pie, Sweet and Sour, Shaker, *79*, 81
Chicken
  Breasts, Garlic-Stuffed Fried, 105, *106*
  Fingers, Sesame, 24, *27*
  Fried, Peanut-Coated, 76, *78*
  John's Famous "Amediteroccan," *19*, 20
  Mom's Simple Simon, 196
  Creamed, and Mushrooms with Tarragon,
    Waffle Topping, *126*, 127
  Paella, New World, 120, *122*
  with Pineapple, Grilled Skewered, 70, *72*
  and Ribs, Grilled, Glazed with Raspberry
    Ketchup, 56, *58*
Chicory Salad with Hot Garlic Dressing, 181,
    182
Chili, Cape Cod, with Guacamole, 40, *42*
Chili Cobbler, 197, *198*
Chocolate
  Angel Food Cake with Raspberries, 79, *81*
  Chip Shortbread, *166*, 171
  Chocolate Chocolate Cake, 160, *163*
  -Coated Bananas, Frozen, *103*, 104
  -Dipped Chips, 217
  Fondue, Classic, 123, *123*
  -Glazed Amond Bars, 30, 33
  Holiday Stollen, *162*, 164
  Orange Bittersweet Bites, 218, *219*
  Pineapple Squares, 206, *207*
  -Praline Truffles, *215*, 216
  Whiskey Balls, Al's, *166*, 168
Cider, Hot Buttered, 153
Coca-Cola Cupcakes with Tutti-Frutti
    Coconut Frosting, *103*, 104
Cocktails, 99; Classic, 141–142
Coconut Lace Wafers, 150, *151*
Coleslaw. *See* Salad
Cookies
  Anise-Seed Shortbread, 182, *182*
  Chocolate Chip Shortbread, *166*, 171
  Chocolate-Glazed Amond Bars, 30, 33
  Chocolate Whiskey Balls, Al's, *166*, 168
  Coconut Lace Wafers, 150, *151*
  Cream Cheese Christmas, *166*, 169
  Jam Thumbprints, *166*, 170
  Lemon Meltaways, 30, 33
  Marble Tiles, *166*, 169
  Mochaccino Chip, 74
  Oatmeal Fig Bars, *115*, 117
  Orange Ginger Snaps, *166*, 170
  Pecan Chess Bars, *166*, 171
  Pineapple Chocolate Squares, 206, *207*
  Poppy-Seed Pinwheels, *166*, 168
  quicker dough for, 169
  Rice Crispie Squares, *103*, *103*
  Tarheels, 43, *43*
  Wild Blueberry, Jennifer's, 58, *61*

Corn
  Bread, Caraway, 185, *186*
  on the Cob with Spicy Butter, 84
  Fritters, 65, *66*
  Gazpacho, Ohio Sweet, 52, *54*
  and Oyster Chowder, 130, *130*
  Pudding, Ohio, 201
  and Shrimp Salad in Grilled Tomatoes, 62, 64
  Skillet, with Sage, 94, *96*
  Sticks, Linguiça and Cheddar, 40
  and Zucchini, Grilled Skewered, 57, *58*
Cornmeal Crackers, 130, *132*
Cornmeal, Polenta-Feta Squares, 173, *174*
Crab(meat)
  Creamed Deviled, Waffle Topping, 125, *126*
  Dip, Iva Mae's, 100
  and Goat Cheese Kisses, 146, 149
  Mousse, Leek-Wrapped, 26, *26*
Crackers, Cornmeal, *130*, 132
Cranberry
  -Almond Tart, 154, *156*
  -Glazed Turkey with Pan Gravy, 132, *135*
  -Wild Rice Dressing for Turkey, 133, *135*
  Winter Pudding, *166*, 167
Cream Cheese Christmas Cookies, 166, *169*
Cucumber and Sweet Onion Salad with Lime-Pepper Dressing, 58, *60*
Cupcakes, Coca-Cola, with Tutti-Frutti Coconut Frosting, 103, *104*
Cupcakes, Miniature, Orange-Coconut Upside-Down, 31, *32*
Curried Honey Mustard, 28
Custards, Pumpkin-Rum, Baked in Miniature Pumpkins, 135, *136*

Desserts. See also Cake, Candies, Ice Cream, *name of fruit*, Pie(s), Pudding(s), etc.
  Chocolate Fondue, Classic, 123, *123*
  Dumplings, Grandma Wynn's, 54, *54*
  Mousse Cups, Frozen Sherry, Iva Mae's, 74
  Pumpkin-Rum Custards Baked in Miniature Pumpkins, 135, *136*
  S'mores, 53
  Summer Fruits, Skewered Spiced, 74, *75*
  Trifle, Strawberry Season, 47, *49*
Dip, 100–101
  Bacon-Horseradish, 100
  Black Bean, 100
  Crabmeat, Iva Mae's Hot, 100
  Hot Pizza, 100; Hot Mexican, 100
  Onion, Everyone's Favorite, 101
Dressing. See Turkey Dressing
Drinks. See Beverages
Duck Pâté with Cranberries, 144
Duckling, Grilled Marinated, with Peppery Plum-Mustard Glaze, 93, *94*
Dumplings, Blackberry, Grandma Wynn's, 54, *54*

Eggplant Puree, Tomatoes Stuffed with, 70, *72*
Eggplant Rollatini, Joe's Baked, 196, *198*
Eggs and Ham in Cheddar Sauce, Waffle Topping, *126*, 127
Espresso-Almond Fudge, 219

Fennel, Cabbage and Apple Salad, 17
Fennel-and-Orange Marinated Pork, 113, *114*
Fiddlehead Ferns, how to fix, 37
Fig, Oatmeal Bars, 115, *117*
Focaccia with Two Toppings, 70, *73*
Frozen Daiquiris, 99
Fruit(s). See also *name of fruit*
  Summer, Skewered Spiced, 74, *75*
Fudge, Brown Sugar–Black Walnut, 215, *219*
Fudge, Espresso-Almond, 219

Garlic, Roasted, 108
  Mayonnaise, 25, *27*
  -Stuffed Fried Chicken Breasts, 105, *106*
Garlicky Oven-Braised Beef with Pan-Roasted Vegetables, 15, *16*

Gazpacho, Ohio Sweet Corn, 52, *54*
Ginger Snaps, Orange, *166*, 170
Gingerbread-Apple Upside-Down Cake, 207, *207*
Gingerbread Whole Wheat Waffles, 125, *126*
Goat Cheese and Crab Kisses, *146*, 149
Goat Cheese, Potted Herbed, *119*, 120
Grape-Walnut Pie, 135, *137*
Grapefruit and Romaine Salad, 41, *43*
Grapes, Golden Glazed, 216
Greens, Mixed, Grandma Stapleton's *106*, 108
"Guess Again" Salad, Corinne's, *115*, 116

Ham
  and Eggs in Cheddar Sauce, Waffle Topping, *126*, 127
  and Pork Loaf, Apple-Glazed, 199, *202*
  Zinfandel and Ginger-Glazed, 45, *46*
Hearts of Palm and Avocados with Lime Vinaigrette, 121, *123*
Herb and Garlic Batter Bread, 53
Herb-Marinated Mozzarella with Toasts, 15, *16*
Herbed Cheese Roulades, 30, *32*
Hominy and Limas, Baked, 113, *115*
Hors d'Oeuvres
  Asparagus Tip and Prosciutto Puffs, 27, *29*
  Assorted "Toothpicked," 101, *102*
  Bacon, Chutney and Cheese Canapes, 102, *102*
  Brie en Croute Stuffed with Olives and Peppers, 188, *190*
  Caviar Torte, Black and Red, 145, *147*
  Cherry Tomatoes Stuffed with Roasted Eggplant Puree, 70, *72*
  Crab and Goat Cheese Kisses, *146*, 149
  Crab Mousse, Leek-Wrapped, 26, *26*
  Dips, 100–101
  Duck Pâté with Cranberries, 144
  Focaccia with Two Toppings, 70, *73*
  Grilled Skewered Chicken with Pineapple, 70, *72*
  Grilled Skewered Sausages and Peppers, 69, *70*
  Herb-Marinated Mozzarella, 15, *16*
  Herbed Cheese Roulades, 30, *32*
  Herbed Goat Cheese, Potted, *119*, 120
  Lamb Spring Rolls with Curried Honey Mustard, 27, *28*
  Linguiça and Cheddar Corn Sticks, 40
  Melba Toasts, Black and White, 147, *148*
  Mustard-Deviled Pecans, 144
  Party Mix, Classic, 103
  Pigs-in-Blankets, 101, *102*
  Pork and Scallion Sticks with Plum Ketchup, Spicy, 27, *29*
  Pretzels, Rye and Caraway, 112, *114*
  Prosciutto-Stuffed Mushrooms, 145, *146*
  Salmon and Red Pepper Mousse, *146*, 148
  Sardine and Olive Tapenade, *119*, 120
  Sausage Bundles, 18, *20*
  Sesame Chicken Fingers, 24, *27*
  Sesame-Parmesan Ribbons, 44
  Shrimp, Potted, Island Style, 69, *70*
  Shrimp with Three Dipping Sauces, *147*, 148
  Sugar Snap Peas, Steamed, with Pink Radish and Caviar Dipping Sauce, 25
  Sweet 'n' Sour Porcupine Meatballs, 101, *102*
  Tortellini, Skewered, with Basil-Ginger Dressing, 24, *30*
  Tuna Canapes, Toasted, 102, *102*

Ice Cream
  Baked Frozen Tortonis, *191*, 192
  Banana Chip, 41, *43*
  Orange Zest, 221
  Vanilla Bean, 221
Ice, Minted Watermelon, 58, *61*

Jam Thumbprints, *166*, 170
Jezebel Sauce, 156, *175*

Ketchup, Plum, 29; Raspberry, 57

Lamb, Grilled, Marinated in Merlot, 173, *175*
Lamb Spring Rolls with Honey Mustard, 27, *28*
Lasagne, Rolled with Spinach, Wild Mushrooms and Three Cheeses, 180, *180*
Leek-Wrapped Crab Mousse, 26, *26*
Lemon
  Meltaways, 30, *33*
  Poppy-Seed Cake, Rum-Doused, 149, *151*
  Pudding Cake, Grandma Wynn's, 15, *17*
Lemonade, Hot, 189
Lentil Salad, Lillian's, 198, *204*
Lettuce, Early, Salad with Scallions, 37, *38*
Limas and Hominy, Baked, 113, *115*
Linguiça and Cheddar Corn Sticks, 40
Lobster and New Potato Salad, 77, *78*

Maids of Honour, 163, *164*
Marble Tiles, *166*, 169
Mayonnaise, 221; Roasted Garlic, 25
Meatballs, Porcupine, Sweet 'n' Sour, 101, *102*
Melba Toasts, Black and White, 147, *148*
Mexican Dip, Hot, 100
Mincemeat-Apple Cake, *162*, 167
Minted Watermelon Ice, 58, *61*
Mocha Macadamia Truffles, *150*, 151
Mochaccino Chip Cookies, 74
Mousse Cups, Frozen Sherry, Iva Mae's, 74
Mozzarella, Herb-Marinated, 15, *16*
Mozzarella, Smoked, and Tomato Sandwiches, Pan-Grilled, 53, *55*
Muffins, Zucchini-Basil, 80
Mushrooms, Prosciutto-Stuffed, 145, *146*
Mustard(s)
  Beer, *175*, 176
  Curried Honey, 28
  -Deviled Pecans, 144
  Flavored, 176

Noodle Pudding, Linda's Mom's, 209

Oatmeal Fig Bars, *115*, 117
Olive and Sardine Tapenade, *119*, 120
Onion
  Dip, Everyone's Favorite, 101
  and Pepper Puff-Pastry Straws, 45
  Sweet, and Cucumber Salad with Lime-Pepper Dressing, 58, *60*
  Vidalia, and Arugula Salad, 21
Orange
  Bittersweet Bites, 218, *219*
  -Coconut Upside-Down Cupcakes, 31, *32*
  Coffee Cake, Fran's, 207, *208*
  Ginger Snaps, *166*, 170
  -Pecan Bread, Grilled, 178, *178*
  -Roasted Beets, 82, *84*
  Zest Ice Cream, 221
Orzo Milanese, *191*, 192
Osso Buco with Gremolata, 189, *191*
Oyster and Corn Chowder, 130, *130*

Paella, New World, 120, *122*
Pancakes, Sweet Potato–Apple, 106, *109*
Party Mix, Classic, 103
Pastry, Basic, 220
Pâté, Duck, with Cranberries, 144
Peach Upside-Down Cake, Grandma Stapleton's, 82, *85*
Peanut-Coated Fried Chicken, 76, *78*
Pear(s)
  and apples, fall, *115*, 117
  Bread Pudding, Mary Ann's Spicy, 207, *208*
  -Pecan Tart, 161, *162*
  in Brandy Sauce, Waffle Topping, 128
Peas
  and Cheese Salad, Tom's, 203, *205*
  and Potato Salad with Mint Pesto, 47, *48*
  Sugar Snap, and Asparagus, Steamed with Lemon Butter, 35, *37*
  Sugar Snap, Steamed with Pink Radish and Caviar Dipping Sauce, 25

Pecan(s)
  Cheese Bars, 166, 170
  Crusts, Little Squash Pies in, 115, 116
  Everglazed, 218
  Mustard-Deviled, 144
  Orange Bread, Grilled, 178, 178
  -Pear Tart, 161, 162
  Waffles, 125
Pepper(s)
  Fried, Grandma Stapleton's, 175, 176
  and Orange Relish, 65
  Red, and Salmon Mousse, 146, 148
  Roasted, 64
  and Sausages, Grilled Skewered, 69, 70
  Walnut-and-Mushroom Stuffed, with Red
    Pepper Sauce, Nolan's, 200, 203
  Yellow, Soup, 92, 94
Pie(s). See also Tart(let)s
  Apple Cider, 135, 137
  Basic Pastry for, 220
  Cherry, Sweet and Sour, Shaker, 79, 81
  Grape-Walnut, 135, 137
  Rhubarb, Little, 19, 21
  Spaghetti, Rose's, 202, 203
  Sugar-Cream, 206
Pigs-in-Blankets, 101, 102
Pineapple
  Baked Rummy, 161, 166
  Bread Puddings, Warm, 38, 38
  Chocolate Squares, 206, 207
Pizza Dip, Hot, 100
Plum Ketchup, 29
Plum-Mustard Glaze, Peppery, 93
Polenta-Feta Squares, 173, 174
Popovers, Hot, 135, 136
Poppy-Seed Pinwheels, 166, 168
Pork. See also Ham, Sausage, Spareribs
  and Ham Loaf, Apple-Glazed, 199, 202
  Loin, Fennel-and-Orange Marinated, 113,
    114
  and Scallion Sticks, Spicy, 27, 29
  Stew, Huron County, 184, 186
Potato(es). See also Sweet Potato
  and Cabbage Casserole, Favorite, 201
  Home-Fried, with Garlic and Herbs, 82, 84
  Idaho, Salad with Boiled Dressing, 205
  New, and Lobster Salad, 77, 78
  and Pea Salad with Mint Pesto, 47, 48
  Scalloped New, with Stilton and Sage, 37
Pretzels, Rye and Caraway, 112, 114
Prosciutto and Asparagus Tip Puffs, 27, 29
Prosciutto-Stuffed Mushrooms, 145, 146
Pudding(s)
  Bavarian Christmas, 165, 166
  Bread, Pear, Mary Ann's Spicy, 207, 208
  Bread, Warm Pineapple, 38, 38
  Butterscotch, with Maple-Butterscotch
    Sauce, Steamed, 186, 186
  Carrot, 200
  Corn, Ohio, 201
  Cranberry Winter, 166, 167
  Noodle, Linda's Mom's, 209
  Rice, Jean's Molded, 209
  Tomato, Mom's Winter, 175, 177
Pumpkin, Pureed, 137
Pumpkin-Rum Custards Baked in Miniature
  Pumpkins, 135, 136
Punch. See Beverages

Radish, Pink, and Caviar Dipping Sauce, 25
Raspberry Camembert Cheese, 215, 216
Raspberry Ketchup, 57
Relish, Orange and Pepper, 65
Rhubarb Pies, Little, 19, 21
Rice. See also Wild Rice
  Crispie Squares, 103, 103
  Pudding, Jean's Molded, 209
  Waffles, Charleston, 124, 126
Romaine and Grapefruit Salad, 41, 43
Root Vegetables and Brussels Sprouts with
  Wild Mushroom Butter, 134, 135
Rye and Caraway Pretzels, 112, 114

Saffron and Wild Rice with Pignoli, 19, 21
Salad
  Arugula and Vidalia Onion, 21
  Beet and Apple Slaw, 78, 80
  Beet and Carrot, Julienned, 47, 48
  Beet Perfection, Jan's, 199, 204
  Bulgur Wheat, 58, 60
  Cabbage, Fennel and Apple with Walnut
    Vinaigrette, 17
  Cabbage Slaw with Pineapple Horseradish
    Dressing, Quick, 156
  Cajun Coleslaw, Stephanie's, 185, 187
  Cheese and Peas, Tom's, 203, 205
  Chicory, with Garlic Dressing, 181, 182
  "Crazy," Uncle John's, 77, 78
  Cucumber and Sweet Onion, with Lime-
    Pepper Dressing, 58, 60
  Green Beans, in Tomato Vinaigrette, 47, 49
  "Guess Again," Corinne's, 115, 116
  Hearts of Palm and Avocados with Lime
    Vinaigrette, 121, 123
  Lentil, Lillian's, 198, 204
  Lettuce with Shredded Scallions, 37, 38
  Lobster and New Potato, 77, 78
  Potato, Idaho, with Boiled Dressing, 205
  Potato and Pea, with Mint Pesto, 47, 48
  Romaine and Grapefruit, 41, 43
  Shrimp and Corn in Grilled Tomatoes, 62,
    64
  Spinach, with Pears and Pignoli, 191, 192
  White Bean and Cauliflower, 175, 177
  Wild Rice and Vegetable, 87, 89
Salmon and Red Pepper Mousse, 146, 148
Sandwiches, Smoked Mozzarella and Tomato,
  53, 55
Sardine and Olive Tapenade, 119, 120
Sauce
  Cucumber-Dill, Dipping, 147, 148
  Garlic Mayonnaise, Roasted, 25
  Jezebel, 156, 175
  Pink Radish and Caviar, Dipping, 25
  Plum Ketchup, 29
  Raspberry Ketchup, 57
  Red Pepper–Caper Mayonnaise, Dipping,
    147, 148
  Tarragon Mustard, Dipping, 147, 148
Sausage(s)
  Bundles, 18, 20
  Grilled Assorted, 175, 176
  and Peppers, Grilled Skewered, 69, 70
Seafood. See also name of seafood
  Cape Cod Chili with Guacamole, 40, 42
  Paella, New World, 120, 122
Sesame
  Chicken Fingers, with Roasted Garlic
    Mayonnaise, 24, 27
  Crunch, 218, 219
  -Parmesan Ribbons, 44
Sherry Mousse Cups, Iva Mae's Frozen, 74
Shortbread. See Cookies
Shrimp
  and Corn Salad in Grilled Tomatoes, 62, 64
  Jumbo, with Three Dipping Sauces, 147,
    148
  Potted, Island Style, 69, 70
S'mores, 53
Soup
  Brown Bean, Ries's Dutch, 152, 154
  Corn and Oyster Chowder, 130, 130
  Ohio Sweet Corn Gazpacho, 52, 54
  Spring Greens, 35, 36
  Yellow Pepper, 92, 94
Sour Cream–Buttermilk Waffles, 125, 126
Spaghetti Pie, Rose's, 202, 203
Spareribs, Grilled Chicken and Ribs Glazed
  with Raspberry Ketchup, 56, 58
Spinach Salad with Pears and Pignoli, 191, 192
Spring Greens Soup, 35, 36
Spring Rolls, Lamb, with Honey Mustard, 27,
  28
Squash. See also Zucchini
  Butternut, and Yams, Gratin of, 134, 135

Pies in Pecan Crusts, Little, 115, 116
Stilton-Walnut Torte, 214, 215
Stollen, Chocolate Holiday, 162, 164
Strawberry(ies)
  -Apple Cobbler, 67, 67
  with Hazelnut Cream, 150, 151
  Season Trifle, 47, 49
Sugar-Cream Pie, 206
Sweet Potato–Apple Pancakes, 106, 109
Sweet 'n' Sour Porcupine Meatballs, 101, 102
Swiss Steak, Paula's Oven-Braised, 197
Swordfish Steaks, Grilled Peppered, with
  Orange and Pepper Relish, 64, 66

Tangerines in Sambuca and Rum, Iced, 181,
  182
Tapenade, Sardine and Olive, 119, 120
Tarheel Cookies, 43, 43
Tart(lets). See also Pie
  Almond, Maids of Honour, 163, 164
  Apple, with Nutmeg-Scented Orange
    Custard, 94, 96
  Cranberry Almond, 154, 156
  Pear-Pecan, 161, 162
  Squash Pies in Pecan Crusts, 115, 116
Tomato(es)
  Cherry, Stuffed with Eggplant Puree, 70, 72
  Grilled, Shrimp and Corn Salad in, 62, 64
  Plum, Grilled, with Grilled Cheese-Stuffed
    Pita Wedges, 86, 88
  Pudding, Mom's Winter, 175, 177
Tortellini, with Basil-Ginger Dressing, 24, 30
Tortonis, Baked Frozen, 191, 192
Trifle, Strawberry Season, 47, 49
Triple-Grain Brown Bread, 153, 154
Trout, Grilled, with Mushrooms and Wild
  Thyme, 87, 88
Truffles. See Candies
Tuna Canapes, Toasted, 102, 102
Turkey, Cranberry-Glazed, with Pan Gravy,
  132, 135
Turkey Dressing, Wild Rice–Cranberry,
  133, 135

Vanilla Bean Ice Cream, 221
Veal Medallions with Wild Mushrooms and
  Herbs, Sautéed, 35, 36
Veal, Osso Buco with Gremolata, 189, 191
Vegetable(s). See also name of vegetable
  Greens, Mixed, Grandma Stapleton's, 106,
    108
  Root, and Brussels Sprouts Steamed with
    Wild Mushroom Butter, 134, 135
  and Wild Rice Salad, 87, 89
Vinaigrette. See also Salad
  Red or White Wine, 220; Balsamic, 220

Waffles
  Charleston Rice, 124, 126
  Pecan, 125
  Sour Cream–Buttermilk, 125, 126
  tips for making, 127
  Whole Wheat Gingerbread, 125, 126
Watercress, Sautéed, with Pecans, 94, 94
Watermelon Ice, Minted, 58, 61
Whiskey Balls, Chocolate, Al's, 166, 168
Whiskey Sours, Blender, 99, 99
Whole Wheat Gingerbread Waffles, 125, 126
Wild Rice
  -Cranberry Dressing for Turkey, 133, 135
  and Saffron Rice with Pignoli, 19, 21
  and Vegetable Salad, 87, 89
Wine Drinks. See Beverages

Yams and Butternut Squash, Gratin, 134, 135
Yellow Pepper Soup, 92, 94

Zinfandel and Ginger-Glazed Ham, 45, 46
Zucchini-Basil Muffins, 80
Zucchini and Corn, Grilled Skewered, 57, 58